OLD MEN CAN'T WAIT

SIMON GANDOLFI was born in London in 1933. After military service served as a subaltern in the 16th/5th Lancers, at the age of 18, early friendships with the co-directors of the cult movie, *Performance*, introduced him to the wider world of the arts, and actor Anthony Quayle encouraged him to write his first novel, *Even With the Shutters Closed*. He has been privileged in making writing and travel his primary occupations and [...] experiencing a variety of cultures [...] and the Indian subconti[nent...] ba for four years befor[e...]

Arcadia Books Ltd
139 Highlever Road
London W10 6PH

www.arcadiabooks.co.uk

First published in the United Kingdom in ebook format 2013
This edition published 2015
Copyright © Simon Gandolfi 2013

A catalogue record for this book is available from the British Library.

ISBN 978-1-910050-61-3

Typeset in Garamond by MacGuru Ltd
Printed and bound by CPI Group (UK) Ltd, Croydon CR0 4YY

Arcadia Books supports English PEN *www.englishpen.org* and
The Book Trade Charity *www.btbs.org*

ARCADIA BOOKS DISTRIBUTORS ARE AS FOLLOWS:

in the UK and elsewhere in Europe:
Macmillan Distribution Ltd
Brunel Road
Houndmills
Basingstoke
Hants RG21 6XS

in the USA and Canada:
Dufour Editions
PO Box 7
Chester Springs
PA, 19425

in Australia/New Zealand:
NewSouth Books
University of New South Wales
Sydney NSW 2052

OLD MEN CAN'T WAIT

A Septuagenarian Odyssey Through the Americas

SIMON GANDOLFI

A

For three wonderful women:
My wife, Bernadette,
My daughter, Anya,
My saviour, Graciela Abbat Agostinelli

PROLOGUE

TIERRA DEL FUEGO
Tuesday, 7 August 2007

I got hit by a truck today – three trucks if you count the two trucks on the main truck's trailer. An attention-grabbing start and humorous, in a perverse sort of way.

Writing the full truth is less easy.

Firstly, why would a reasonably sane man in his mid-seventies, overweight and having suffered two heart attacks, set out to ride from Tierra del Fuego to New York on a small motorcycle? Fear of decrepitude has much to do with it. My wife is younger than me by almost thirty years. I fear her reaction, should I become a doddery old man, and I suspect that our late-teenaged sons find me an embarrassment. I am mistaken for their granddad – or an old vagabond. So is this journey an attempt to prove to myself and to my family that I can hack it? Or simply an escape from the 'me' who grows grumpy and geriatric in a Hereford cottage: mediocre writer, inadequate lover, out-of-touch and out-dated dad.

Of course there is the positive side: I have always relished travel through foreign lands and find liberating the escape into a foreign language. When speaking English I am marked as a product of private education with an accompanying presumption of conservative opinions and prejudices. I become classless when speaking French or Spanish; my voice lightens. I smile more readily, am more courteous, more patient, less given to irritation.

My steed is a Honda 125 Cargo built in Manaus, Brazil – the classic pizza-delivery bike, single seat, single cylinder and kick-start.

I bought the Honda new two years ago in Veracruz, Mexico, and rode south 16,000 kilometres through Central and South America to Ushuaia at the tip of Argentine Tierra del Fuego, where the bike has been in storage for the past six months.

I fly from London to Buenos Aires and take the double-decker bus south. The distance is 3,000 kilometres. The bed seats on the lower deck are occupied by mature citizens. We frown at occasional bursts of upper-deck jollity before retiring into hibernation, from which we stir fatalistically at pit stops to refuel on water, coffee and empanadas. Departing Buenos Aires Wednesday evening, we reach Rio Gallegos, capital of Santa Cruz Province, early Friday. A connection departs immediately for the Magellan Channel and on across Tierra del Fuego to Ushuaia.

Silesian missionaries founded Ushuaia in 1893 on the steep north shore of the Beagle channel. Timber and sheep *estancias* fuelled growth into a muddy slum of weatherboard bungalows, sheering sheds and lumber mills. Bungalows and sheds rotted in the rain or surrendered to the frequent gales. The modern town is an unplanned concrete ribbon. Nature is the redeeming feature. Views south across the channel to the white peaks of Isla Navarino are magnificent. The Cerro Martial Mountains behind the town offer an adequate ski resort in winter and summer trekking for ardent masochists. Cruise ships sail for Cape Horn.

Paulo's workshop is a myth-teller's paradise, where bikers collect on winter evenings to boast of vanquished dangers. Oil cans and tool boxes serve as chairs round the stove; *maté* is the drink of choice. To prepare *maté*, pour boiling water over rancid grass, and sip through a metal straw.

Paulo services my Honda and fits fresh tyres. Late July and the pass above Ushuaia is snow and rutted ice – impassable to motorcycles. A truck driver will deliver the bike 200 kilometres north to Rio Grande. The driver is sure that I can ride safely from Rio Grande to the Chilean frontier, then west for Puerto Natales from whence the ferry sails the fjords and islands north to Puerto Mont. Ahead will stretch a road journey across thirteen nations...

TIERRA DEL FUEGO

The white peaks and black rock of Tierra del Fuego's mountains tower above dark pine forests. North stretches bleak moorland of tufted grass and peat bog, small burns and tarns. Clarity of light foreshortens distances and hills seem no more than ridges sculpted and scoured by incessant gales. To the east lies a slate grey sea scummed with foam. Sheep quiver in the cold. Wind fluffs the tails of a few sad ostriches. Raptors perch on fence posts. Guanacos patrol the road edge in search of a lift to anywhere else. Wild geese and tourists enjoy Tierra del Fuego. Argentines loathe the place. Graciela Abbat is the exception.

Graciela owns the Hostel Argentino in Rio Grande. She is mid-forties, small, lithe, black curls, black eyes; imagine a mountain cat, tranquil at rest, fearsome when on the move. Our connection is a single November evening at the end of my ride south from Mexico. Graciela and I sat in the hotel kitchen and talked intimately late into the night. Graciela criticised us tourists for merely skimming the surface of the countries we visit and made me promise to return, that she would introduce me to the true Tierra del Fuego.

Thus Rio Grande was on my itinerary.

Nothing kind can be said of Rio Grande. The town serves Tierra del Fuego's oil field and has doubled in size over the past few years. Wide straight streets are accelerators for icy squalls. Architecture is concrete box. Rare survivor from the 1920s, Hostel Argentino is a low, L-shaped tin shack. A gloss coating of canary yellow is Graciela's failed attempt at cheerfulness. Backpackers are summer's clientele. Winter is for oil workers. I am to sleep in Graciela's studio.

The studio is out back of the hotel in a garden of log piles, frozen mud and snowdrifts. The studio is new. The bed is new. The mattress is the best I've slept on in Hispanic America. Heating works. Bathroom gleams – unfortunately without water. Excavating a burst pipe must wait for warmer weather. Graciela has moved back to her old room in the hotel.

This is the tale of a journey so I will be brief in describing my four days of preparation in Rio Grande. By day I ride short distances along the sea front – tentatively and without confidence. Fear keeps me awake at night, fear that I am too old for the journey, too unfit. Only in the evening do I relax and share vast helpings of beef at the kitchen table, splash red wine into waiting glasses, listen to tales of politicians' malfeasance, join in raucous following of televised football matches. Sunday I am invited to a barbeque. I leave Monday morning.

I dress in three sets of Alpinestar's thermal underwear, pyjama bottoms, cargo trousers, biker boots. On top are further layers of Alpinestar, three T-shirts, cord shirt, two jerseys, leather bomber jacket. Over all comes a zippered pale-blue thermal work-suit bought on sale half-price in Ushuaia and I wear two pairs of gloves. Elastic ties hold a small suitcase above a top box clipped to the cargo rack. I wheel the bike alongside a concrete block and mount it. Half a dozen well-wishers watch as I heave a leg over the saddle. Two kicks on the starter and the engine buzzes.

Graciela kisses me on both cheeks. 'Be careful, Little Grandfather.'
'Certainly… '

Helmet on, goggles lowered over my bifocals and off I wobble. Imagine a large, pale, grey-bearded blue balloon…

The two-lane black top follows the coast out of town: low grey sky, grey-green ocean. Riding at fifty kilometres per hour together with a temperature of zero centigrade gives a wind chill factor of minus twenty-two degrees. I sit upright; to avoid cramp, grip lightly on the controls. The bike purrs happily. My confidence grows with the miles. This is easy, pleasurable. Why did I worry? Why do I always worry?

The road turns inland, rounds a bluff and climbs. Fresh snow sprinkles the heights. I hadn't expected snow. Oil workers at the Argentino had reported the road clear so it must have fallen overnight.

I should turn back.

I ride slowly onward.

Why?

Because my greatest fear is of being thought a coward, losing what my youngest sons refer to as street cred. The barbeque party yesterday was to wish me farewell; Graciela's kiss on the cheek this morning was reward for the intrepid traveller. Turn back and I become a laughing stock. Such are my adolescent thoughts as the road climbs. Snow has melted beneath truck tyres on the lower slope, sheet ice at the crest. The bike slews to the right. Leaning to the left is automatic. The wheels shoot sideways and my left shoulder slams the ice. I scrabble from beneath the bike, try lifting it. The bike slides away. I untie the suitcase, release the top box and drag the bike sideways to the verge. There, in the snow, I lift it upright, set the stand and reload my baggage. The effort leaves me huffing and puffing. Only a fool would continue. No fool like an old fool … My only excuse is that the Automobile Club of Argentina has a hotel at the frontier. I am a paid-up member of the club. Fifty miles from Rio Grande and I have ridden thirty. Surely I can make it. Ride where the trucks haven't compressed the snow…

The road dips and the going is easier. Then comes the next climb. I fall again. The first car in twenty minutes passes as I heave the bike upright. This is the oil field and a nodding donkey watches as I reload. I fall a third time, each fall on my left shoulder.

A pickup stops; the driver asks if I'm OK.

Fine, I lie. How far to the frontier?

Over the next crest.

The driver will drop my baggage at the Customs Post. Unburdened, riding is easier. The road dips towards the sea. No more ice. I park at the ACA hotel. No rooms. Sleeping in the lobby is forbidden.

I haven't the strength to argue.

Sensible would be to park the bike at the Customs Post and catch a lift back to Rio Grande. The left leg of the thermal suit flaps open, the zip ripped. Perhaps I am suffering from the beginnings of hypothermia – or am too exhausted to think. I ask a Customs officer what chance there is of cadging a lift on a truck to Porto Venir on the West coast of Chile's Tierra del Fuego.

Possibly at the Chilean frontier, a further ten miles.

The road heads inland. The first few miles are gravel – sea level and no snow, easy. To continue was sensible. Then the road climbs. An ice rink…

Better try the snow verge. The front wheel slams into an open drain. I scramble to my feet, unload the bike, heave it out of the drain and back on to the road. The frontier is a further three miles. An Argentine police officer in a Volvo saloon stops to ask whether I need help.

'I'll be fine,' I say and fall twice more, each time on my left shoulder. Tempting to surrender, lie on the ice, let the cold take me – or a passing driver. However, even to surrender demands a decision.

I ride at a slow walking speed, both feet on the ice. A truck klaxon bellows behind. I try to swerve off the road but have no control. The rear wheel crumples as the truck hits. The bike slews. The truck's fender hits my right leg. The bike tips. My left shoulder smacks the ice. I am astride the bike and trapped beneath the fender. The truck slides some forty metres before the trailer's rear wheels slew off the road. The trailer is loaded with two truck tractors. The driver clambers down from the cab. He is Argentine: grey-haired and in his early fifties. He expects to find me dead. Relief brings him close to tears. He asks if I'm hurt. I'm not sure. I need to rest a while. A couple of minutes pass before I try moving my limbs. The limbs function. The driver and his mate prise the bike loose, lift me to my feet, hold me upright.

I mumble what every English gentleman of my generation mumbles in such circumstances. 'Please excuse me. I'm so sorry. All my fault…'

Two young Chilean police roar up in a double cab 4×4 pickup. The Argentine in the Volvo saloon reported that I was in trouble.

The cops ask if I am OK.

I say: 'Yes, that I think so.'

The cops wish to arrest the truck driver.

Convincing the cops that I am culpable takes a while. The driver holds me in his arms, hugs me and names me Brother. Better he calls me an irresponsible old fool.

I take a first step towards the pickup. A spike twists inside my right ankle. Fortunately the cops are supporting me.

'I think I've broken something,' I say and giggle. Note the claim to responsibility: Catholic guilt.

The cops chair-lift me to the rear seat of the pickup and dump my suitcase, box and smashed bike in the back. Thoughtful young men, they decide to return me to Argentina where a nurse staffs a frontier medical post and state hospitals are free. Unsaid is the thrill of fish-tailing the pickup at speed on the frozen road.

The young Chilean cop drives one-handed. The truck skids and slides through ruts in packed snow. The speedo quivers around 120 kilometres. My little Honda makes 100 kilometres downhill with a tail wind.

'What are you trying to do?' I ask. 'Kill me? Can't you leave that to the Argentines?'

I continue with such inane remarks and find them hilarious. We reach the Argentine frontier. The cops carry me into the first aid post. The nurse is a kindly grandma. My two Chilean cops, two young Argentine cops and an older sergeant watch as the nurse checks my temperature, pulse and blood pressure.

I ask whether I am alive.

A Chilean cop says, 'You shouldn't be.'

I say, 'It's something to boast of, being hit by three trucks.'

My hysteria infects the watching police officers. Raucous describes the scene as the nurse removes my thermal suit. An Argentine cop grips my leg. The nurse unzips and removes my boot and cuts through three sets of Alpinestar's slinky thermal underwear. The ankle is puffy.

'It's probably just a sprain,' I say.

The nurse pokes and I yelp.

The five cops nod in agreement with whatever thoughts they share.

Argentina and Chile are in almost permanent dispute. Chile aided the Brits in the Malvinas/Falklands War. How come these cops are friends?

The sergeant says, 'Enmity is for politicians.'

The nurse binds my ankle. The cops chair-lift me to the ambulance and load my baggage. The nurse straps me to a stretcher and holds my hand. Having my hand held is good. We discuss children and grandchildren and the decline in respect showed to mature citizens by the younger generation. The driver hits a rut. The nurse falls on me – a second assault.

Riding the eighty kilometres from Rio Grande took six hours. The return takes sixty minutes. I am wheeled into the hospital and X-rayed from head to toe. I hate being X-rayed: the doctors may discover something truly frightening.

The X-ray technician reports that my ankle is broken. I am wheeled to a doctor's office. The doctor is middle-aged and somewhat careworn. He says, 'You have damaged your thorax.'

'My ankle.'

'No, your thorax.'

'My ankle,' I insist.

The X-rays arrive. The doctor holds them to the light. 'Your ankle is broken.'

I am about to reply, 'No, my thorax.'

The door slams open. Graciela…

She grabs my ear lobe, shakes. 'So, Little Grandfather, now what have you done?'

'Nothing,' I say – nursery denial.

'Broken his ankle,' the doctor says – such betrayal!

'What were you doing?' Graciela demands. The tone of voice is exasperated mother.

'There was ice on the road,' I say.

'Why didn't you turn back?' Graciela knows the answer. 'Men,' she exclaims. 'You're seventy, Old Man. When are you going to grow up?'

Silence.

The consultant orthopaedic surgeon arrives and studies the X-rays. The truck sheared the round bit of what I consider to be the ankle bone. The surgeon advises pinning and wiring the bone – plaster for two months, a further month of minimum activity. The explanation is for Graciela. I am a non-person – a situation with which children are familiar.

Pointless to address the surgeon. I ask Graciela the cost.

The surgeon shrugs, and to Graciela, says, 'His insurance will pay.'

Graciela sniffs disdain. 'Insurance for an old fool travelling by motorbike?'

To me she says, 'I wish for a second opinion.' And to the surgeon, 'When must we decide?'

'One day, two days at most…'

The surgeon applies a temporary cast. I am wheeled to Graciela's car. Graciela collects my backpack and biker box and drives to the Hostel Argentino. Two oversized oil riggers carry me from the car. A small lobby gives on to a big living room warmed by a wood stove. The kitchen boasts the original wood-fired range converted to natural gas. The kitchen table seats a dozen. The riggers settle me in the corner, back to the range. They assure Graciela that the previous night's snow was the first in almost a fortnight; that I met with bad luck.

Graciela doesn't believe in luck. 'He's an old idiot,' she says.

Argentines are argumentative. No one argues with Graciela.

She fills a mug with coffee. My hands shake. 'Don't spill,' she says. I shouldn't be here. 'I'm sorry,' I say. 'I'm a nuisance.'

'You try to be a nuisance,' says Graciela. 'Better sleep in my room where I can keep an eye on you.'

A single bed is carried through to Graciela's bedroom. I am carried through to Graciela's bedroom. Graciela is expert in dealing with the physically impaired; she has a grown daughter confined to a wheelchair. I am stripped, washed, clothed in my striped pyjamas and put to bed. An upright chair makes do as a walking frame. 'No more accidents,' Graciela commands. 'You must go to the bathroom, bang on the door. Someone will help.'

I lie in bed and wonder at my fortune, yes, that I am alive and so little damaged – but far more, to find myself in the care of such friends. Why should they, these Argentines, each with his or her problems, treat an old Englishman as if he were one of their own?

2
RIO GRANDE

I wake sweating and delay as long as I dare before easing out of bed. The upright chair is my walking frame, slide and hop, slide and hop. Progress is slow. I am in need of speed, acutely aware of Graciela asleep in her own bed, and that I am an intrusion.

I abandon the chair outside the bathroom, close the door and hop the last two metres. My balance is poor at the best of times. On one leg, I'm nervous of missing the pan. I'm nervous of making a noise. Shake, shake, then hop and slide the chair back to bed where I lie on my back and worry.

Countless non-worriers have advised me over the years that nothing is achieved by worrying – also that an obsessive sense of guilt is puerile.

Less puerile than telling a worrier not to worry? Or chiding a Catholic for his sense of guilt?

So, yes, I worry.

I worry about what I can tell Bernadette to assuage her concerns. And I worry, as always, about money. And about being a failure – how else can you describe ending a six- or seven-month bike ride on the first day?

If I have the operation here, what will it cost? Two months in plaster; two months' diminution of my already slender funds. A month's convalescence – further financial seepage. And the cost of rebuilding the bike … Can it be rebuilt? Or do I give up now, and catch a flight home? No book written, no articles – no possible excuse for further travel. Accept my age. Surrender.

Meanwhile Graciela snores gently – more a purr than a proper snore. And bed is a prison. I want to move, or turn on the light and read – anything to stop the tightening spiral of questions, none of them answerable at two in the morning – nor at three o'clock – nor at four o'clock.

My third bathroom safari: the chair catches on an uneven floorboard and bangs Graciela's bed. Graciela switches on her bedside light. A small slight woman in a sleeveless nightgown should appear vulnerable. I feel vulnerable.

Graciela says that I am sleeping in her room so that she can help me to the bathroom. I reply that I hate waking her. Graciela says that having a chair bang her bed is a more stressful than being asked quietly for assistance. And she says that I snore – not a soft purr.

Graciela has many friends. One is the orthopaedic surgeon she has summoned to offer a second opinion on the ankle. In his early sixties, Pepe Gonzalez is a one-legged barrel of a man, blued-eyed, grey bristle beard, wispy hair. He divides his life between a medical practice in Buenos Aires and a 17,000-hectare *estancia* in Tierra del Fuego. Grazing is poor in Tierra del Fuego; so is the climate – 200 hectares feeds a skinny steer, so 17,000 hectares is a smallholding. Pepe inspects the *estancia* on horseback. In Buenos Aires he rides a rebuilt 1970s Triumph Bonneville: the missing leg was victim of a bike crash.

I sit with my back to the kitchen range while Pepe examines the X-rays. My age concerns him. He advises against pinning; operating will delay recovery; two months in plaster could transform me into a shuffling old man. Better a cast for four to five weeks, a further month of careful use. Pepe will arrange a meeting with the hospital consultant. Meanwhile I must exercise the leg without putting weight on the foot. Pepe demonstrates the exercises: lie on my back, lift the leg to the count of ten, hold the leg up, then lower to the count of ten.

Pepe has brought aluminium crutches manufactured in the People's Republic of China. I am not good on crutches. My balance is uncertain. Maybe the painkillers are to blame. Or am I merely nervous at having to email Bernadette and my daughter, Anya? Keep it light…

Beloved B, I took a slight spill yesterday. Not much damage but delayed a few days …

Or is honesty the best policy?

Got run down by a truck transporting two trucks on its trailer. Ankle broken. Bike requires rebuilding…

Graciela's ex-future *novio*, Fernando, has driven to the frontier in his pickup to collect the bike. Fernando is a contract maintenance engineer and probably a few years younger than Graciela. He is a strong, slender man, big-eyed, black hair thinning. Briefly married, he cares for a nursery-age daughter. Graciela imagined him early in their relationship as a future husband. She now accepts that Fernando will never remarry. Thus the ex-future – and *novio* – because Fernando remains her lover. He is a central link in Graciela's inner circle. Xavier, the driller, is another. Xavier has been working oil rigs for nearly thirty years. He is a short man with a permanent twinkle in bright blue eyes, clipped grey beard, and lopsided smile.

Xavier and Fernando unload my Honda into the back porch at the Hostel Argentino. The rear wheel is crumpled, rear forks twisted, mudguard splintered, and mirrors shattered. The left footrest and gear lever require straightening; clutch and brake levers are twisted, handlebars out of true.

News of my crash has spread through the biker community via the Internet. Dakar Motos is a way station for foreign bikers passing through Buenos Aires. The owner, Javier, has emailed, offering to repair the bike. Thus a possible future takes shape: five weeks in plaster, bus across Argentine and Chilean Tierra del Fuego to Puerto Natales, passenger ferry north through Chile's fjords to Puerto Montt and bus north to Santiago. From Santiago I can bus east to Buenos Aires, collect the bike and continue up through Uruguay into Brazil and on through Venezuela. Easy…

My Argentine cousins in Buenos Aires have read my blog of the accident and email that I must fly direct to Buenos Aires. A second email of commiseration comes from the manager of the hotel that is my Buenos Aires home from home, the Gran Hotel España. Graciela is away at lunchtime tending to her daughter. I hop to the corner restaurant with four of the inner circle as my guests: Fernando, Xavier, Pedro and Carlos. Pedro is a forty-year-old electronics technician specialising in security systems. He wears his hair midway down his back and cultivates the swagger of a pirate. Carlos studies engineering at the Technical College attached to the oil refinery.

Carlos and Xavier order churasco: a plate-sized chunk of grilled meat surmounted by two fried eggs and piled with mammoth potato chips. Fernando prefers Milanese, with eggs and chips. The Milanese is two thick slices of breaded veal each folded in two to fit the plate. Pirate Pedro and I stick with the midday special: spaghetti with meat sauce plus a hunk of stewed beef.

Pepe arrives from his *estancia* and drives me to the hospital. Doctor Lopez is the consultant. The two men examine the latest X-rays. A small shift of the bone is evident. Lopez again advocates screw and wire, but now a full cast for three months and a further month of rehab. Pepe argues that I am seventy-four; that I don't have four months; that keeping me immobile is a recipe for disaster.

Pepe lost his right leg from above the knee. A stroke lessened the feeling in the right hand and he no longer operates (except on sheep). He does run a large *estancia*, rides his Triumph Bonneville or a horse. He has a medical practice specialising in long-term rehabilitation. He is closer to my age than Lopez, suffers from the same impatience with his own physical frailties and is an expert on living life to the full. Take Pepe's advice and I may limp a little; however, I will complete this journey and produce a new book.

Choose the screw and wire and I risk an old man's shuffle – and no book. I am a writer: no book is a disaster. Doctor Lopez is aggrieved and forbids Pepe use of the hospital's facilities. Pepe builds the new cast in the Hostel Argentino's kitchen, more of a boot with a wooden arch support and rubber heel. The plaster requires two full days to dry. Once dry, I can rest the heel on the ground, though not put weight on the foot. Balancing will be easier. Pepe says I can travel in less than four weeks, more than three weeks. He will get me a wheelchair. Have I made the right decision? Time will tell.

I am occupying the spare bed in Graciela's bedroom. A further three weeks is a massive imposition. Pepe and I speak English together. I tell him that I must find somewhere to stay. Pepe translates for Graciela.

Graciela says, 'Why do you want to make my life more difficult, Old Man? In my room, you are convenient.'

I try to express my thanks.

Pepe squeezes my hand. 'Simon, it is impolite to thank friends.'

I find that I am weeping. So much for the phlegmatic Brit.

On my first visit, Graciela criticised travellers for seldom experiencing more than the surface of the countries through which we pass. What am I taught by three weeks in the kitchen corner? Argentina has suffered two major catastrophes in recent times: defeat in the Falklands/Malvinas ended ten years of brutal Military rule, then came the collapse of the economy. Riding south last year, I never heard people discuss the Military years nor the crash. Even now I am the one to lead the conversation. Three women sit across the table.

'We wish to forget,' says one.

The other two nod their agreement. 'There is so much that we wish to forget'

Silence apart from the suck of tin straws in maté…

X tells of his father, a writer, arrested during the Military dictatorship and condemned to ten years in jail. Police ransacked the family home once or twice a month, broke china, smashed toys, ripped books, and deliberately imprinted their prisoner's children with fear. At the change of government, the father was released under amnesty. X is a close friend of Graciela. They have known each other for a dozen years. X has never talked to Graciela of his childhood and of his father's imprisonment.

Two men in their twenties plonk a bottle of red wine on the table.

They are bright kids, cheerful and ready to party. They are down from the north selling holidays for schools. Teachers are on strike today – no work. They talk of the north as bordering on Paraguay and Bolivia where, they say, people are dying of hunger. One young man says, 'In some countries, governments murder their people. Ours is the most cruel – it kills all hope.'

A cab driver sips maté. He is in his fifties and from a small town near Mendoza. He and his wife have been in Tierra del Fuego for six weeks. She works in a shop. He drives from seven in the evening to seven in the morning. Back home there is no work for fifty-year-olds. They had a good life before the financial crash. He was a teller in a bank. She clerked for a lawyer. They owned a small house in town and a weekend cottage. They saved. They contributed to a pension plan. Their children expected to attend university. The crash came and the good life ended. In those two years only the rich survived financially, those with hoarded capital hidden abroad, and adroit politicians. The present president made a fortune in real estate.

The cab driver and his wife speak quietly to each other, cook for each other on the range, touch each other frequently through need for reassurance that something other than despair exists. He relates their history without bitterness. Bitterness demands emotional energy.

Sunday lunch for Graciela's inner circle is in the garage at the home of the ex-future *novio*. A charcoal grill runs full width of the back wall. The table is laden with bottles of wine. Present are a head of department in the state government together with his pregnant wife and a two-year-old granddaughter. Other guests include a third-generation lawyer. The lawyer denounces endemic corruption. The official is embedded within the system. The confrontation across the table is indirect and I almost miss it. The ex-future is turning meat on the grill. Pirate Pedro opens bottles. The official's pregnant wife feeds their granddaughter. Xavier twinkles. The lawyer pushes his chair back and is gone.

How bad is corruption here in Tierra del Fuego? The previous governor created 7,000 non-existent jobs for supporters. The governor, his wife and brother-in-law are charged with illicit enrichment. The province is bankrupt and begging funds from federal government.

Rio Grande has the feel of an island in the vast empty spaces of Tierra del Fuego. Islands are closed communities. We are four in the pub on Saturday night, three men and Graciela. Pub? So the street sign says. The oblong space is in a new building. Rental as a hardware store or shoe shop would seem more suitable. Pub it is. We sit at a corner table beneath photographs of Rio Grande in the thirties. Two nondescript young men sit at the bar. They attempt humour with the bar woman and with the waitress. The humour is ignored. Will the young men realise eventually that they will never belong, never be insiders?

Graciela, Xavier and Pirate Pedro are insiders.

The publican kisses Graciela and chats.

Other customers pay respects.

Pirate Pedro fetches a cable from his truck for the music system.

Graciela watches her younger son (twenty-one) complete an application form at the kitchen table. For Graciela this is a rare moment of relaxation. She is content to watch and love. Maternal, she points to an empty box on the form.

I might be watching Bernadette and our eldest boy, Josh. At what age do sons stop bringing home their application forms for Mum's advice? And do mums ever have sufficient energy to stay awake during a film on TV or showing of a DVD? Bernadette and I have been together for nearly thirty years. I don't recall Bernadette ever staying awake through an entire film on television. Graciela slept through three showings of *The Last King of Scotland* last week. Yesterday she nodded off to *Apocalypto*.

I slip out late in the evening to collect a couple of beers from the corner restaurant and leave my jacket on the back of a restaurant chair. I return for it later. The lights are dimmed. A bunch of kids are swilling beer and already midway drunk. One of them demands my nationality. English? To whom do the Malvinas belong? Argentina, right?

I say, 'To those who live there.'

'No, no. The Malvinas are Argentina.'

I reply that Argentina has possessions far more valuable than the islands – the best footballers in the world.

Confrontation evaporates.

Each hour I lie on my bed and do leg lifts. Today I achieve three consecutive series of thirty lifts. While exercising, I cogitate on an article I have been asked to write on the difference between young travellers and oldies. Young travellers journey alone by day and gather in the evening to swap war stories. Oldies enjoy exploring in a group by day with a knowledgeable guide and separate in the evening into couples and foursomes. Arrogant generalisation...

Pepe has visited the barber for a haircut. The result resembles Tierra del Fuego pastures: short and blown tufty by the wind.

Pepe asks if my ankle hurts.

How to differentiate between ache and pain?

Pepe believes in direct action. He wears work boots. He swings his artificial leg and hacks the underside of my foot. 'Does that hurt?'

'No.'

He raps me on the ankle. 'Does that hurt?'

'No.'

'Good,' he says.

I say, 'Sometimes it aches in the night.'

'Of course it does,' says Pepe. 'It rests against hard plaster.'

I feel foolish.

Party time at the Hostel Argentino: Xavier, the oil driller, is barbequing chickens in the yard. We are celebrating the arrival of two Spanish pedal bikers from Valencia. The bikers have ridden the mountain route from Buenos Aires via Bariloche, Monson and Calfate, then across into Chile and back via Porvenir to Rio Grande. Tomorrow they will head for Ushuaia. One is a salesman, early forties, handsome, voluble, lots of charm. The forty-day bike ride makes a great tale for his customers and will boost sales. The second biker is younger by ten years, an odd-job man in the modern sense: basic electrician, basic plumber, painter and decorator, simple carpentry. He is the more thoughtful of the two and talks little. The Spaniards complain of ruthless Argentine truck drivers, of being forced off the road. I prefer a different image: the driver who held me in his arms and called me brother.

My neighbour at table eats two whole chickens. I drink more than one glass of red wine and hop off to bed.

The Spaniards party to five in the morning. They are on the road at seven. Such men were the conquistadors…

The gang have driven me over to the pub for a change of scene. Tierra del Fuego is populated by incomers. Most are men: women take their pick. Three young women sit at the bar. One believes herself too tall. She watches another young woman dressed in a pale beige work-suit play the coquette, displaying her shape, pursing her lips for a kiss from a tall, handsome *novio*. Yet there is a hollow core to her confidence. She wields her beauty, yet knows that she is not beautiful, merely moderately pleasing – condemned to play a different role outside Tierra del Fuego. Perhaps a wallflower…

The tall young woman is envious, yet sees the hollowness.

Pepe has brought a wheelchair. It is a 2008 model drop-head sports-coupé of a chair. I do spins. I weave between the tables in the hotel lounge. I make for the kitchen. The wooden doorsill is a vertical barrier one centimetre in height. Buff! I back up and attack the sill at speed. Double Buff!

Graciela, the ex-future and his daughter (six), schoolteacher Luisa and I spend the weekend in a beachfront cabin on Lake Fagnano, midway between Rio Grande and Ushuaia. Our host is a serial lunatic. As a teenager he rode a 50cc scooter from Buenos Aires to Ushuaia: 3,000 kilometres. Aged forty, he circumnavigated Lake Fagnano solo on a pedalo. The lake fills a narrow trench in the mountains and is 117 kilometres long. It runs west to east. The prevailing wind blasts from west to east. The weather changes in minutes, dead calm to a gale, bright sunshine to driving snow. Little wonder that Roberto Daniel Berbel is known locally as Robo Loco.

White peaks rise above pine forest while the light continually changes on the lake, as does the colour of the water: dark blue, light blue, slate grey, pale smoky grey. Birds of prey spiral leisurely overhead. A brace of duck, feet splayed, skid into land on the dark, silky-surfaced lagoon that lies behind the strip of paddocks along the foreshore. Graciela and Luisa play cards in the cabin. The ex-future tends a meat mountain on the outdoor barbeque while his daughter plays a complicated game with small dolls. I am outdoors in my wheelchair. Graciela has wrapped me in a grey blanket. A continual swell breaks and sucks at the pebble beach. The blanket makes me feel old. I am old. Tough shit…

We sit on solid benches at a solid wooden table in the log cabin. An enormous wood stove warms us. As does red wine. We snack on a sausage or two. Then we eat meat. We eat more meat. Then we seriously eat meat. First comes the thin end of the skirt. Then the middle thickness. Finally the thick end. Finally? A steer has two skirts. We recommence at the thin end of the second skirt – surely cholesterol suicide; though Doctor Pepe claims that Tierra del Fuego meat is cholesterol free because animals have to range across such immense distances in search of fodder. Pepe is a meat producer…

Glutted, we drink more red wine and listen to Robo Loco's guitar, his harmonica and his patter. He possesses all the party tricks and performs them with brilliant élan. The ex-future's daughter is in heaven as he pulls his mouth askew with a long black hair plucked from schoolteacher Luisa's head.

And I am in heaven. I am amongst friends. Robo Loco presents me with a copy of his book recounting the pedalo marathon. The gang adds signatures and comments to the front page. I lie in bed and listen to three sets of gentle snores and worry that the crutches will slip on the tiles when I make the next trip to the bathroom.

We drive back to Rio Grande the following night in heavy snow. The ex-future is a good driver and we are safe in his big double-cab pickup.

Safe? Trucks scare me.

Weird, I will be happy to be back in the Hostel Argentino tucked up in my own bed in Graciela's room with my foot propped up on a stiff pillow.

My own bed, that's the weird bit: pretending to be home because I want so badly to be home with Bernadette and the boys.

I am on television this afternoon. The programme is broadcast live. The compère is a gaucho poet in the true Argentine tradition: early sixties, thin as a stick, white moustache, black Basque beret, silk neck scarf fastened with a silver-gilt brooch. The gaucho poet has been conversing with trees and horses, red wine and cigarettes for fifty years. His voice carries a hoarse rhythm as he talks to the camera of nature's gifts and nature's cruelties, while I cruelly picture bit-part actors in the B-movie westerns of my youth.

An elderly guitarist plays a classical introduction. Later he plays a great tango. Most of the programme is focused on the English writer with the leg in plaster. I worry that I am using the wrong verb tenses.

Later the musician asks for my thoughts on the Malvinas.

Duck and run…

The editor has brought me a CD of my television appearance. I have never watched myself perform in Spanish. My manner is disturbingly familiar. Where have I seen that exaggerated raise of eyebrows, the opening wide of eyes, hands spread to proffer a self-evident truth to a captive audience? The conceit that invests a superior being?

Truth is unavoidable.

We were resident in Cuba in the nineties. The Commandante's four-hour speeches have left their imprint.

Fidel, over the years, became a caricature of Fidel.

I am a caricature of the caricature.

I haven't shaved since the accident. Woolly is the image. Xavier drives me to a front-room hairdresser. The hairdresser is in Spain for three months. Her replacement is an overweight teenager.

Retreating would hurt the girl's feelings and might hurt Xavier's feelings. I recall being equally imprisoned by guilt when visiting historic churches on the southern leg of this journey. Enter during a service; the priest remarks an unfamiliar face. Leave before the service ends and he may obsess into the night: did he fail to save a soul from eternal damnation? Rather than cause such anxiety, I have, in one day, attended three masses, a funeral and an elevation of the Eucharist. How can I now deny a teenage hope-to-be coiffure?

The beard first: the girl approaches with an electric trimmer. Zip and a bald patch marks my right cheek.

I confess to the same error ten years ago when trimming our youngest son's hair. Jed remains unforgiving. I am more liberal. I say, 'That isn't quite what I imagined.'

The girl says, 'This is the first time I've cut a beard.'

Her tone suggests that the blame is mine.

The bald patch is too wide to hide. Shaving my cheeks is the only option. I commandeer the clippers.

The girl is forlorn. I imagine her going on an eating jag. She says, 'Can I cut your hair?'

'A very light trim. Very light,' I insist.

Snip go the scissors. Blood drips from a gash in her palm. She emits a small screech and vanishes in search of a bandage.

Xavier and I muffle hysterical laughter.

Xavier produces a cold beer from his satchel – a true friend.

For his birthday, the ex-future is our guest for lunch at the Hostel Argentino. How to describe an Argentine birthday lunch? Immense heaps of beef, a vast chocolate cake, red wine, innumerable toasts and the Spanish version of 'Happy Birthday'.

A large concrete notice outside a government building on the next block to the Hostel Argentino boasts the legend:

> **GOBIERNO DE TIERRA**
> **DEL FUEGO**
> **ANTARTIDO, E ISLAS**
> **DEL ATLANTICO SUR**

LaLa Land would be more appropriate…

And I have been invited to a televised meeting of academics. Surely the Malvinas/Falklands will be discussed, so I run a practice session with one of the organisers.

My knowledge of Argentina is very limited.

Are people suffering from hunger?

Is the independence and integrity of the judicial system assured?

Is the government clean of corruption?

If not, surely Argentines should have more pressing aims than acquiring a few boggy islands…

I have been uninvited.

I am a manic depressive. I have learnt tricks that snap the mental circling. Ski a black run, reach the bottom, ski it again. An hour and your only worry is whether your legs will hold up. A depression has threatened over the past couple of days. I can't ski. I can't even travel. Morose, I sit with my back against the kitchen stove.

A young doctor and her *novio* present me with CDs of tango and the *Misa Criolla* and a beautifully illustrated edition of the great poem of Argentina's gauchos, *Martin Fierro*. The edition includes the English translation and a dictionary of gaucho slang.

The doctor holds me in her arms while I weep.

Damn these Argentinians. How dare I be depressed? I am so fortunate, so privileged…

Xavier drives us to the Chinese restaurant for prawns at midday. The restaurant is closed. It was closed for lunch last week.

'Chinese work 365 days in the year,' declares Xavier. 'These aren't proper Chinese.'

Observation from the corner by the old iron kitchen range: *Marginales* is the Argentine word for those who were called hippies in my youth. Modern *marginales* carry mobile phones.

The truck ran me down on 7 August. Today is Wednesday, 5 September. Pepe has a steak knife, scissors and newspaper. He bangs my cast. 'Any pain?'

'Not on the broken side,' I reply.

Pepe is uninterested in pain on the unbroken side. He saws the cast, splits it and taps the broken bone. 'Pain?'

'No,' I say.

'Stand,' says Pepe.

I stand.

'Any pain?'

'No,' I say.

Pepe gives me a bear hug. No more cast. He wraps the leg in an elastic bandage. I must walk with the aid of crutches for a while.

I thank him.

Pepe says, 'Thank yourself,' and taps his temple. 'You did the curing. Cure comes from the head.'

If so, Pepe governed my thoughts with his energy and determination. He gave me belief.

How do I feel?

Immensely grateful. Immensely relieved. I have been scared of coming out of this as an invalid and a drag on my beloved wife.

That's enough truth. Anyone for tango?

My healed bone is Pepe's victory, proof that he was correct in his argument with Doctor Lopez. He rewards me with dinner at the Posado de los Sauces, Rio Grande's most expensive restaurant (though I don't see the menu). Food is unquestionably fine. They serve fish. Fresh fish. Fish that has never seen the inside of a freezer!

Pepe orders for me black hake, a south Atlantic fish caught deep on long line. The fish is perfectly grilled, the steamed vegetables are crisp, wine (a ten-year-old red Malbec) is divine.

The guests at other tables?

Estancia owners, visiting foreign businessmen, upper echelon oil executives – a different world from the Hostel Argentino.

Less naturally tanned complexion? Yes, of course.

I walk alone to the bank. The bank is two blocks uphill the far side of the six-lane Avenida San Martin. I use the crutches at the inter-sections and for support while taking a short rest. A security guard beckons me to the head of the queue at the cash machine. From the bank, I take a cab on a shopping spree: two pairs of boxer shorts, shampoo and a couple of throwaway razors.

Happiness is an email from Javier at Dakar Motos reporting the arrival of the Honda in Buenos Aires. What more to write from the kitchen at the Hostel Argentino? This will be my last weekend and I am hosting a thank-you barbeque. Xavier takes me shopping. I suggest ten chickens. Javier says five. These aren't battery-bred half-water English supermarket chickens. These are free-range chickens raised at a Catholic mission outside of town: solid meat, size of a mini-turkey.

Then to the butcher for ten kilos of Tierra del Fuego beef at 1.30 dollars a kilo.

For the ladies I select a kilo of strawberries and fresh cream.

Argentine strawberries are huge.

Argentine apples and pears are the size of a small melon.

Big back home and you eat fruit without taste. Not so in

Argentina. Best apples I have ever tasted. Great pears. Delicious grapes. Superb strawberries.

Each new act of kindness adds to the pain of separation and to the guilt of wishing to be gone. Saturday the Argentine Pumas whip France in the opening match of the Rugby World Cup and Carlos from the Petroleum school drives me to his *novia's* home for beer, tapas and conversation. Graciela cooks a delicious stew of squid and shrimp. Sunday I join in devouring a final meat mountain with the Sunday gang at the ex-future's car port. Mobile-phone *marginales* present me with a freshly crocheted black wool hat.

A final drink at the pub: an oil-company truck driver leans across the table. He is a big man, not yet drunk but getting there: 'You think you understand us, Old Man. You think that we would care for any stranger. No, this was for you, because of you, who you are…'

I pretend to study the drink menu, hand shading my eyes. I will be gone in the morning. How will I cope? And what he says is untrue. Argentinians dream of being tough tango heavyweights. They are real softies and would care for any traveller.

My last night of sleep at the Argentino: soft purrs come from Graciela's bed. I recall the vile headlines in the British yellow press during the Falklands/Malvinas War. *A good Argie is a dead Argie.* Much of the British press is owned by foreigners and tax evaders of very dubious morality. Odd that successive governments should permit such people to manipulate public opinion. Murdoch terrorised Prime Minister Blair. Will Prime Minister Brown, child of the manse, be more courageous?

3
CHILE

My grandson, Charlie-Boo, has been told of the accident. He refers to me now as Grandpa Oops. Grandpa Oops is back on the road – though travelling with crutches. Weight is the enemy – both mine and my backpack. Too undisciplined to diet effectively, I have been ruthless in discarding clothes, shoes, books, even my precious Toughbook laptop (indestructible, but weighed a ton).

Tecni Austral runs a bus service from Rio Grande to Punta Arenas six days a week. The bus leaves in the morning at nine o'clock and arrives at five in the afternoon. The fare is twenty-five dollars. The bus is half empty. A double seat to the rear enables me to prop my feet up.

We climb the last hill before the Chilean border, the hill where the truck ran me down. I am an old familiar to Immigration and Customs at both Argentine and Chilean frontiers – no queues for Grandfather Hoppity-hop, merely congratulations at being mobile.

This is my goodbye to Tierra del Fuego, goodbye to dear friends. The sky is washed in every shade of grey from charcoal to near white. Rain softens the greens and greys of the moors. Hills on the eastern horizon glow topaz blue. The dirt road follows a valley through hills reminiscent of the Scottish borders. Wind and weather have rounded every crest. Burns overflow their banks. The lee side of a hill has collapsed under the weight of rain to leave a curved pink cliff rising from the fallen waves of grassed earth. Fifteen *guanacos* stand on a ridge by the roadside; wild geese face west into the wind;

Hereford cattle face east towards our homeland. Spring approaches: geese pair; freshly sheared sheep cringe beneath low scrub; *gauchos* are bulbous in rain suits worn over puffer jackets and pants. Meeting a truck, the bus driver slows. Not so the truck driver – not so any truck driver. A small drive-on ferry crosses the Straits of Magellan. Sun sneaks between the clouds and transforms the sea into a shimmering sheet of aluminium foil, pale side up.

The bus stops on the same block as the Tourist Bureau (a change bureau operates on the corner). The young lady at the tourist bureau calls Hostel Taty's House at Maipu 1070. Walking the half mile from the Tourist Bureau, I tire on the last block – pain in the ankle and back of the calf.

Hostel owners come in three categories: those who offer the absolute minimum; those who calculate a reasonable norm; a very few who truly care for their guests and add those small touches that make the guest feel at home. Claudia is the best of the third category – vases of dried spring flowers in bedroom and bathroom, scented candles, thick towels…

Claudia warns that restaurants open at eight o'clock. I doze a while before heading up O'Higgins on the hour. Everything is closed. An adolescent mixture of stubbornness and stupidity drives me on. Pain increases. Finally I surrender and retrace my steps. The ankle has disguised itself as a red football. Better to forgo dinner, sprawl in the glory of a warm bed and watch soaps on cable.

PUNTA ARENAS
Tuesday, 11 September

I soak in a hot bath this morning. The ankle is back to normal, back of the calf a little stiff. Breakfast awaits me in the kitchen. Claudia finds me answering mail on the computer in the sitting room.

'You're up early.'

'Quarter past nine?'

'Quarter past eight,' Claudia corrects.

Time in Chile is an hour behind Argentina. No wonder I found restaurants closed last night.

I am impertinent in judging a town on the evidence of a single day. I have hobbled a few blocks, bought tickets for bus and ferry, found a bank that accepts my VISA card (Banco Santander). El Chocolate is a chocolateria, a block from the main square. I sit at a table in the window, sip hot chocolate, people-watch and read the newspaper. The hot chocolate is orgasmic, townsfolk appear happy and busy and better dressed than in Rio Grande.

Evidence of optimism? Trees newly planted in gardens and in the sidewalk (people plant trees because they believe in a future). Freshly dug flower beds are a further sign; builders at work embellishing homes; parks free of rubbish. People want to be here: most people in Rio Grande want to be somewhere else. No building in Rio Grande is worthy of a second look; no one cares. People are proud of Punta Arenas, proud of the architecture. The nineteenth-century founders of the first *estancias* built splendid mansions on the back of a boom in wool. The cathedral is charming. So are the Town Hall and the Officers' Club. Modern domestic architecture is simple and in keeping with the past: clapboard, corrugated pitched roofs, dormer windows, fresh paint. Better yet are avenues of trees, squares shaded by trees, gardens with trees. On this spring day the waters of the Straits of Magellan sparkle blue in sunshine at the south end of every street, the first emerald shoots glow on garden shrubs, roses are in bud; drivers halt to allow me time to cross at intersections. Such acts of courtesy are jewels in an old man's journey. I ask a cab driver where he would eat fish the day before payday. He drives me to the waterfront. Three worn stone steps lead up to a four-table workman's café where a delicious shellfish stew and jug of red wine set me back three dollars.

Thank you, people of Punta Arenas, thank you for a great day.

PUERTO NATALES
Wednesday, 12 September

Late morning and I am one of a dozen passengers riding the bus north from Punta Arenas to Puerto Natales. This is a rolling land of vast haciendas where sheep, freshly shorn, glow white in spring sunshine. Ten or fifteen miles separate each hacienda. Small, white-washed cottages by the roadside signal a dirt track to shearing sheds and the red roofs of the owner or manager's house part hidden by conifers. The land is better cared for than in Argentine Patagonia, grazing improved, fences well maintained. Snowy peaks glitter in the distance. Sad is the sparseness of ancient pines – all that remains of the glorious forest that once cloaked this land.

European settlers decimated the forest. They were less intent (or less successful) in laying waste to the indigenous population. A majority of bus passengers are of mixed race – short in stature, square-bodied, bronze of skin. Country stores are scarce and stock few goods. Passengers carry laden shopping bags. How often do they visit town? I gather courage and talk with a woman across the aisle. A weathered face disguises her age – somewhere between thirty and fifty, features more far-east Asian than Caucasian, faded jeans, cherry-red puffer jacket, home-knitted wool beanie, rough stubby hands folded in her lap. Her husband, a shepherd, earns the minimum basic wage of approximately 240 dollars a month. They have four children: three girls and a boy. One girl and the boy are at high school in Punta Arenas. In term time they live with the woman's sister, an auxiliary (cleaner?) at the hospital. The woman doesn't speak of the other girls.

Late afternoon and pupils from a country primary school board the bus. They talk quietly amongst themselves. A girl sits beside the woman – thus ends our conversation. They leave the bus at the next hacienda. Others drop off in ones and twos. I watch a lone boy, satchel over his shoulder, duck through a fence and trot uphill across a paddock. He is dwarfed by the space. No houses are in sight. How far must he walk? Why do I spoil a good day with unanswerable concerns?

Puerto Natales is the base for tourists exploring the immense forests, granite mountains, glaciers and ice fields that comprise one of the most spectacular wildernesses of the Americas. Puerto Natales is also the port for the ferry that runs a thousand kilometres north through the islands to Puerto Montt. Foreigners and outsiders own most of the businesses. Few locals have capital and banks charge twenty per cent on a business loan or mortgage – surely extortionate in a stable economy with low inflation?

Casa Cecilia is a clean comfortable way station on the tourist route. The owners (Cecilia is Chilean; her husband, Werner, is Swiss) are helpful beyond the call of duty. Werner's bread baked for breakfast is delicious. I circle the main square, drink beer, chat with a portly citizen and am directed to a pleasant restaurant where I order a half-bottle of red and a grilled fillet of hake. Fish is a rarity on Argentine menus: eating fish in the land of beef is unpatriotic.

PUERTO NATALES
Thursday, 13 September

Passengers board the ferry to Puerto Montt this evening at eight o'clock. A tourist with two good legs would spend the day touring the national park, admiring massive trees, gazing at volcanoes, frozen lakes, waterfalls. Unfortunately even the closest highlights are a good walk from the track.

I explore the town on crutches; photograph a couple of cute tin cottages and the church. I walk too far and eat a mediocre lunch in a restaurant packed with locals. Better is a sybaritic chocolateria a block back from the waterfront where I glut on a chocolate brownie served with alcoholic cream and excellent coffee. Better still is the welcome on board the ferry. Our guide for the voyage is a young woman. She shoulders my pack and leads me up the car ramp to a cabin with private bath opposite the lounge restaurant. The cabin is two grades up from that for which I paid! I have four berths to myself, and a large window. Water is piping hot in the shower; the lavatory flushes. To bed early, we sail at dawn.

Friday, 14 September

I am cruising the fjords and channels of southern Chile on a private yacht – so it seems. Off-season and we are twelve tourists on a car and truck ferry with accommodation and crew for 200 passengers. We sail at first light. The ferry creeps between islets, the channel a bare eighty metres wide. Each island is a Japanese garden of rock tufted with bonsai. The shore is as perfect in proportion and differs only in scale. Above tower the mountains. Rock and snow and ice glow in the early sun. The sea is mirror smooth. Duck and moorhens momentarily crease perfect reflections.

Vast meals of adequate quality are served at a cafeteria in the lounge/dining room: breakfast at eight o'clock, lunch at one-thirty, supper at seven-thirty. Cabins vary in price from dormitory to upper-deck swank. Oldies earn a twenty per cent discount. A guide offers a commentary on geography, fauna and flora in Spanish and English. The ferry sails Friday morning. Arrival in Puerto Montt depends on weather, but sometime between midnight, Sunday, and noon on Monday.

Out of season would be best for the mature traveller, or the traveller with a distaste for crowds. I have travelled much of my life; the beauty of these fjords is staggering. As always in Patagonia, the light is extraordinary. Neither house nor other sign of man besmirches the forested shore. Snow peaks tower above the forest. I find a sheltered corner on the upper deck and gaze and gaze and gaze. Our guide seeks me out with a cup of coffee or a titbit. A French scientist fetches me for meals and for films and lectures. Discovering that I am tri-lingual, he has co-opted me as his translator. English infuriates him.

He is insistent on the superiority of French culture and language (he speaks no other), yet carries four CDs of blues, jazz, and The Doors, which he demands the purser play over the speaker system.

Saturday, 15 September

I wipe the condensation from my window and watch a launch chug across the water. It's four a.m., and twenty or so street lights signal habitation. The ferry lies off the one village in 1,000 kilometres, the village after which the ferry is named: Puerto Eden. Fishing for king crab sustains a community of some 100 people. Some are *mestizo* descendants of the original inhabitants. Those 'Indians' also lived from the sea. Women dived naked for molluscs in water a few degrees above freezing while men fished from canoes. Civilisation came to decimate them with disease, despair and alcohol.

I try to imagine the lives of these modern inhabitants for whom the ferry passing twice a week is the sole physical contact with the outside world. Do they watch television, seek relationships on the Internet? Is there a preponderance of men or women? What happens to the children? Where are they schooled? Do a privileged few head north to high school in Puerto Montt – or south to Puerto Natales? How many of those students return? What are the feelings of the parents as they watch the children board the launch? Schooling is the Long Goodbye...

A statue of the Virgin Mary stands on the rocky shore of English Channel. The Virgin protects sailors navigating the currents swirling through the narrows from the open sea. A wrecked Greek sugar ship from the 1920s perches on a rock mid-channel. The wreck is a droll monument to cupidity. The Greek captain loaded a cargo of sugar in Brazil, sold it in Uruguay, then rammed the ship on the rock. He expected the ship to sink. It stuck, balanced on the pinnacle. The captain reported the loss of the ship to the insurers and claimed for the cargo, which he swore had melted into the sea. The insurers enquired as to the whereabouts of the sugar sacks. Had the sacks melted?

The French scientist reports that a friend voyaged on the *Puerto Eden* last year. Rain fell continually: the coast was barely visible. Today the coast glows in sunlight, snow peaks glitter, not a cloud and the slightest puff of wind.

Midday and we face a notoriously stormy sea passage across the Bay of Pain. Twelve hours before we regain shelter. The ferry carries a male medical assistant who issues pills to combat seasickness. Our guide advises us to stay on deck in the open air; should we suffer badly, take to our cabins and lie in the foetal position.

A dozen heifers moo occasionally in an open truck on the upper vehicle deck. Their ancestors came from Herefordshire – as do I. Are they given pills? The ferry edges out from behind the islands. We meet a gentle swell. This is the calmest passage the crew can recall.

Sunday provides a third morning of brilliant sunshine. I share the bridge deck with two University of Cambridge students and a charming Belgian woman. The Belgian scans the sea through binoculars. Both she and one of the students are indefatigable in their search for marine mammals. Whales head their list. One student's parents are immigrants from Japan and own a Japanese restaurant off Piccadilly on Half Moon Street. I have walked past the restaurant, glanced with longing through the window, accepted the financial realities that forbid my entrance. The second student studies physics. He longs to study music.

Later I talk with a young couple from the US. The young man is a maths student at Cambridge. He has a grant to study at Cal Tech over the summer. Maths and physics have always fascinated me: that a mathematician or physicist can have a totally original thought, think where no one has ever thought before.

The maths student should be writing a commentary on an equation. He doesn't understand the equation and doubts that he has the mind for original thought. His girlfriend studies chemistry at Cal Tech. She has forgotten to bring notes for her summer project. Both are deeply depressed. They cling to their open laptops as torpedoed sailors cling to a life raft.

Cloud finally closes in as we sail up the east coast of Chiloe Island. Chiloe suffers or enjoys an average of 300 days of rain each year and we view the coast through a thin drizzle. The Belgian woman and the Cambridge student of Japanese descent are on whale watch (unsuccessful). The student reads the temperature from a large thermometer screwed to the bridge bulkhead: three degrees centigrade above freezing. Good. I have been shivering and feared that I might be sickening for something. Reluctant to desert my two companions, I crunch myself into a corner.

Our last dinner on board and we have entered a war zone. Music is the fuse. The Frenchman is incensed by the non-Japanese Brit student's opinion of the blues. The Frenchman is totally ignorant of the student's opinion. The student is a typical Brit; ten years of school French yet he remains monosyllabic. The Frenchman is typical in loathing the supremacy of the English language. He wishes me to translate his contempt for the Brit student's musical taste and knowledge. I have been translating with good grace for three days. The student of Japanese parentage and I are enjoying our own conversation. The Frenchman departs for bed in a huff. Too bad: he is a nice man, intelligent, though somewhat dogmatic (a quality often apparent within the scientific community). His wife left him a few years back – not for another man. Perhaps the Frenchman's retirement drove her out. No longer a few evenings and weekends: *The full Monté*.

The weather has been exceptional. We dock in Puerto Montt twelve hours ahead of schedule. Disembarkation is after breakfast on Monday morning. We bid our farewells. The Frenchman is cool. The British students are immensely polite. The two students from the US mooch in their private huddle of near despair. I catch a cab to the bus station.

Monday, 17 September

At over half a million acres, Lago Llanquihue is Chile's second largest lake. I am heading for a small town at the head of the lake, Puerto Octay. The road passes through rolling country reminiscent of my own Herefordshire, a country of small paddocks and woodland, of dairy cattle, sheep, fruit trees. Mimosa and daffodils glow in the spring sun. Orchards are pink with blossom, roses and camellias in bud. Early magnolias are already fading. Werner of Casa Cecilia in Puerto Natales has made a reservation for me at Hostel Zapato Amarillo. The owner, another Swiss German, awaits my arrival at Puerto Octay's bus station. Hostel Amarillo (Yellow Boot) comprises a family house, a bunk house and a rental bungalow. The wooden buildings are new and set in a meadow. I am greeted by children, dogs, chickens and a sheep.

Tuesday, 18 September

I am eating proper family breakfast: a family of mother, father and two children. These are the owners and builders of Zapato Amarillo. I have slept in a comfortable bed under a goose-down duvet beside an immaculate bathroom. Everything functions, everything fits, everything is very Swiss: it has been designed and built by a Swiss mechanical engineer. These must be the only doors in Hispanic America that shut with a slight whoosh of expelled air. Breakfast is enormous and frighteningly healthy: fresh baked bread, hand-churned butter, homemade jams, eggs from free-range hens. Dominic, eleven, is an artist. His sister, four, is a minx. I am a boring old man and thoroughly content…

German settlers founded Puerto Octay in 1850 or thereabout. Chile is a Catholic country and the Germans were Catholic – so they claimed. They built Catholic churches in proof of their Catholicism and were rewarded with land grants. Chilean nationality confirmed, they shed their camouflage and built Lutheran churches. With so many churches, what joy to discover that Puerto Octay's one up-market hotel originated as a brothel…

The lakeside Hotel Centinela occupies the tip of the peninsula that shelters the town. The big salon retains the feel of an Austrian turn-of-the-century hunting lodge – monster fireplace, wood panelling and stag heads. Imagine those early Catholic-Lutherans (or Lutheran-Catholics) lolling in leather armchairs round the log fire, meerschaum pipes, pewter tankards, lederhosen that leave the knees bare. Imagine young indigenous girls dressed in dirndls – or did the brothel-owner import plump pseudo-Catholic blondes from Austria?

My hosts at the Yellow Boot have arranged for an elderly gentleman to show me the countryside. He drives an equally elderly eight-seat minibus. We make a fine threesome, creaky but functional. I am in questioning mood. Agricultural land sells for 1,500,000 pesos a hectare – 3,000 dollars. Dairy farming is profitable on farms of a hundred hectares or more. Twenty grand builds a good house such as the Yellow Boot. The monthly minimum wage is around 240 dollars, a wage on which a Buddhist monk would starve. Chile's government is centre left. Last week two government ministers were appointed to the Supreme Court; meanwhile, the non-socialist cardinal officiated at a family memorial Mass for General Pinochet.

My elderly driver follows the lakeshore through country that holds continual reminders of northern Europe: rolling hills, green paddocks, trees, dairy cattle, wooden barns and houses. Away on the lake's east coast, two monster volcanoes dominate the placid waters. Both are capped in snow. Osorno is a perfect cone. Calbuco is a shattered mess.

Spanish Jews who converted to Catholicism in the sixteenth century are known to historians as *conversos*. Lutheran *conversos* founded a tiny village midway down the lake between Puerto Octay and Frutillar. They built the first small church on the landward side of the road; the second some years later exactly opposite. The churches are built of wood. Catholic and Lutheran, they are indistinguishable. We pass a small hillside cemetery shaded by fine trees. Snowdrops and daffodils have spread between the gravestones.

The Catholic church in the English village of Hanley Swan was paid for by my paternal great-grandfather soon after Catholic Emancipation (end of the Persecution). Members of the Church of England immediately built a bigger church with a taller steeple. Their church is short on charm. Ours is pretty; I shall be buried in the graveyard.

Wednesday, 19 September

Forced to travel by bus rather than bike is a prison sentence. I am heading north. Valdivia is today's destination and I have chosen a country bus in preference to the express coach. Such buses give an illusion of freedom. I could get off at any of a hundred halts. I don't through my own choice or through indolence or nervousness at finding myself stranded – or because I am on crutches and fear that my ankle will collapse if I walk too far. I shouldn't complain: I get a pensioner's discount and the view changes.

We travel through a flat, fertile dairy country of green paddocks and woodland. Rain falls steadily. A black-and-white saddleback sow snouts up a patch of mud beside a small hovel. A woman shod in rubber boots and dressed in a torn blue puffer jacket stands outside the hovel and watches the bus go by. A farm track leads to a large farmhouse. We pass more roadside hovels and another track to a substantial house and farm buildings. I would enjoy writing that the bigger the farm, the more vile the hovels. The opposite is true.

The bus heads towards the coast down a river valley between hills planted with eucalyptus. Eucalyptus drains all goodness from the soil; soil becomes friable and is eroded by rain. The ugly scars of this erosion are visible where trees have been felled.

Valdivia is an ugly city in a beautiful location on the delta of two rivers. The city was founded by Spaniards in the sixteenth century and flattened by an earthquake in 1960. What remain of the old are a fine university and a reputation for seafood.

Entering a town by bike, I head for the centre, enquire of locals for a clean family hotel, check comfort and price. On crutches I must consult guidebooks. Airesbuenos International Hostel is recommended. I telephone for a reservation. My room is on the ground floor. Thirty dollars is the most costly of my nights in Chile. Light comes from an energy-saving bulb draped in one of those round Japanese paper shades made in China. The light is too dim for reading anything other than big print. I have to get out of bed to turn the light on or off. The lounge area is a training ground for expeditions to the Antarctic. Backpacker hostels are invariably a rip-off for anything other than a dorm bed. And all the guests are foreigners. Why travel…?

Sadly I have arrived on Chile's national day. Rain falls steadily. Restaurants are closed. Best I can do is a fake Chinese at the city centre shopping mall: barely edible shrimp with bean sprouts and rice.

VALDIVIA
Thursday, 20 September

My room at the Airesbuenos International Hostel faces the main road. Trucks head for market before dawn – old trucks with defective silencers and rattling bodywork. I uncurl from between damp sheets. The electrical wiring to the shower's water heater is lethal. Water dribbles barely warm. Breakfast is powdered coffee, no milk and factory-baked sliced white bread that remains soggy even when toasted.

Rain drizzles from a grey sky. I ride a bus to the waterfront, buy a newspaper, find a café. Divine Italian espresso is the hallmark of Argentina. Southern Chile is Germanic. Some of my best friends are Germans. Germans brew good beer. Coffee? Not that I've noticed…

As to the news, reports of yesterday's celebrations of Chilean Independence predominate. Generals and colonels monopolise the front page. A regiment goose-steps across the next. In turning the pages of the newspaper, I dislodge my crutches. The crutches clatter to the floor. A squall blasts rain against the café window. I am not doing well.

A youngish couple enter the café. By their clothes, I surmise they are middle income. I watch from behind my paper as they peel off raincoats. The woman's coat has a hood. She is fair-haired, clear skin pink this morning from wind and rain. I bid them good morning. The woman asks my nationality. She seems a pleasant woman, friendly and open. Her husband is a notary. They are on holiday from further south. I slip General Pinochet into our conversation. She tells me that foreigners don't understand: Pinochet saved Chile from a Communist Dictatorship; Allende surrounded himself with foreigners, Russians, Cubans, East Germans, all Communists. The woman's husband sits beside her. He withdraws a little as his wife speaks, leaning back to hide his face from his wife while, with his eyes, he begs for understanding of the silence that makes him an accomplice to his wife's opinions. Guilt or embarrassment or generosity makes him insist on paying for my coffee.

I lunch beside the fish market at La Perla del Sur. Paila de Marisco is Chile's national dish, shellfish stew. Good? Yes. Great? No.

Later I discuss General Pinochet with a young man at another café. How can Chileans continue in their allegiance to the good General despite his now-known plundering of the National Exchequer. The young man assures me that some have changed their opinions. However the General's true supporters either ignore the evidence or believe the evidence is fraudulent.

Meanwhile Pinochet remains a *good chap* for some of my fellow Brits.

The rain turns to thin drizzle and I walk (hop) along the waterfront to the fish market. Heaps of monster clams and mussels cover concrete slabs. Cormorants and gulls hop on the parapet and lunge the instant a stallholder turns his back. Yesterday I travelled through mile after mile of eucalyptus plantations. Boatmen tell me that the rivers are polluted by pulp factories.

Two oarsmen scull by in racing shells.

Drizzle turns to rain.

I am cold. My ankle aches. Valdivia is depressing. Or I am depressed by Valdivia.

I might cheer up were the sun out and joyfully optimistic students milled in the streets and cafés. I eat grilled fish for supper and drink an excellent local beer blessed with the Real Ale insignia. Back at the hostel I chat with a bright and funny young American woman from San Francisco teaching English at a Chilean school. Her mother is Mexican. She is familiar with Mexico and Central America. Chile depresses her. The food depresses her – particularly the bread. Her companion is Chinese teaching Mandarin at the same school. The Chinese loathes Chilean food, especially the bread. She complains that bread isn't part of her home diet, yet Chinese bread is infinitely preferable to Chile's variety.

I will travel north to Temuco in the morning.

TEMUCO
Friday, 21 September

I travel by express bus to Temuco. We ride through mile after mile of eucalyptus plantation, trees that destroy the land, food for paper mills that pollute the rivers. Rain dribbles down the windows; visibility is minimal. We stop for a bathroom break. Coffee is a teaspoon of tasteless brown powder stirred in tepid water.

Temuco is an industrial city. It is magnificently ugly. It could win prizes for ugliness. Even the central square is ugly. I have consulted two guidebooks. Both recommend that travellers don't stop. I am here to stay a night in Chile's oldest hotel, the Continental. Established in 1888, my guidebooks report that nothing has changed. I telephoned yesterday for a reservation. No one answered. I sent a fax.

I give my destination to the cab driver at the bus terminal. The cab driver is nonplussed. He radios base to be told that the Continental has been closed for a year. The driver takes me to a modern hotel in the city centre with a thirty-dollar room rate. An elderly woman with a kind face runs reception. I suggest a pensioner's discount and she drops the price to twelve dollars. Next stop, the Tourist Bureau in search of trees...

Chile boasts two of the oldest living tree species in the world. Alerce and Araucaria. Both species will live for two to four thousand years and grow to sixty metres in height. Alerce are the Redwoods of Chile and exceed six metres in girth. Araucaria is the monkey-puzzle tree favoured by Victorian gardeners. I long for giants in their natural habitat.

Crutches forbade me the natural glories surrounding Puerto Natales. Now the Tourist Bureau forbids me the forests of Parque Nacional Conguillio. National Parks are unsuitable for hoppity old men on crutches. Defeated, I book myself a seat on the morning bus for Buenos Aires.

One bright jewel in a rainy day: a charming bandstand.

The best I can do for dinner is vicuña soup.

I talk with three immensely tall Afro-Americans in the hotel's minute lobby. They are pro basketball players on the Temuco team. They hate Temuco. They hate the hotel; they hate the climate; they hate the food.

I lie in bed and wonder where Temuco rates in the pro basketball league.

And I wonder how the rebuild of my little Honda progresses at Dakar Motos in Buenos Aires. Travelling by bus has transformed me into a gloom-laden misery...

Saturday, 22 September

I am crossing South America by coach – eighty dollars from Temuco to Buenos Aires via Neguyen for a fully reclining seat. Mile upon mile of eucalyptus brings me close to tears. Trees are planted in what were rich pasturelands and on hillsides already scarred by soil erosion. We climb into the Andes and finally escape the rain. Eucalyptus gives way to plantations of spruce, more food for paper mills. We emerge from a long tunnel to the fringe of the snowline. The bus stops briefly at a charming mountain village, Lonquiney. This is tourism country, country hotels, bungalows to rent, saddle horses in paddocks and, joy of joy, those familiars of my Scottish childhood, blackface sheep.

Snow-ploughs have left piles of snow along the road edge. The bus slushes through fresh snow. We cross a plain below sun-brilliant peaks. A thin scattering of monkey puzzle trees stands dark in the snow. More trees… Ahead lies the Chilean border post. My crutches earn me sympathy and a place at the head of the queue. I chat with a young Chilean woman studying Hotel Management and Tourism at a college in Buenos Aires. Back in the bus and we drive on through a sparse forest of Araucaria. Dark giants rising from the snow, the trees are splendid here in their natural habitat rather than imprisoned in an English suburban garden.

4
BUENOS AIRES

Buenos Aires is a delightful city of impressive avenues, classic buildings, excellent restaurants and a coffee house at most intersections.
For much of the architecture, imagine central Paris. The Gran Hotel
España is my home from home. The Gran Hotel is not grand. It
does have charm. Half a block off the Avenida de Mayo, it occupies a
small fine *fin de siècle* building with stained glass, a surfeit of marble
and two small, somewhat shuddery elevators. The radiators are hot;
so is the water.

A workman's café is perfect for my first night in the city. One
of a dozen men in their early thirties, bank clerks and insurance
clerks, offers me a stool at their table. The men briefly boast of sexual
exploits before switching to football.

I ask which is most important to an Argentine. Fifty-fifty is the
answer – though one man adds that a football match lasts two hours.

In what condition will I find my Honda? Dakar Motos is a forty-
minute ride on the suburban railway. Champion procrastinator, I
have my beard trimmed first at a barber's palace on the Avenida de
Mayo. In earlier years, the pre-Peron years of affluence, all thirty
chairs would have been occupied while a dozen bootblacks burnished shoes. Only two elderly barbers remain; gold leaf and paintwork peels; mould disfigures mirrors.

I stroll the sidewalk in bright sunlight, buy *La Nacion* at a kiosk,
order coffee and croissant at a coffee house. An elderly tweed-suited
gentleman at the next table enquires my nationality. My first visit?
Do I admire the city?

'So much has changed,' he says. 'In my childhood, every Porteno fancied himself an English gentleman. Peron brought us back to reality. We are working-class Italians.'

Thank you, Italy. Argentina serves the finest coffee in the Americas. Sad that Italy and Argentina are incapable of producing equally fine politicians. Sit at a café, sip coffee and enjoy the illusion of being in a major capital, stable and tranquil. Read the news and reality seeps through. A fresh poll reports that ninety-six per cent of Argentines believe the judicial system corrupt; ninety-eight per cent believe the politicians corrupt. Striking fishermen have blockaded the main fishing port and torched the processing plants. Pickets block highways and close all but one bridge into Uruguay. Why? Because direct action is as Argentine as beefsteak. And because a presidential election approaches. The main candidates are followers of Peron – Peronistas. The official Peronista candidate is the present president's wife. There is an opposition Peronista candidate and there are dissident Peronista candidates. Those of us with memories and an interest in foreign affairs recall Peron as something of a buffoon, a lesser Mussolini, wrecker of the seventh largest economy in the world. Our children know only the stage or film version of *Evita*.

And, yes, the economy once again heads for disaster. The government has been falsifying the inflation figures. A minister has resigned after the discovery of a horde of illicit US dollars hidden in her bathroom. A loyalist union leader's chauffeur is caught on television firing a pistol at supporters of an opposing candidate.

Such details delight the manager of the Gran Hotel España. He practised law before the crash. He says of Argentina: 'Honesty in a politician is a miracle. Only the foolish expect miracles.'

Dakar Motos is in the outer suburb of Florida. Tin and cardboard hovels crowd wasteland along the suburban rail track; beyond rise apartment buildings of a different world where sun shimmers on glass walls and air-conditioners purr. On train and bus, Argentine men invariably offer their seats to women and the elderly – if only

Londoners were as courteous. And Argentines show interest in their fellow passengers. I am asked where I come from. My age? Am I married? Children? What does my family think of my travelling alone and by motorcycle?

I reply, as always, that millions of people ride to work each day. I merely ride further. As to danger, I have met with nothing but kindness: witness Dakar Motos. The owners, Javier and Sandra, have created a haven for foreign bikers. Travellers can work on their bikes, sleep in a bunkroom, camp in the garden. BMWs, KTMs and Africa Twins crowd the workshop. My baby Honda sits on a pedestal minus rear wheel and rear suspension. Javier will have it ready in a week. He assures me that the cost will be reasonable. He is a tall, slim, dark smiling man in his late thirties, jeans and T-shirt, boots. Sandra is a few years younger, equally slim and similarly dressed. Bikes are their passion; every holiday is an expedition.

Ballet and opera are my passions. Buenos Aires has both. I can afford neither and make do with a jazz club at the rear of a high-tech music store. The band is an all-white Brazilian trio playing Portuguese sob music for a fur-coat clientele, cashmere sweaters, up-market perfume, gold-bullion jewellery. The music should be played softly. The trio has discovered mikes.

Better entertainment is a café frequented by Goths. Argentine Goths are divided into tribes and sub-tribes and dissident branches of sub-tribes. All Goths wear black. Serious Goths wear leather knee boots. Less committed sub-tribes wear boots only to mid calf and with canvas uppers. Festooning laces are obligatory.

Seriously committed Goths shave one side of the head and spray the other half in red and silvery-grey streaks. The spray kills all life in the hair. Add a chalked white face, blackened eyes and lips and you have a weird semi-mobile late-teenage corpse.

Multiple silver lip ornaments are common amongst 100 per cent Goth women. How do they kiss? And imagine having to scissor a woman free from a lover's genitalia. However the true Goth shows no interest in sex – nor interest in anything other than his or her appearance. Drink is a single beer split amongst many. Conversation is a short sentence followed by minutes of silence.

Men of an unpainted sub-tribe wear their hair spread in waves down their backs. Once settled, they barely move for fear of disturbing the display. This sub-tribe *is* interested in sex. And there are vivacious sub-tribes, Goths dressed in black but with more in their lives than dressing up. These Goths chatter amongst themselves and even interchange remarks with other sub-tribes. I ask one of the vivacious to explain the classifications. He replies that it is very complicated.

The same is true of Peronistas.

Pepe, the orthopaedic surgeon, is in the city. We were in a cab earlier today on the way to an art exhibition. Pepe insisted I recount every detail of my accident.

'I've heard your jokes,' he said. 'The accident wasn't a joke. Hide from the truth and you store up trouble for yourself.'

Joking is more comfortable than truth: how it is to be hit by three trucks – orthopaedic trucks because my back hasn't hurt since the accident and I was in continual pain for months prior to being hit.

The accident wasn't a joke. I should be dead. That I am alive is almost inexplicable.

I was riding on ice on a dead straight gentle climb, perfect visibility. A driver coming from behind would have seen me from a mile back. I would have been a dot in the road, then a man on a bike and finally a man on a bike travelling at a few kilometres an hour, a biker scrabbling for purchase on the ice with his feet and clearly with minimal control. The truck driver was frightened of losing traction and didn't slow. He sounded his klaxon to warn me to get off the road. I was in panic and attempting to get off the road when he hit me. I heard the plastic above the rear wheel shattering. I remember my shoulder hitting the ice and the black fender above me and knowing that I was about to die. I remember sliding and remember worrying that the truck would crush my chest: that I might live and what a mess that would be for Bernadette. Something gripped behind my right knee. Whatever held me snapped and I slid to the left with the wheels now directly behind my skull. The truck slid and slid and I kept thinking why doesn't the driver brake? Why doesn't he slow? I knew as we slid that I would feel the wheels press against the back of my head. There would be a few seconds of sliding with the tyre pressing. I was fully conscious and knew that I would feel it all happen quite slowly and I knew that I would be aware all the time of what was happening until the tyres finally mounted up over my skull and crushed it. The truck's trailer slewed off the road. The rear wheels sunk through the snow into the ditch and the truck stopped. Two electrical cables to the klaxon saved me. The klaxon was behind my knee. The klaxon mounts snapped. The cables held.

I began to shake as I recounted this to Pepe. I had to ask the cab driver to stop and I threw up in the gutter. I have been feeling increasingly shaky as I write. I suppose that I am suffering delayed shock … And being alone now, no longer with Graciela and the guys at the Hostel Argentino, I don't have to maintain an act. The tough upper-lip Brit…

Fortunately I have family in the city to proffer emotional shelter, Anglo–Argentine cousins of my generation. Tony is the elder. A bluff colonial Brit of the old school, rancher and polo player, he is also a prize-winning naval historian. Published by Chatham House, his *Nelson's Favourite* is meticulously researched and beautifully written. In my dotage, I will take my autographed copy down from the shelf and stroke the cover as book lovers do, and think myself privileged to have known the author.

Tony's younger brother, Brian and his wife, Carmen, emailed me after the accident, worrying and fussing, wanting me to stay at their home while I healed, be checked over by Buenos Aires doctors. They hold family dinners most Thursdays at their town house. Twelve of us sit at a square table: my cousin and his wife, their daughter and two sons, the sons' wives and a blonde English girl for whom statuesque or trouble are equally accurate descriptions – though trouble is paramount.

Calle Florida is Buenos Aires´ main shopping street. Top-end shops specialise in smart country clothes for people who never visit the country: Mid-market Suburban Golf Club smart. I buy a denim shirt to wear at Javier's and Sandra's Saturday *assado*. Mostly I feel a fraud in the company of fellow bikers. Real bikers don't ride baby Hondas.

An Argentine biker, early forties, fair-haired and heavy, comments on my accident. Supporter of the Military, he is a man of strong views. Everything has gone to hell since the return to democracy. Kids lack discipline. They don't work. They don't study. They drink, fuck, take dope. Parents are as bad, lazy, always expecting a handout. I met a Texan biker of similar views in Dallas last year. I listen in silence, drink red wine, eat meat and hold my peace…

A neat, slim East German in his thirties is the only other foreigner present. A computer engineer, he works as a consultant for a couple of years, then wanders Latin America for a year on a big BMW. Friends back home think him crazy to forego all that money he could be earning and hoarding in the bank. Ming, who I rode with for a while through Colombia and Peru last year, would understand; Ming was on a runner from Hewlett Packard. And there was the Pole I met in Porto Bello, Panama. The Pole was director of a software company in Boston, Mass. He spotted a FOR SALE sign on a small sailboat while having lunch with a client in a restaurant overlooking a marina. He walked down to the marina after lunch, bought the sailboat and never returned to the office.

What do these men have in common?

High-earning capacity and discovery that money isn't a sufficient goal. Nor is it a satisfactory foundation for society: there has to be more. The East German talks of social morality while I wonder why I haven't pressed Javier to have the Honda ready.

I am too settled at the Gran Hotel España, too comfortable within a protective routine: breakfast at a corner café on the Avenida de Mayo, work in an Internet café with helpful staff, lunch of hot and sour soup at a cheap Chinese restaurant with a glass of red wine from a bottle the waiter keeps for me on a shelf behind the cash register; an ankle-testing stroll on crutches in the afternoons, perhaps a museum; more work followed by a cinema and late meal at the workman's café; once or twice a week a family lunch or dinner.

I have been avoiding newspapers for the past few days. Local politics is too depressing. Only a miracle can stop the present president's wife becoming Argentina's next president. A weekend opinion poll reports that the two greatest concerns of the voters are economic instability and corruption. The same poll reports that only 2.7 per cent of the electorate will vote for the president's wife believing in her honesty. Meanwhile newspapers report that nearly two billion US dollars has been spent by the president without parliamentary permission or oversight. Much of the funds are reputed (by the newspapers) to have been channelled through the minister closest to the president, a Senor de Vido: thus a common joke that Argentina is a *nacion devido*. I, a foreigner, have no reason to believe the reports are other than scurrilous.

A younger cousin in government service is entrusted with the integrity of the coming elections. Government salaries are small by any standard; he is a highly qualified lawyer and would be a high earner in the private sector. His reasoning: that a better future demands that people of integrity serve the country. Integrity is both admirable and dangerous.

I have enjoyed a celebratory lunch of *Callos a la Madrilena* and a big glass of excellent Malbec in the beautiful dining room at the Club España. The celebration? I have sorted all the photographs of last year's journey and sent those that are relevant to my publisher. I have completed the final editing on a piece for Elli Cobb at *Lonely Planet* for an anthology to be published in August and I have emailed my column. I expect to see a halo when looking in the mirror.

And Javier has left a message that the Honda is ready. I have run out of excuses for further delay.

Once more riding the suburban train to Florida: I bring a slab of beef and bottles of wine. Javier collects me at the station. A rainy lunch hour in the suburbs offers safety for my first ride since the smash. The butt-ends of my crutches fit in a plastic cup mounted on the rear chassis; bungee rubbers hold the crutches upright against the rear carrier. Three kicks and the engine starts. I creep down almost deserted streets. How do I feel? Too nervous to ride to the city centre … Better wait for Sunday midday when traffic will be minimal, truck traffic non-existent. How to explain to Javier without being thought a coward?

He waits on the sidewalk. Sandra, fearless Amazon, sits astride a new trail bike.

'How did it go?'

'Great,' I say.

Actual cost of repairs is ridiculously small. Such is the advantage of riding a small bike manufactured within the South American Customs Union. Spares are available…

Add Javier's and Sandra's generosity and I am a very fortunate old man.

Writing novels, my characters suffered. Reporting is more dangerous. I must raise my own head above the parapet. In writing of family what do I include? What do I exclude?

My cousins, Carmen and Brian, give a small farewell-to-Buenos-Aires dinner for me. I am deeply touched that Tony comes. He is not well and climbing the three flights of the circular stairway to the living room demands great determination. A third brother, Robin, is invited for the first time in decades. My presence is an attempt at healing a family rift caused by Robin's support for the Military dictatorship of the eighties. A butler hovers at the dinner table, cutlery gleams, great bowls of flowers on the sideboard, light limpid on the roof garden – Anglo-Argentines at ease, so civilised, so comfortable, so secure.

I am discussing film with Brian's and Carmen's daughter and miss the catalyst to war.

'You are a disgrace,' Brian storms at his brother, Robin. 'You disgraced the family. Never will you enter this house again.'

Robin's wife sits stone-faced.

Such is the aftermath of Argentina's dictatorship, even for the financially secure: families sundered, 30,000 disappeared, self-righteous murderers and torturers at ease in the neighbourhood café, suspicion, shame…

Today, Sunday, I must ride the bike back from Dakar Motos to the city centre. The autopista scares me. I am scared of a truck or a car smashing into my rear. Rain threatens which doesn't help. I imagine slippery road surfaces and being unable to see clearly through fogged spectacles.

I take the metro and suburban train out to Florida. Eight of us eat a great *assado* in the workshop at Dakar Motos. The meat is cooked by Javier. Preparing the salad is more time consuming – women's work, no applause.

An Argentine rose grower drives us to the pizza parlour to watch the England–France rugby match on television. The rose grower helps run his family's nursery in Ecuador. He hopes to remain a biker but carries a thick scent of inevitable marriage, four wheels, four kids, an expanding paunch and executive desk.

The rugby football match is a breath-taker right to the final whistle.

Lots of hugs and I saddle up and head for the city.

Clouds have cleared. Evening sunshine glints on wet tar. Drivers weave lane to lane on the autopista, overtake on the inside, flash lights to express impatience and ill temper.

I reach the Avenida de Mayo. The Gran Hotel España is one block off to the left. I park on the sidewalk, take the elevator, lie on my bed. Only 40,000 kilometres to New York. My hand shakes as I pick up the telephone and dial Dakar Motos to thank Sandra and Javier, two more in my Pantheon of Argentine saints…

I drop by the Internet café to say goodbye. The manager has prepared three opera CDs as a farewell gift.

BUENOS AIRES
Monday, 15 October

The great ride begins: my destination, Cousin Carmen's hacienda in Uruguay. I am up at dawn, shower, pack, load the bike, bid farewell to the staff at the Gran Hotel España. Full of confidence, I ride down to the ferry port, clear Immigration and wait to board the ferry. A junior Customs officer inspects my documents. The documents are photocopies. They are accompanied by an official statement that the originals were eaten by sheep in Tierra del Fuego. The statement is signed by a senior Argentine police officer with a sense of humour and decorated with a splendid variety of stamps. Unfortunately the dates on the statement and in my passport differ. The bike has over-stayed its welcome by eight days. Today is a national holiday. The Customs officer's superior is away. Government offices are closed. I ride back to the Hotel España. The manager giggles happily as I drag my gear to the elevator. I call Carmen and Brian that I will be a couple of days late for dinner.

BUENOS AIRES
Tuesday, 16 October

Foreigners travel in terror of Hispanic American officialdom. The section head at the Customs office is Maria de Angeles, a woman of good looks, and amiable disposition. She listens patiently to my tale of woe, admires my police statement, even adds a few stamps – and composes a partially true but legally acceptable explanation for my oversight. I sign a dossier in three directions. Maria de Angeles permits me to kiss her hand. I am free to leave Argentina.

TO URUGUAY
Wednesday, 17 October

The ferry company, Buquebus, runs fast boats and slow boats across the River Plate to Uruguay. I choose the slow boat to Colonia. The fare including the Baby Honda is forty-eight dollars. New and gleaming apartment buildings dominate the Buenos Aires waterfront. Most developers and apartment owners are foreign. Few Argentines can afford the prices. Of those that can, few would risk their savings within Argentina. Mortgages? In pesos? Don't be silly. The president has announced a ceiling on bank rates. The ceiling is ten per cent below the true rate of inflation. Banks aren't lending. Argentines hold their breath, close their ears and eyes and await disaster.

5

URUGUAY

For Brits the Thames is a major river. For South Americans it would seem little more than a small stream. The river crossing from Buenos Aires to Colonia is a three-hour voyage. The upper deck saloon on the ferry has comfortable chairs and splendid views of the Rio Plato. I sit beside a plump lady in her eighties, black silk dress with a white lace V, blued hair piled high. She is visiting a friend in Montevideo. The friend is frail and in her early nineties. My companion celebrated a replacement hip last year by touring much of Europe. She was four years old when her father and mother emigrated to Argentina. In her father's youth the family village was part of the Austro-Hungarian Empire. It became Italian after the First World War, Yugoslav after the Second World War. Now it is Slovenia and she travels abroad on a EU passport.

Her eldest son's daughter, twenty-three, had an emergency operation last week. My companion telephoned her granddaughter this morning.

Her son answered the telephone. Her granddaughter was resting.

'I'll wait,' she said.

Her son put down the telephone.

He hasn't spoken to his mother in nine years.

She doesn't know why.

There was no fight, no argument. He simply ceased talking to her.

Why are we so cruel?

The Uruguayan river coast is gentle, no distant mountains. Colonia is equally gentle. The heart of the town is humble Hispanic colonial:

small whitewashed houses, cobbled streets, shaded squares. Cars queue in three lines. I complete an Immigration fiche. A Uruguayan Customs officer rips off the original, hands me the copy and waves me through. I suspect that I should say, 'Wait a minute. Don't I need my passport stamped or register the temporary import of the Honda?'

What will happen when I try to leave Uruguay?

Weren't my difficulties in leaving Argentina sufficient?

Two tour coaches follow me out of Colonia. Fearful, I watch them in the mirror and have to break hard to avoid running a red light. Out of town a straight highway shaded by palm trees flows over gentle hills. I slow and ease on to the hard shoulder. The coach drivers wave as they swish by.

Carmen's *estancia* is 360 kilometres north across a wispy pampas of smooth slopes and dips dotted with groves of shade trees. Small birds with black plumage feed on the verge; eared-doves abound, coveys of partridge. Cows are mostly white-faced Herefords. Country roads are mostly straight; some stretches, the tar is beginning to peel. Truck drivers are courteous and the few cars are driven sensibly. Solitary horsemen raise a hand in salutation. The sun shines – perfect biker weather. My confidence seeps back. I edge the speed up to ninety kilometres per hour. The final ten kilometres are dirt. My tyres are new knobblies and the Honda holds rock steady.

An avenue of tall eucalyptus throws bars of shadow across the approach to Estancia Los Tajamares. Breeze-fluffed ostriches watch as I turn down the farm track between fenced paddocks. The modern house is low and ochre. Floribunda roses and lavender scent the evening. Lawns surround a small swimming pool. Sunset paints in shimmering orange two ponds in a dip below a hibiscus hedge. Two Alsatians and a dappled gun dog bark greetings. A man in a beret and black work trousers gathered at the ankle introduces himself as Rafael and reports that my cousins are out walking. I dump my bags in an open-plan living space. Hip-high cupboards and a rack for wine glasses divide a big kitchen from the dining area. Sofas and armchairs face an open fire of smouldering logs.

A roofed area the pool-end of the house is open at both sides to channel the breeze. Rafael has lit charcoal in an oven built into the end wall. The dogs start up a racket. Brian and Carmen come strolling down the track. Youngest of the brothers, Brian is my junior by nearly twenty years. Carmen is younger. Dressed in soft browns and fawns, they seem to me very small in the vastness of the pampas – babes out of the wood. Yet if South America's beef industry has a royal family, they are it. Carmen's paternal great-grandfather founded Uruguay's Fray Bentos canning industry in the 1860s. Brian's maternal great-grandfather shipped the first frozen beef from Argentina to England in the 1880s.

Six of us eat pizzas baked in the wood oven. Rafael is gardener and handyman. His partner, Sylvia, cooks and cares for the house. The *estancia* gaucho, Trinidad, is mid-forties, a shy man given to few words. I have ridden a full day and surmounted the fear barrier; the wine is excellent; I feel great.

ESTANCIA LOS TAJAMARES
Thursday, 18 October

Trinidad is saddling his horse. He wishes me good morning – nothing more – tone little above a whisper. Even his smile is quiet, his face dark and grooved by wind and sun. Unmarried, he lives in a room behind the hacienda and takes his evening meal with Sylvia and Rafael. I wonder that one man on horseback can manage more than a thousand acres of pasture. The acreage is unimportant. Important is the number of cows.

Carmen's elder sister, Cecilia, inherited an equal acreage with the original homestead of Las Canadas at its centre. The homestead is a repository of Uruguay's history with family portraits numbering a president and Uruguay's great poet laureate, Juan Zorrilla de San Martin. Furniture is polished wood, comfortably battered leather chairs and sofas, old-fashioned bathtubs. While Carmen talks with the staff, I explore the outbuildings and discover a model-A Ford on flat tyres.

The *estancia* is run as a tourist operation. Cecilia provides sufficient horses to mount a cavalry regiment, swimming in a spring-fed pond, traditional country meals cooked in a wood oven and on a wood stove or outdoors on the parrilla. Be a gaucho for a week, learn to spin the *estancia*'s wool, whitewash a wall or paint a picture. Seventy euros *per diem* is cheap for the privilege of sharing in Uruguay's past. Go elsewhere should you desire air-conditioning, television and fast food.

The closest railway station to the *estancias* of Los Tajamares and Las Canadas is at the township of France. France is not very big. Don't tell the French. We are touring the family's holdings by car. Carmen is at the wheel. We stop on a ridge and look down over paddocks and through trees to a pristine lake of brilliant blue. Sheep float in the water. I wonder whether I am in Heaven or hallucinating.

Carmen drives on down the dirt road and through the trees. The lake is a deep carpet of blue flowers. A slight breeze stirs the surface. White woolly sheep munch happily.

ESTANCIA LOS TAJAMARES
Friday, 19 October

I have a touch of bronchitis. My bedroom windows open to a shaded terrace and the lawn. From my bed, I watch tiny hummingbirds dip their beaks in citrus blossoms. A bird with a yellow breast finds a worm in the lawn. A small white bird sits on a fence post. Vast open paddocks stretch beyond the fence to the distant horizon. Carmen chides me for not taking care of myself. Brian pampers me with Vitamin C. Silvia heats water and I sit at the kitchen table with a towel over my head and inhale the steam. Bronchitis doesn't feel so bad in Paradise.

ESTANCIA LOS TAJAMARES
Saturday, 20 October

Brian and Carmen have departed for the vet in Montevideo with a very small, very sick miniature Yorkshire terrier. The dog belongs to their daughters. Brian and Carmen care for it. We have a Border terrier at home that belongs to our two sons. Bernadette cares for it.

A covey of five partridge peck the far side of the garden fence. Carmen should plant a pear tree. Coughing hurts. My nose runs. So do my eyes. I sit with a roll of lavatory paper in my lap and watch the final of the Rugby World Cup on satellite television. The players are obscenely fit. I drink vast amounts of ascorbic acid, inhale water vapour with my head under a towel; the steam eases my chest.

LOS TAJAMARES
Sunday, 21 October

Rain falls much of the day. I have been working on the Internet with Clare at The Friday Project. Clare is copy-editing my first travel book due for publication next March. Extraordinary to communicate with someone in London while on a South American *estancia*, some fifty miles from the nearest small town. The electricity cuts out occasionally and I lose the satellite connection. Clare's comments on various chapters get lost in the ether.

A glass door opens from the study on to a terrace. The dogs sit on the terrace and watch me type. The dogs want me to take them for a walk and try to make me feel guilty. I already feel guilty at staying so many days at Los Tajamares. Carmen called Sylvia and Raffa this morning with orders that I wasn't to leave until I felt absolutely fit. Old men seldom feel absolutely fit; I would be here forever. I do the steam and towel routine, drink ascorbic acid, and try not to cough. Sylvia fusses, prepares coffee and cooks too much lunch. As a cook, she is great taster and complains that her already ample butt spreads the more she cooks. I suggest that a poached egg would be perfect for dinner. She seems disappointed.

LOS TAJAMARES
Monday, 22 October

Five ostriches stalk past the house and down the slope towards the two ponds. Camera ready, I wait for them to look in my direction. I whistle and shout. Shouting makes me cough and the ostriches pay no attention. I curse them for being snobs. Long necks, they would be easy victims of the guillotine.

Back in the kitchen I drape a towel over my head and inhale steam – and recall that ostriches are reputed to bury their heads in the sand. Communication between my publisher's server and Hotmail remains somewhat haphazard. Some emails have been delayed a day, few come in the order in which they were posted. Pray God the final chapters come through. I am determined to leave for Brazil tomorrow.

The book and the emails contain many dangerous words. To list a few: Bush, Blair, terrorist, liars, torture, Halliburton, corruption. Clare and I suspect that *they* are reading our mail. I have advised Clare to put a couple of bolsters in the bed and sleep on the floor for a while – better yet, move in with an elderly paid-up member of the Tory party with an annual subscription to the *Daily Telegraph*.

While waiting for mail from Clare, I skim the news. DynCorp (*We serve to make the World a better place*) is a splendid US corporation, very similar to Halliburton. DynCorp is training the Iraqi police. Keeping records is an essential part of police work. DynCorp is unable to produce records for 1.2 billion US dollars of government funds.

Nor can DynCorp explain why it built an Olympic-sized swimming pool in Iraq and purchased a bunch of top of the line executive trailers – you know, those vast lush bedmobiles movie stars cavort in on location. DynCorp also train the Afghan police. Both Afghan and Iraqi police are notoriously corrupt – DynCorp must feel right at home. And DynCorp runs the anti-cocaine aerial spraying in Colombia, another nice little earner. Over the past twelve months DynCorp shares have fluctuated between ten and fifteen dollars. If the president and board bought and sold at the correct moment, they should be wealthy. Perhaps they can stop mislaying government funds.

TO BRAZIL
Tuesday, 23 October

I slept well. My chest feels easier. I wrap up well in jerseys and leather bomber jacket and persuade Raffa to release the Honda from the locked garage. The bike starts. Dogs bark and gambol and try eating my hand. I kiss Silvia and Raffa goodbye and head down the grass track to the dirt road. At last I am free of the glorious comforts of Los Tajamares.

I am Latin in that I share the importance given to a wider kinship. Brian and Carmen are cousins at three or four generations' distance. I treasure our relationship. And I hate them. I hate them because I will miss them and suffer year by year the separation of continents. Hopefully their young and mine will meet and discover this same sense of mutual belonging.

A good road with few cars or trucks runs straight north to Brazil across gently undulating country. I rode south last year through Peru and Bolivia. Rubbish littered the landscape, lay heaped beside the roads and surrounded every town. Uruguay is clean. Expanding forestry is the tragedy – the dreaded Australian eucalyptus, devourer of soil, harbinger of erosion. I inhale their scent carefully for fear of irritating my lungs. A lone white heron watches me from a creek. Traffic cones narrow the road on the outskirts of the frontier town of Santo Do Livramento.

Uruguayan cops wave me through a barrier. How could I tell that I had entered Brazil? I spend the next three hours hunting Immigration and Customs while a team of single-seat planes do aerobatics overhead. Drivers watch the planes in preference to the road. All directions given me lead to a main road closed for a fiesta. Finally I discover Uruguayan Customs and Immigration back behind the original barrier. Brazilian Immigration is thirty blocks on into town. Customs is five kilometres out of town.

6

BRAZIL

Brazilian Customs officers are similar to my wife in doubting my ability to enter correct information on a government form. The Customs officers at Santo Do Livramento do the writing. The head man speaks good Spanish and is an Anglophile. His daughter stayed six weeks in Cambridge, England, on a language course and found the English kind and more sincere than Brazilians, though much less outgoing. She commented that kissing is a commonplace greeting between Brazilians; the English shake hands.

The head man adds that Brits are invariably polite while people from the US are rude and arrogant.

I counter that he has been lucky in the Brits he's met and unlucky in North Americans.

He condemns Argentines as equally rude and arrogant: Argentines believe they *are* the best while Brazilians are always *trying* to come first.

With much laughter, the Customs officers recommend a Mama Esperanza as the best hotel. I retort that I am too old to harbour sexual *esperanzas*. A room in a central hotel costs twenty-seven dollars; the bedspread is dirty and the shower tray overflows; long hair, presumably female, blocks the outflow. Future travellers should follow the Customs officers' advice.

In the lobby I chat with a Spanish-speaking overweight Brazilian in a beige linen suit. He owns a small factory the Uruguayan side of town. He complains that the government in Uruguay pays a subsistence benefit to the unemployed. Pay double the unemployment benefit or Uruguayans won't work. Double is 400 dollars a month. The Brazilian factory owner denounces Uruguayans for their greed.

TOWARDS PORTO ALEGRE
Wednesday, 24 October

I wake in a new country. The bedspread smells. So does the carpet. I wear sandals to the bathroom. Complimentary breakfast is a stale pastry and powdered coffee. Only one ATM machine in town accepts foreign plastic. I slide my card into the slot. The machine spits it out. Panic!

A lady bank clerk reports that the machine is doing something to itself. The machine continues doing things to itself for an hour. Meanwhile I search unsuccessfully for a bookshop that stocks road maps. Finally the ATM relents and I ride out of town. Most travellers head for the coast. I prefer to avoid the tourist route by travelling across Brazil's heartland to visit Brasilia before heading west to Porto Velho on the Madeira River.

First impression, Brazil countryside is less tidy than Uruguay. Even those privileged Uruguayans who own vast acreages are aware that theirs is a small country and they husband every morsel. Brazil is vast; ten acres here or there is unimportant. Argentina is similar – so is much of the US.

I stop at a petrol station a short way out of town and ask a smartly dressed woman in a shiny off-roader for advice on which road to take to Brasilia. Head directly east to the coast, she advises. Southern Brazil is poor and uninteresting. The coast is rich. I will enjoy the coast. The roads are good. I can ride the littoral all the way north to São Paulo before heading inland to Brasilia.

I stop at a Federal Police post. Which road do they recommend? Head directly east to the coast.

Stubborn, I turn north at a town called Bage.

The road crosses hills of dry scrub and stunted trees. Every mile or so an optimist has tilled a small patch of dry earth. Stones are the only crop.

An iguana scurries across the road. An hour later a second iguana scurries across the road. Both iguanas cross left to right. Is this significant?

Meanwhile the road continues over dry hills, no clouds, harsh sun, immense distances – 100 kilometres to get anywhere. Get to anywhere and it might as well be nowhere – unless a gypsum mine talcum-powdering the landscape excites you. How will I cope with the mammoth ride from Brasilia to Manaus and on across the Amazon forest to Venezuela – 5,000 kilometres?

The road climbs a ridge. The view from the crest is spectacular – though similar to the views that depressed me at the ten previous crests. A flashback to a crystal dawn in Mexico last year has wrought the miracle: riding the Pacific coast, surf bursting on empty beaches, scent of frangipani. Suddenly I am in tune with the country and the road and the bike. The few trucks are harmless, travelling at approximately my speed. A side turning promises a town, food, perhaps a cold beer.

The town is three hovels and a petrol station with an attached restaurant. A dilapidated notice advertises the restaurant for sale. The waiter has the charm of a concentration camp guard. The menu offers steak with an egg or steak without an egg. Vegetables?

No.

Rice?

No.

Beans?

No.

And no beer.

The steak is gristle. The egg is edible. Bottled water is warm with a rusty cap.

Back to the main road and more dry hills until the East-West highway to Porto Alegre. The country is instantly greener with vast fields of wheat and rice interspersed with equally vast cattle paddocks, timber plantations along the hills, grain silos as dominant as Apollo missiles. Shameful that people suffer hunger amongst such agricultural plenty.

Two iguanas today and a lone white heron yesterday; now a second heron rises from a pond below the highway and flies very slowly across a patch of marsh. A billboard advertises Hampshire Down sheep for sale and I have ridden 400 kilometres…

Minas do Leão is a small clean town 130 kilometres inland from the coast. A small park is pretty. The architecture is nothing. I find a clean hotel with parking, big towels, hot water and a comfortable mattress. Pricing a country takes a few days. I paid twenty-seven dollars last night. I pay seventeen tonight. Dinner is chicken disaster.

I try to converse with other guests. I have been assured countless times that speaking Spanish will enable me to get by in Brazil. Yes, at grunt level. I want conversation.

LITTORAL
Thursday, 25 October

On the road early and ride for two hours before hitting a six-lane highway bypassing Porto Alegre. The highway runs for forty kilometres up the littoral before degenerating into a federal government project, kilometre after kilometre, diversion following diversion. Laden trucks bull their way past. A long stretch follows the landward side of a lagoon. Precipitous hills close in on the highway; the hills accelerate the on-shore wind off the lagoon where twin lines of giant aliens disguised as wind turbines stand sentry. Sit upright in the saddle and the headwind cuts my speed by half; crouching low over the petrol tank is exhausting and gives me a bellyache.

The lagoon ends and the highway draws close to the shore. At last the wonderful beaches of Brazil – though barely visible beyond the chaotic sprawl of high rise apartment buildings, warehouses, car lots and petrol stations, slow fast-food outlets cloaked in construction dust, manufacturers of concrete beams and conduit.

Of what am I reminded? The worst of the Costa Brava.

A restaurant on the banks of a small artificial lake advertises fruit of the sea.

Parked cars and half the tables occupied is encouraging. I order a cold beer and the eleven-dollar *completo*. I would get into a conversation anywhere but Brazil. Here even eavesdropping is unproductive. As to food: tasteless black bean sludge; tasteless wet shrimp sludge; a tasteless sludge that presumably contains fish; tasteless semi-dry crab sludge; three fried minnows – two of which are excellent while the third is disgusting; soggy fried potatoes; salad of exhausted lettuce; edible rice.

Clouds gather while I shunt unwanted food round my plate. Ride an hour and the hills draw ever closer to the sea. A low retaining wall separates the road from the beach. The beach is golden sand, perfect to photograph. My camera batteries are flat. A light rain falls steadily and steadily…

Dusk draws in as I ride into a small town. I search the coastal side of the highway for a hotel. Houses are small and neat and long established. Open skiffs stir tiredly at a fisherman's quay beside a Cooperative's cold store. The scent of wet sawdust drifts from a boatyard where a carvel-planked fishing boat sits on a cradle above the slipway. Shutters close a sidewalk café. The few people on the street are reminders of peasant Portugal or southern Italy. Strangers are presumed either criminal or perverts. Hotels? None. I must cross the highway to the new town.

The hotel is on a dirt parking lot. A room with a highway view costs seven dollars paid in advance. A padlock serves for the smashed door lock. One naked light bulb hangs from the ceiling; the switch is by the door. A thin nylon sheet covers a spiky mattress. Squashed mosquitoes spatter the walls. Dirt rims the shower tray. Light two anti-bug incense coils, spray the bed with insecticide and pray. Dinner downstairs is inedible steak, egg fried in grease, untrustworthy salad. Brazil can only improve…

CURITIBA
Friday, 26 October

A four-lane highway climbs inland through a lush landscape of dairy farms and forest. The air is fresh and sparkling. I fill up with petrol that contains an additive. The bike loves the petrol. We whizz up steep inclines. The land flattens on the approach to Curitiba, capital of Paraná Province. I stop at a bank in hope of an obliging ATM. Whoever did the welding for Dakar Motos welded the bike's side stand at the wrong angle and I don't have sufficient strength, when astride the saddle, to raise the bike on the main stand. I try and fall and break the camera – my fault for carrying it in the side pocket of my cargo pants.

Gleeful apprentice mechanics at a Honda showroom service the bike in their lunch hour. They replace the stand at cost and charge three dollars for the oil. Such kindness restores enthusiasm. I determine to love Brazil.

I ride to the city's historic quarter only to be disappointed by a few blocks of nineteenth-century pretty. The rest of the city is highrise. I don't like cities. I go up to London on the early morning train for a three-day visit and invariably catch the afternoon train home. So why am I staying in Curitiba? I try talking with a man at the café where I drink coffee and soda water. We soon give up on the attempt.

Brazilians, surrounded by Spanish speakers, have determined to resist the slightest encroachment. And, if I can't communicate, why am I in Brazil? Because I want to see Brasilia and cross the Amazon forest.

The highway to Brasilia runs north from Ponta Grossa, the self-styled *Princesa dos Campos* – Princess of the Fields. This upland countryside is breathtaking. Imagine the perfect English landscape of rolling hills, fields and woodland. Multiply by ten the size of the fields and paddocks and woodland; multiply by ten the height of contours. Wheat glows gold in late afternoon sunshine as I approach the town. New factories and warehouses and granaries abound on the outskirts – all financed by agricultural wealth.

The town is an unplanned hotchpotch of modern bungalows and tower blocks of negligible architectural merit. Sidewalks are pretty: black sets inlaid with white or white sets inlaid with black. I find a fifteen-dollar room with a good mattress and excellent towels. The Internet is free in an air-conditioned lobby. I have twenty-eight emails, one from the Honda apprentices with an attached photograph – great kids. And Bernadette sends love and encouragement and news of our boys. The rest are queries from the publisher and include final proofs that require immediate study. I shall be here tomorrow. The receptionist recommends a restaurant two blocks from the hotel. The menu offers steak with an egg or steak without an egg. The egg is edible.

PONTA GROSSA
Saturday, 27 October

I was up in the night with bad cramps in my thighs. A white-jacketed expert at a homeopathic store prescribes quinine (one pill to be taken before bed), while a regular pharmacist fills my heart medication prescription. I am alive.

In the US I was warned repeatedly that Latin America was dangerous. Business-class Mexicans wondered that I survived their bandit-infested sierras. In Brazil I am warned against travelling through the interior. The advice came first from the smart woman in the off-roader at the petrol station and from the Federales. A cop in Curitiba gave the same advice as does the hotel-keeper here in Ponta Grossa. This morning I am warned by a federal cop on a motorbike. For Brasilia you must ride up the coast to São Paulo before turning inland.

A huge dogleg, why? Is the interior dangerous? Are there brigands? Is the road so bad?

The cop shrugs. 'Everyone travels via the coast.'
Not this fat old Brit. Swimsuits don't suit my figure…

TO BRASILIA
Sunday, 28 October

I leave at dawn and head due north into forbidden territory. One short stretch of road is calamitous – probably federal punishment for a recalcitrant local politico. The rest is excellent, much of it four-lane carriageway with little traffic prior to São José do Rio Preto. Countryside is dry scrub and Texas ranch land. Cattle are skinny hump-necked Zebu.

I pull into a petrol station at one-thirty, fill the tank and park in the shade by the open-fronted cafeteria. The truck park is full. Sunday lunch is all you can eat for six dollars: help yourself from the buffet to salads and vegetables, rice and beans, stews. Waiters tour with big skewers of beef, pork, lamb, mammoth sausages and grilled pineapple. The pineapple is excellent.

A small truck driver with bow legs wears baggy shorts and a Manaus T-shirt. He has never been to Manaus. A big truck driver in jeans and a plain shirt has driven from Manaus this week. He was held up for six days by floods.

Or he may have been on a calamitous six-day surfing holiday – translating from Brazilian Portuguese to my Cuban Spanish is an inexact science – the only certainty, that water featured and wasn't fun.

Communicating, however inadequately, with the truck drivers has rekindled my enthusiasm – back on the bike and ride till dusk. Weary, I pull into a petrol station with an empty truck park and a single-floor hotel, no village, tall shade trees, a couple of shacks. The hotel is shut. Perhaps it was built before trucks had beds. The petrol pump attendant sends a small boy running to one of the shacks and a woman brings a key. The ten-dollar room is half the size of a squash court, cold-water bathroom with rusting fixtures, double bed with clean linen, mosquito netting on the window. The roof extends over a front terrace overlooking the road. I sit alone on an iron chair at an iron table. The woman brings a cold beer. A few trucks pull in. Drivers shower at the back then gather on the terrace. An elderly man (my age?) walks over from the shacks. He points to the Honda's registration plate. 'Mexico… '

'Mexico,' I agree.

Where am I going?

Brasilia, Porto Velho, Manaus, Venezuela, New York…

More questions, unintelligible – as is the conversation when the drivers invite me to join them. Children sit on the edge of the terrace and swing their legs. The woman serves bowls of beef stew with beans. The occasional truck or car passes. Frogs croak and cicadas rub their wings. I have ridden 700 kilometres, a record on the Honda, and am blissfully content.

TO BRASILIA
Monday, 29 October

A further 600 kilometres to Brasilia necessitates another dawn departure. I stop a moment to gaze down over treetops floating on a sea of short-lived mist. Each day is hotter than the last and I ride in T-shirt and cotton trousers across a dry landscape of short trees and cactus and clumps of wispy grass. Fences sag, Zebu cattle show their ribs. Breakfast at a nothing café in a straggly hamlet, lunch at another.

Traffic builds up and agricultural land improves as the road approaches the city of Goiânia, capital of Goiás State. The highway bypasses the city with only 200 kilometres further to Brasilia.

Motels mark the approach to urban Brazil. Brazilian motels are short-stop conveniences for short-time lovers. Drivers enter directly into a garage, pay through a hole in the wall and receive free prophylactics. The prophylactics are advertised on roadside billboards – as are saunas, hydro spas, naughty movies, cascades and a swimming pool. Many of the motels are named after cities in the US. Miami is a favourite. Dallas and Lilith are common, as are Ecstasy, Orgasmic and Love. I spot a Mama Maria's on the approach to Brasilia – the hydro-spa is tempting after a long day in the saddle. Sadly I am too shy to ask whether singles are permitted – or if so, does the manager immediately telephone for a service provider. Is refusing the service proof of some vile perversion earning instant expulsion?

BRASILIA
Tuesday, 30 October

Brasilia is a creation of the fifties. Architecture is concrete brutalist; each building sited according to a master plan created by Professor Lucio Costa. Government ministries form a glass and concrete avenue in the Ministry sector; Embassies in the Embassy sector shelter behind tall walls; hotels cluster cheek by jowl in the hotel sector, all of them expensive (by my standards).

Great swathes of parched parkland separate the sectors. Did Professor Lucio Costa fail to consider the months of drought? Or did he imagine an irrigation system greening his open spaces and cooling the air? Brasilia overlooks a vast artificial lake so surely water is available. What do I know? I am merely an old Brit passing through…

Culture, in my youth, was considered an important aspect of the national image. Poets and erudite novelists represented Britain as officers of the British Council. Lawrence Durrell's *The Alexandria Quartet* was a product of his posting to Egypt. Transfer to Cyprus produced the equally brilliant *Bitter Lemons*. Today I visit the British Council offices in Brasilia. No Brits on the staff. The manager is a young and exceedingly beautiful Brazilian woman and child of Thatcherism with a degree in business administration.

BRASILIA
Wednesday, 31 October

The Mexican Embassy in Brasilia is a fine example of brutalist architecture. An Olmec head in front of the Embassy is equally brutalist and a brilliant juxtaposition. Lawns are watered emerald. Barcelona chairs around a square glass-topped table in the atrium create a calm meeting place. I wear black cargo pants and my Buenos Aires denim shirt. My companion teases that I have cast myself as an ageing Kerouac.

He is a silver-haired Savile Row symphony in a jacket of lightweight tweed, check shirt, silk tie with red ladybirds on a primrose background, grey flannels with turn-ups, burnished brogues. He is the Mexican cultural attaché. He is immensely cultured. He does not have a degree in business administration. In her nightmares, Mrs Thatcher must have imagined British Embassies staffed with such men; men who read books, attend concerts, study history, promote philosophies.

We discuss the Conquest and the Christianising of Mexico. The cultural attaché mentions the Madonna of Guadalupe. I am a fan of the Madonna. I wear two images of her round my neck and a lapel badge. The medallions were donated by a Colombian wholesaler of wind-cured hams; a Mexican dentist's wife gave me the lapel badge. They were gifts to keep me safe on my journey. I was wearing all three when the truck struck together with a gold Saint Christopher given to me by my brother and sister-in-law. I suffered one hell of a crash and survived.

Our conversation retreats historically from the Madonna to the Aztec enthusiasm for human sacrifice. My companion wishes me to believe that those about to be sacrificed were joyful at such honour.

I beg him to imagine.

The victim clambers up the pyramid.

The steps are steep with shallow treads – the angle designed to ensure that his dead body rolls back down.

At the summit, a priest gouges out his heart with a stone scalpel. Does the victim's bowels let go? I must check with a medical expert on this last point – if I can find an expert on hearts being gouged out.

Down tumbles the corpse.

Imagine the pyramid covered in blood and shit.

Imagine the stink.

Then imagine millions of flies.

Flies rise in a black cloud each time a fresh body tumbles down the steps and would have buzzed around the victim as he climbed.

Honour? No, sir. I don't think so.

The cultural attaché quotes witnesses of the period. I argue that witnesses hadn't had their hearts gouged out; added to which casting doubt on the joys of heart surgery earned you a one-way ticket up the pyramid.

The cultural attaché suggests a historian I should seek when next in Mexico City. I doubt that the charming young lady with a degree in business administration who manages the British Council in Brasilia could name a historian.

Salman Rushdie is the most important and least parochial of modern British writers. His work touches on dangerous territory. Islamic fanatics have issued fatwa against him. He is equal anathema to backwoods Tories. He spent years unable to walk to the corner shop without police protection.

Our ex-Foreign Minister, Jack Straw, recently remarked that he was incapable of reading Salman Rushdie's work. In any other European country, such a confession would make of the Minister a laughing stock. For Brits, culture is suspect.

BRASILIA
Thursday, 1 November

Understanding Brasilia's master plan simplifies navigation. Distances from sector to sector make a vehicle obligatory. Jobseeking demands a major trek in one direction or another. How do the poor manage? Perhaps Professor Lucio Costa believed that Brazil's wealth would consign poverty to history. Corner shops and cafés don't feature in his grand design. Arrive fifteen minutes early for an appointment and you either sit in the car and broil or squat under a shade tree that provides too little shade.

The Metropolitan Cathedral stands on an island surrounded by urban thruways. The Cathedral is built in the shape of a crown. The design is drawn from the Crown of Thorns. The image is trite. The building is weak. I long for the majestic simplicity of a sixteenth-century Christian/Islamic dome. And I could do without the thruways. Thruways fail as aids to contemplation.

However Brazilians appear impervious to noise. They shout consistently and their language sounds brutal. At first I presumed that they were quarrelling. However their use of language is mirrored in their behaviour. They show little courtesy.

I wondered whether this perception was a misconception arising from my lack of Portuguese. Ankle swollen, I take my crutches for a walk to the shopping centre this evening. In Buenos Aires, Argentinians would have made way for me, offered to help me at the curb. Here I am twice jostled off the sidewalk.

Are Brazilians aware of being impolite?

Do Argentinians recognise that they are courteous?

TO PORTO VELHO
Friday/Saturday, 2/3 November

Enough of the café-free designer city, I am out of here by midday. Given the vastness of their country, Brazilians have little need to look beyond their frontiers – nor do they evince much curiosity. A car pulls in at a roadside café. The driver is a journalist specialising in internal tourism. He speaks to me briefly and only to display his command of English to his companions.

According to Wikipedia, Cuiabá is located in the exact centre of South America. To Brazilians it is known as the Gateway to the Amazon. I pass the city on the second evening and find a small hotel by the roadside.

TO PORTO VELHO
Sunday, 4 November

Ahead lies the Amazon Highway, 1,500 kilometres to Porto Velho. I halt every 150 kilometres for a bottle of water and coffee and break for Sunday lunch at an outdoor restaurant on the outskirts of a small town. The place is packed, tables often pulled together to seat groups of friends, relatives or neighbours – mostly farmers.

I face a table occupied by Mum, Dad, two daughters and a son. The daughters are early teens. The boy is a couple of years younger. He is a good-looking kid with fair, sun-streaked hair. He sits slouched deep in his chair. Parents will recognize the attitude: *Why did you bring me here? You must hate me. Why did you bother having me?*

The girls finish eating first and find school friends to chat with.

The boy sinks deeper in his chair.

The parents are seated diagonally to each other either side of the table. They ran out of conversation years back. Dad finally reads Mum something off the label on a big bottle of Coke. Whatever he reads fails to elicit a response.

The boy leaves.

Dad shifts seats to sit directly opposite Mum. Shifting seats doesn't help.

He gets up and pays the bill at the cashier's counter.

Had Bernadette been present, she would have kicked me under the table and told me not to stare. Staring is what writers do. People fascinate us.

Brazilians improve the further west I ride. So does the food. I pull off the highway into a small town this evening. Nondescript would be a polite term for the architecture. Sidewalks are tatty, so are the road surfaces. The grass in the square hasn't been cut in a year and is strewn with drink cans and plastic bags; rubbish stifles open drains. A couple of pedal bikers and a woman walking a dog take time to direct me to the only hotel. The hotel is run-down or never come up. The two women running the hotel are kind and helpful and work at communicating. I shower and change into clean clothes. The women point me to a restaurant where I devour great fish soup outdoors at the standard white plastic table. The temperature and humidity are a little high for perfect comfort. Not that I care. I am content. I have stumbled on a place of which I can find nothing good to write except that it has a pleasant and friendly feel. What joy after Brasilia…

TO PORTO VELHO
Monday, 5 November

Each village in Hispanic America offers a fresh opportunity for conversation, to learn something of the territory. Deaf and dumb in Brazil, I ride ever onward: 800 kilometres yesterday, twelve and a half hours in the saddle and a new, totally pointless, personal record. Today I leave soon after first light and face a mere 700 kilometres to Porto Velho. Early mornings are misty and cool and beautiful. Trees appear out of the mist, miracles of survival in an agricultural landscape of cattle ranch and freshly sown cereals. The agricultural wealth is worshipped in granary cathedrals of galvanised tin. Dark clouds offer a brief relief from the sun.

A rain squall strikes. The clouds clear and my clothes dry as I ride.

A small fluttering of yellow butterflies is remarkable only because these are the first I have noticed in two weeks of travel through Brazil. Once noticed, the scarcity nags. And bird life is minimal: none of the doves and pods of small blackbirds on the road side, partridge, quail – to all of which I became accustomed in Uruguay.

The road enters a stretch of forest. A small animal with a ringed tail darts across the road. Later, in a second stretch of forest, I spot a plump red animal with fine legs, size of a medium dog, possibly a deer. Orange-painted spray aircraft are common. Do orange planes spray Agent Orange?

I pass three dead Zebu steers during the day – not a vulture in sight. Is Zebu beef too tough for vultures? Or have Brazilian vultures emigrated to glut themselves on Peruvian rubbish? I miss the white-faced Herefords of my native land, so common in Uruguay and Argentina. I picture those small fields back home, slopes smoothed by centuries of toil and passion. And I think of those vast fields in the US, not a single tree planted, no attempt to please the eye. The soil is beggared, natural nutrients replaced by greater and greater quantities of chemical fertiliser; topsoil becomes increasingly friable; a gust of wind blows it away.

Most farms in Brazil look cared for. Arable fields are contour-ploughed to protect the soil. On ranches, trees shade the cattle. Sadly there is a long stretch at the approach to Porto Velho resembling a war zone, every tree crudely felled, jagged stumps enveloped by termite mounds. Such are the frontiers of the Amazon forest…

PORTO VELHO
Tuesday, 6 November

I was fortunate in being treated by a one-legged orthopaedic surgeon in Rio Grande. I am about to be saved by a one-eyed, defrocked, Baptist minister in Porto Velho.

Porto Velho is a city of half a million inhabitants and slopes gently towards the east bank of the Rio Madeira. The centre is a grid of wide, unshaded avenues sun-dipped in shimmering mirage. The occasional not very high high-rise sprouts above banal houses of concrete-block. The rest is an unplanned shanty town.

I have ridden 2,500 kilometres from Brasilia in four days. Heat and humidity are oppressive. The comfort of an air-conditioned room at the Hotel Centro is a self-awarded reward. The concierge at the hotel warns that much of the road south to Manaus is dirt and impassable after heavy rains. A riverboat is the alternative.

The river is the basis for Porto Velho's existence. To the south it marks the frontier between Brazil and Bolivia and flows 900 kilometres north into the Amazon at Manaus. The road down to the river is a retreat from modern concrete to daub and tin shacks, a higgledy-piggledy market, relics of the long-deceased Madeira-Mamoré railway and a few decrepit warehouses. The near vertical banks of the river plunge fifty feet to the water where a few scruffy wooden boats lie alongside a floating dock. Sad trees shade a short row of concrete huts at the top of the bank to the left of the road. The huts have counters on two sides and serve bad food and cold drinks. To the right a fence keeps riffraff out of a marginally higher class of bar where happier trees shade plastic chairs and tables.

I sip cold lemonade at one of the cheap bars and watch stevedores hump sacks from a boat up steps cut in the dirt. A scrawny self-styled shipping agent sits beside me. I had imagined a Mississippi paddle steamer. The agent offers passage on a steel cargo barge pushed by a wooden tug. The tug is painted white and has two decks and a tiny wheelhouse up top that resembles an accessory to a doll's house. The barge is black and without shade; oil puddles the deck. The agent says the voyage will take four days and I must buy food and a hammock.

Surely there must be boats with cabins?

'Possibly one boat, though only every two weeks,' reluctantly admits the agent. Late rains are to blame. The river is fifteen metres below its high water mark and only the one boat is of sufficiently shallow draft. The boat sailed yesterday. I must wait at least two weeks or travel by barge.

I am suspicious of this information. The Footprint guidebook lists four good boats. Have they sunk? And I wish the agent would stop picking his nose. In need of cash, I retreat to the hotel where the concierge directs me to a bank with an ATM machine. I insert my card. The machine merely smiles. I am on foot. I walk from bank to bank. I even take a cab out to a supermarket with ATM machines. None accept my card. I am hot, soaked with sweat and desperate. My ankle has become a football gouged by a marlin spike. At a Western Union office I am advised that banks in Porto Velho don't accept foreign plastic; wiring funds is the only solution. In walks a burly citizen of the US, early forties, one glass eye: John, the defrocked Baptist missionary.

He is a man of miracles – firstly that his rusty, wing-crumpled Volkswagen starts and runs. I've seen cleaner cars used as a chicken house around the back of a dirt-poor dirt farm. We drive back to the river where bar-keeps and stevedores greet him as a chum. A different shipping agent confirms that a boat sailed yesterday from Manaus. Via John I reserve a cabin for the return voyage on Saturday. Driving to the Hotel Centro we stop at a traffic light. An obese blonde woman on the sidewalk bids goodbye to an obviously American older male in a short-sleeved check shirt.

'My dad and sister-in-law,' John says as the woman waddles across the street.

'And my brother,' John adds, as she heaves herself into the passenger seat of a Ford pickup driven by a fat crew-cut.

Both John's dad and brother are Baptist missionaries in town. They haven't spoken to John in years. Nor has his mother.

John's sin was to exchange an equally obese blonde wife from the Bible Belt for a dark-skinned Brazilian. This history emerges slowly: that his father and brother, mother, wife and sister-in-law retain from their blue-collar Southern upbringing a disdain for Brazilian miscegenation and maintain a magisterial isolation from their congregations; John's feelings of imprisonment and oppression within the family; finding freedom in voyages downriver to succour small communities and so on to Manaus for supplies and succumbing to the city's fleshpots; the downward spiral into drink; John's wife leaves for the US and John's father expels him from the Baptist community.

His present wife saved him.

I imagine a plump dusky sexy juvenile. She is a slim dark-skinned *mestiza*, two years John's senior. A single mother, she met John at the church he built.

As a missionary, he earned 9,000 dollars monthly. She was raising a child on less than 300.

Her steadfastness restored his hope.

Defrocked, he has joined the Brazilian economy and earns less than 800 dollars teaching English at a private language academy. Their home fronts a dirt lane bordering a shanty town. Walls are concrete block, painted cement floors, tin roof. Doorways to the two bedrooms are curtained. A bathroom has a lavatory and shower that drains through a hole in the wall. The kitchen is equipped with a two-ring gas stove and small electric fridge. The sink is outdoors in the yard. Furniture is the cheap end of plastic.

PORTO VELHO
Wednesday, 7 November

English is a prerequisite for a good job in modern Brazil. To learn English, a student must attend private school. Only the privileged can afford private education; thus the advantaged extend their advantage. The CNA language academy has 1,200 students of all ages from primary school to adult. Baptist John introduces me to the Japanese/Brazilian administrator, Aya Imajo. Thus I find myself conducting two classes a day in conversational English. I expect the unfamiliar, foreign (whatever that is). Instead I am reminded instantly of summer brunch back home on the lawn with all our sons and their friends visiting for the Big Chill music festival. These are the same young, eager, sun-bronzed faces, the same jeans, T-shirts, trainers, headphones – though the girls are marginally smarter.

I strive to bridge the same generation gap.

'Are you all at university?' I ask each in turn. 'What do you study?'

Business Administration wins narrowly over Law. Psychology comes third (mostly women students), Medicine fourth (also mostly women); one lone Maths student, none in the Sciences. History appears absent from university curricula. One student (male) intends working in government in the hope of changing something. The rest are scornful of public service; everything government touches is corrupt; Brazil is the most corrupt country in the Americas; however good your intentions, you soon get sucked into the quagmire.

Amidst much laughter, they illustrate both corruption and incompetence. Construction of a massive new hydro-electric plant upriver is imminent. Porto Velho must absorb 50,000 new workers. The city is already short of hospital beds and schools; two giant shopping malls are the only new construction approved by the government.

PORTO VELHO
Friday, 9 November

Three days and I have become a familiar figure on the twice-daily ride to college. I belong, however temporarily, have made the grade, become a proper adult with a proper job. People greet me with a wave or smile. An elderly lady sends a coconut cake to the college.

I entered Brazil in a state of total ignorance. Without the students I would have remained ignorant. They have been very patient in answering questions and opened to me a very small window into the Brazil that lies below the façade we tourists experience.

Three students, Jorge, Daniel and Natasha, have invited me for dinner at an excellent fish restaurant. What do we discuss? Politics and corruption…

What do I want to discuss? Where are the Afro-Brazilians?

A teacher, Brito, small, late-twenties and gay, is the only Afro-Brazilian at the academy. Black in Porto Velho is a medium negative. Gay is a full negative. Brito imagines Holland as a liberal paradise and has a Dutch tourist visa. Long hours and living with his mother has enabled him to save for a return flight – though he hopes to stay indefinitely. I give him telephone numbers of close friends in Rotterdam and Amsterdam.

PORTO VELHO
Saturday, 10 November

The riverboat is late. Baptist John assures me that it will dock tonight and sail Sunday evening. We drive upriver in his Volkswagen to a restaurant overlooking the Cachoeira de Santo rapids. The rapids are navigable in high water; now grey boulders bask in the sun. I had hoped for mini bikini voluptuousness; one more disappointment…

Late evening I sit at a sidewalk café. My companion is a senior economist in the Department of Planning and Development. He is sound on economics, weak at explanations of local flora. Thus I remain bewildered as to whether the local non-alcoholic drink he orders is extracted from a root or a fruit or, possibly, a cactus.

In three days I have questioned approximately 140 students; fifty-eight are studying for degrees in Law. I ask my companion why lawyers are in such high demand.

He smiles sweetly. 'To negotiate the bribes… '

DOS HERMANOS
Wednesday, 14 November

I have been sailing down the Rio Madeira aboard the riverboat, *Dos Hermanos* for three days. I occupy one of eight cabins, four each side, directly behind the wheelhouse on the upper deck. The cabin is one metre fifty wide by two metres long and has an upper and lower berth. Mattresses are concrete coir, no sheets. I was promised sheets. I was also promised a fan. I have a fan. The fan is broken. For ventilation I tie one end of a shoelace to the cabin door-handle and the other end to my knife. I jam the knife in the bulkhead. The door opens towards the ship's bow; shortening or lengthening the shoelace governs the current of cool air funnelled off the river into the cabin. I share the cabin with large cockroaches. Cockroaches dislike daylight (as do vampires). At night I hear them scurrying across the deck – the roaches...

Non-cabin passengers sling hammocks from hooks in the solid canopy that shades the afterdeck. Minimum standing room separates the hammocks. The only clear space is by the bar. I make friends with a charming young Spanish couple. The Spaniards' hammocks are equipped with mosquito nets. They own a solar cigarette lighter, a variety of mini solar lanterns, knives, forks, spoons, plates. They lend me a bed sheet. I store their cameras under my bunk at night. I sleep an hour, thread my way between hammocks to the lavatories in the stern, sleep a further hour: such is my nightly routine. A woman cleans and unblocks the lavatories each morning. Get up early and you may enjoy a clean seat.

The Madeira River is a small stream when compared to the Amazon. The water is yellowish brown. We are seldom further than sixty metres from one bank or the other. I wake at dawn and watch, through the part-open cabin door, jungle slip by on the west bank. Jungle is green and mostly trees. I get out of bed and circle the wheelhouse to view the east bank. The east bank is jungle. East bank jungle is indistinguishable from west bank jungle. I return to bed. I wake again at eight o'clock and look at jungle. The jungle is similar to the jungle I watched at dawn. I brush my teeth, wash and go find my Spanish friends, Diego and Victoria. They have slept badly. They are watching jungle. We watch jungle together for an hour. I ask Victoria whether nine-thirty is too early for a cold beer. Victoria says that a cold beer is desirable when watching jungle. We drink a cold beer every two hours. At night I swallow Paracetamol every two hours.

This is sensible jungle discipline.

Food is provided. Medium loathsome is an apt description. We make do with equally loathsome, though marginally cleaner, toasted ham and cheese sandwiches from the bar. Sometimes we photograph jungle. Each photograph is markedly similar to the previous ones.

And we try to ignore Brazilian pop blaring through massive speakers.

Brazilian pop must be an acquired taste – though you would have to live for many years to acquire it. Songs have an affinity with the jungle in that each song is indistinguishable from the previous song and will be indistinguishable from the next. Songsters are backed by blond or dyed-blond women in mini shorts and bras. The women prance rather than dance. Their actions are ugly and have little to do with the music. Every few minutes they bend over and waggle their buttocks at the cameras.

Diego believes that Brazil exports all its good music.

Or is good music illegal on riverboats? (I am typing this in a Manaus Internet café. The music is charming).

Diego, Victoria and I are joined for breakfast (cheese toasties) the first day by an eighty-year-old German. The German is delighted to meet fellow Europeans. He has been resident in Brazil since 1949. During the Second World War he served in the SS. He wasn't aware of atrocities. No German knew of the death camps. *Particularly those serving in the SS?*

This German was captured by Americans in the Spring Offensive of 1945. He did not remove his SS insignia from his uniform. An American officer cut the insignia off, no doubt intending to sell them back home: SS memorabilia are much sought for and fetch a good price in the US.

The German came to Brazil immediately on being released from de-Nazification camp. In Brazil he had an operation on his nose. The anaesthetist asked how many Jews the German gassed. The German laughs at the memory of such a stupid question. Germans knew nothing of gassing Jews (*an army miraculously free of barrack room gossip?*).

The German has been recounting this version of events for so many years that he may believe it. However he senses that Victoria and I believe him to be a liar. Not only a liar, we believe him to be a piece of moral shit.

He keeps his distance for the remainder of the voyage.

Later we are joined by a tall, thin Brazilian with a grey beard. He is a Franciscan friar awaiting a visa for Angola. He is amused by Diego's anti-clericism and lack of belief. A rainstorm thrashes the river in the afternoon. Diego and the friar photograph the storm. The friar captures a perfect picture of lightning forking through black cloud. The friar is delighted with his photograph. He smiles as he tells Diego that when to press the shutter button is a matter of faith.

A boy spends much of his time with us. He is fourteen, tall for his age, good-looking and intelligent. He speaks excellent Spanish. He learnt the language in Lima, Peru, where he resided for nine months. Now he is travelling to Guiana to learn English. He travels alone and never talks of any family. He changes clothes three times a day and is always smartly dressed in sports shirts and pants. One of his T-shirts is Australian. We wonder where he gets his money and worry that he sells himself. Diego teaches him magic tricks; the boy learns quickly.

An attractive woman in her early twenties enters my cabin. I am seated on my bunk. She squats on the deck. She tells me that God is love and that God is on my side. She tells me that God is patient: he will wait for me to come to him. She tells me this at great length. For punctuation, she kisses my hand. I understand one word in ten – however the meaning seems clear.

Brits are embarrassed by fervour and we keep God private. Not knowing where to look, I look into her eyes and attempt to portray understanding and spiritual oneness. Twenty minutes of looking into her eyes leaves me exhausted. The woman kisses my hand once again and departs. I sit on my bunk and watch the jungle. When watching jungle, bugs come to mind. However jungle is soothing at a safe distance. I like trees and green is a calming colour…

MANAUS
Wednesday, 14 November

Two branches of the Amazon meet upstream from Manaus, the almost black water of the Rio Negro and the pale ochre of the Solimões. The two rivers flow side by side yet separate in the same vast riverbed for some twenty kilometres. Crossing the meeting of the waters, the *Dos Hermanos* docks alongside three other riverboats and is engulfed by a raucous mob of porters, relatives and putative thieves.

The Palace Hotel is a short ride uphill from the river port. My room overlooks the city's ochre and white cathedral. The air-conditioning functions and the mattress is adequate. I stand under the shower for thirty minutes and watch the grime of the voyage flow down the drain.

In Argentina, dining before ten o'clock in the evening is unusual. Manaus is different: eight-thirty and the only place open is Japanese. Every other nation has worked at perfecting the cooking of rice so that the grains remain separate. Japanese have perfected gluey rice, which they sculpt in pretty designs. The Japanese have also perfected the art of serving the minimum amount of food for the maximum amount of money. My dinner is inadequate and viciously over-priced.

I check my mail at an Internet café and consider posting a photograph of the meetings of the waters. Manaus is 1,600 kilometres upriver from anywhere. The Internet connection flows against the current. Uploading photographs is for fantasists

My fantasies are better indulged sitting at an outdoor café facing across the plaza dominated by the Theatre of the Americas. The cathedral enjoys the simplicity associated with Jesuit architecture. The Theatre of the Americas is majestic Italianate romanticism. Listening to operas at this theatre is an opera buff's dream. It has been my dream for months. The theatre is hosting a documentary film festival. Men are erecting Christmas decorations.

I sip a cold beer and try to forget the Japanese restaurant bill. A dozen gay young men hug and kiss and hold hands. The guys are enjoying themselves and seem unafraid of being mugged: perhaps Manaus is the gay capital of Brazil (I haven't been to the coast). Three young women at another table giggle amongst themselves. One of the women smiles at me. The woman probably mistakes me for Papa Noel. I sip a second cold beer and forgive the theatre for showing documentary movies that I don't want to watch. I will attend a classical concert on Saturday night. Meanwhile I might as well order a third cold beer and contemplate moonlight glinting on the theatre's golden cupola.

MANAUS
Thursday, 15 November

I am invited to dinner by a young couple, friends of student friends made in Porto Velho. We drive along a bluff above the Amazon. Apartment blocks for the rich line the shore side of the road. Apartments sell for upward of a million dollars. Where does the money come from? Hush…

We eat delicious fish at an outdoor restaurant above a river beach. Pale-skinned dancers prance on stage. The dancers are dressed in Hollywood jungle-tribe outfits: bare feet, feather headdresses, mini skirts.

Imagine an indigenous family straying from the jungle in their canoe. What would they think of the dancers and apartment blocks?

My young host claims that Brazilians are lazy: Brazilians expect Brazil's wealth of natural resources to provide for them by magic. My host is a good Catholic and works for charities in his spare time. He ignores red lights and drives to my hotel the wrong way up a one-way street.

MANAUS
Friday, 16 November

Guests at the Hotel Palace in Manaus enjoy television at breakfast. The breakfast is ample and comes free with the room. Television programmes are either cartoons or beach volleyball. Beach volleyball is the sport of the people. The cost is minimal: a patch of sand, ball, net – and designer shades.

My bike was built at the Honda factory here in Manaus. I ride out to the factory this afternoon. Manoel Antonio Libório dos Santos, Director of Production, is my bike's daddy. Manoel summons a cosmetic surgeon and manicurist. They change the rear wheel and the drive sprocket and the petrol tank and the mirrors. I forbid the changing of the rear wheel fairing; the black web of repairs is the biker equivalent of German duelling scars.

A Japanese Brazilian, Mario Okubo, and Francisca Viana – both from the Department of Institutional Relations (whatever that is) – conduct me on a factory tour. Manaus is 1,000 kilometres from anywhere. It is in the middle of the Amazon forest. Surely an odd place to site a vast factory? Taxes are the explanation. Manaus is a tax-free zone. The Honda factory employs 8,000 workers in three shifts. All employees, whether executives or on the assembly line, wear the same white overalls with HONDA embroidered on the breast pocket. A new bike comes off the assembly line every 50 seconds – 6,000 bikes a day, thirteen models. Bikes are exported downriver to more than sixty countries and Honda sells 1,200,000 bikes a year inside Brazil in a market of 1,500,000. That is one big market slice. As with the US, Brazil has an internal market capable of sustaining manufacturing. Workers on the assembly line earn 800 reals monthly – well over double the minimum wage. They receive pensions, injury insurance and medical benefits. They don't appear hurried or pressured. What would I know?

Mario Okubo complains of the threat from China. Chinese workers have no security, no benefits. No country can compete with Chinese labour prices. The Chinese are undercutting home manufacturing throughout the developing world. They are forcing factories into bankruptcy. They are nullifying twenty years of slow improvement in living standards. The Chinese government is Communist and claims to support workers worldwide.

Imagine those elderly members of the Presidium in their smart dark Western suits standing to sing 'The Internationale' before drinking their morning tea. The Chinese translation of 'The Internationale' is on Wikipedia…

There is a type of bar, café, restaurant on the periphery of the art world. Maybe it includes a gallery or is owned by the younger sister of an art critic. It is a place where knowing the help by name gets you served less slowly – though probably with the wrong order – and insiders are expected to leave a larger than normal tip.

My editor at HarperCollins, New York, took me to such a place some years back. I recall that the waiter was a Michael and wore a red shirt. Such places are an invention of the US. A gypsy society without roots, North Americans crave the illusion of belonging and of friendships – hence their habit of abbreviating first names. My brother, Antony, becomes a Tone while I am Si.

The desire to belong fosters restaurant guides, which our New York friends study eagerly to discover what place is *in*. They then trek right across town to eat food similar to that available at restaurants on their own block, but at twice the cost.

Celebrity cooks are a further menace.

I enjoy cooking. I read cookery books and watch cookery programmes on television. I do not want to shake the hand of a celebrity cook at his restaurant. He should be in the kitchen. I want to eat his food and enjoy the company of my companions.

What started this rant? The Café Galeria do Lago opposite the theatre in Manaus…

MANAUS
Saturday, 17 November

I am in love with the theatre plaza. Pollard trees surround the square and shade stone benches. The pavement is a mosaic of white and black squiggles. A monument to the five continents commands the centre. And such joyful juxtapositions: a short-time hotel, a strip joint, the restored house of a music historian, a church, a bar with tables that spread off the narrow sidewalk into the street.

Sad that office buildings block the river breeze.

Musicians play competitively inharmonious noise on an outdoor stage. Brazilians have little grace in their movements and few are beautiful – I compare with Cuba and the Dominican Republic. On the boat I found only one woman to photograph for her looks. Perhaps all the beautiful people and all those with rhythm live on the coast...

I set out with high cultural intentions for the theatre and a concert this evening. My error is in sitting at a sidewalk table outside Bar Armando for a pre-concert beer. A young copywriter and his girlfriend in marketing hijack me. The girlfriend is a local girl. He is from San Paolo. They have been enjoying an Internet relationship for a while. The physical meeting has gone well. A squad of large empty beer bottles parade on their table. I ignore the warning. A few further beers and I welcome their invitation to visit the girlfriend's mother's bar over in the new city. The mother is in remission after chemo. Her bar has fifty tables outdoors on two levels and serves deliciously fresh river fish. The mother judges her daughter drunk. The daughter is in no state to argue the point. Nor is the boyfriend. Nor am I. We sit next to a Japanese/Brazilian photojournalist and her *novio*, a print journalist specialising in and campaigning on ecology. What do we discuss?

Don't be dumb. This is Brazil. There are only two subjects: endemic corruption and incompetent government.

An hour past midnight and I apologise to the copywriter and

his girlfriend. This was their last night together and I was probably boring and obsessive. The two journalists drive to my hotel. They warn that the area is dangerous. I have been wandering the streets for the past few days without fear.

MANAUS
Sunday, 18 November

I haven't suffered night cramps since taking quinine prescribed by the homoeopathic pharmacist in Porta Grossa – more than three weeks. Most days I wake before six o'clock. Today I sleep through to nine. I deserve a hangover. I feel grand.

Sundays the main shopping street in old town Manaus becomes a vast open-air restaurant. Countless cooks with mobile stoves serve remarkably similar food. A young waitress with dyed yellow hair brings me a plate piled mostly with things that I don't want to eat. A yellow pap is revolting. What I hoped were fried potatoes are an unpleasant stringy tuber – and flour ground from *mandioca* (whatever that is) has the consistency of sharp sand. I eat a little and think of my friend and writer, Cliff Irving. Cliff took a five-day trip down the Amazon and decamped after the first twenty-four hours.

This evening dancers perform folkloric ballet on an outdoor stage in the theatre plaza. The dancers are stronger on charm than expertise. The Amazonian music, vocal and instrumental, is a delight.

As to the dancing – I am reminded of how difficult is the art of choreography. The human body is limited in its movements. Only the greatest choreographers avoid a repetition of motion or gesture that becomes mundane. For me, the most perfect performance is the Cuban ballet's version of *Swan Lake*. Sensual sadness is a winner and only the Cubans make me weep – this from an addict who has seen *Swan Lake* performed in Kiev, St Petersburg, Moscow and London.

Ballet is only one of the attractions on Sunday evening. Actors perform a series of short plays between the twin stairs to the theatre promenade; toddlers speed by on electric trikes; a brightly painted Toy Town train circles the plaza; the beer is cold and the corner café serves delicious smoked fish tarts. Take ten degrees off the temperature and Manaus would be a delightful place to live.

MANAUS
Monday, 19 November

A middle-aged biker couple park a big, decal-clad Yamaha trail bike on the sidewalk outside Armando's Bar. I am drinking a cold beer. I ask how the road is to Boa Vista. They tell me the road is badly potholed. These are Brazilians, inward-looking. They don't ask what bike I ride or where I have come from or where I am headed. A minute kitten stalks a cowardly dachshund; the dachshund retreats between my feet.

EAST ALONG THE AMAZON
Tuesday, 20 November

I ride out of Manaus at dawn. The road north divides at the city outskirts. Ask any Brazilian for Boa Vista and he will point and gesture, 'Direct, direct…'

He or she will tell you this within a hundred metres of the police post that marks the division of the road. Direct takes you parallel with the Amazon.

No, there isn't a sign.

I obey instructions. Were the sun visible, I would know that I am on the wrong road. Mist clings to the trees and I wear my leather jacket against the chill and damp. The knees of my trousers are soaked and my spectacles need wiping frequently. Finally the sun breaks through the mist. I remain in self-denial for a further few kilometres before pulling into a petrol station. 'Boa Vista?'

The pump attendant points back the way I've come. 'Direct, direct…'

I show him the map.

He can't read a map.

A truck pulls in. I show the map to the driver. I am headed for 'Itacoatiara: a nice town, a clean town, a safe town. The road ends at Itacoatiara… '

A further 160 kilometres on the wrong road to visit a small town on the Amazon River?

Sure, why not?

Itacoatiara *is* a nice town, clean, tidy and safe. Teenagers in school uniform ride bikes and motor scooters. A double row of trees attempt to shade the main avenue. The Hotel Amazon overlooks the river. A single room with bath and air conditioning is less than fifteen dollars. You can sit on the terrace and look down on the river and watch the ships and boats. Beer is cold. A variety of river fish are on the menu. Not a bad place to chill for a couple of days…

I ride back towards Manaus and finally find the *straight-on* road to Boa Vista, which is a right-angle turn off what is clearly the main highway. I race a rainstorm for sixty kilometres before pulling in to a roadside restaurant for shelter. The owner insists on showing me a cabana out the back. We are midway to the cabana when the storm explodes. We dash for shelter in a Brazilian poolside gazebo – tin roof, four iron posts, concrete base, iron garden table, four iron chairs. No gap between lightning and thunder – we are the focus of the assault. With so much metal, is the gazebo sensible protection during an electric storm? Or is it a lightning conductor?

My want-to-be host makes a run for a cabana. He opens the door, closes it quickly and dashes to the next cabana; presumably the first has a leaky roof. Wind blasts the downpour in under the gazebo roof. I tip the table and shelter beneath it. Mosquitoes hate wind. My table is the only shelter. Drenched or devoured? Such are the alternatives.

My host returns triumphant; he has killed a snake in the second cabana. He drapes it over a chair. This is a man who wishes me to stay the night. Rain stirs green sludge in the swimming pool. The lawn hasn't been cut in weeks. We are surrounded by trees. Bomb the place for a month with an insecticide cocktail and the bugs would giggle and dance a samba.

Am I ready to see the cabana?

Thank you, but the rain is slackening, I'll be moving on.

God has filled the rainforest with bugs that bite, reptiles that bite, animals that bite and various lethal plants. God is sending us a message. The forest is the planet's lungs – KEEP OUT. This applies to both Brazilian farmers and eco-tourists demanding a real-life jungle experience.

I dwell for a moment on Victoria (she of the boat trip from Porto Velho). Diego has taken her 200 kilometres up an Amazon tributary to an eco-camp on the swampy shores of a lake. Safely home in Cadiz, Spain, she will tell everyone what a great time she had.

Great for masochists…

I am riding in late evening in search of concrete sidewalks, a paved square and air-conditioning. A room in an inn off the highway in Presidente Figueiredo will do. The room has a double bed with a good mattress, clean bathroom, hot water. Room rate is fifteen dollars, less than half the cost of a bug-infested cabana an insane distance from the closest air-conditioner.

Before taking a shower, I hit the room with insecticide. Five minutes under the shower and I am ready to make a body count: six mosquitoes and one fly dead on the bed sheet.

I stroll to the town square, drink cold beer, eat a cheese and ham toastie and people watch. A toddler attempts a runner to the ice cream parlour across the square. The young mother jerks the child back by the arm. The mother is angry and bitter. I feel for her. In Brazil distances are so great; every small town has the feel of being at the end of the line. This awareness is engraved in this young woman's face. She is no more than a kid, yet already trapped, imprisoned, no way out. She could have gone to São Paulo, had a career, become someone (maybe). Now she is condemned by motherhood to be a man's chattel – a man who doesn't bother coming directly home from work (more fun to be had out with the boys). Screw it, she thinks, and eats another slice of chocolate cake…

TO BOA VISTA
Wednesday, 21 November

The road to Boa Vista comes in three grades: reasonable, awful and diabolical. The first and last sections are reasonable together with eighty kilometres in the Indian Reserve. The rest is potholed. Try to slalom the potholes – three swerves max then *Wham!* and you've hit an elephant trap. Two hits and you give up the slalom. Clambering out of potholes rips the tread off the rear tire. Creep is the only method, or follow a local driver. On a bike, following gets grit in your eyes. I hit one pothole hard and lose the box off the back rack. The impact has straightened the hooks on the bungee rubbers holding the box; the hooks and bungees were made in China.

I am surprised at passing a monument acclaiming Brazil's invention of ice hockey. The monument marks the equator. Why with an ice hockey stick projecting from a boulder?

I should carry a tripod and study the camera manual so that I can photograph myself rather than wait for a kindly truck or car driver to oblige. I wait twenty minutes in the heat. This is not heat for basking sun lovers. It is a heat that makes you long for air-conditioning. To hell with waiting. A photograph of the bike at the monument will suffice.

I ride into Boa Vista at dusk and follow signs to the historic centre. Christmas lights decorate the central division of a tree-shaded main street. Kiosks beneath the trees sell cold beer and cold sodas. I ask an elderly gentleman for directions to a hotel. He directs me to a five-star snake pit. I find a two-star hotel on the next block, The

Colonial. The room is panelled in dark varnished wood. I bug spray and shower then collapse and sleep an hour. The hour is too long; I walk back to the street with the kiosks and the lights only to find everything closed except for the Catholic cathedral. The cathedral architecture is modern-peculiar. So is the service. A chubby white priest in spectacles appeals to the congregation to get with the Spirit. The congregation gets – arms waving above their heads, chanting and swaying.

Wow! Where am I? Does the Pope know this stuff is going on?

A woman grabs my hand and drags me into a chanting swaying group. The priest is summoning the Spirit of the Holy Ghost.

'*Espirutu,*' he cries, '*Espirutu, Espirutu…*'

'*Espirutu,*' echoes the congregation '*Espirutu, Espirutu…*'

There is more, of course, but in Portuguese and I don't do Portuguese. Nor am I good at swaying and waving my arms in the air. Such behaviour isn't British.

I escape and watch football on television at a corner kiosk serving fruit juice. Brazil is playing Uruguay. I support Uruguay out of loyalty to my dear cousin, Carmen, and because I don't much like Brazil. Four motorcycle cops pull in to check the score.

BOA VISTA
Thursday, 22 November

The proprietor of the Hotel Colonial dispatches the help to lead me across town to the Honda agency where I have a new rear tyre fitted and buy a new pair of goggles. A surprise awaits me at the hotel. My sister-in-law dropped by. She has a document I must sign. Bernadette has three sisters. All three work in London. I question the receptionist at length in a language he doesn't understand. He replies in a language I don't understand. However the Spanish for sister-in-law is too similar to the Portuguese for confusion.

With a document?

Yes, she had a document.

Will she return?

He doesn't believe so.

Could this be the woman who drew me into the cathedral last night? Is she a religious sister-in-law, our relationship confirmed by the Spirit?

Was the document a papal bull?

Or a plenary indulgence?

Such mysteries are a delightful epitaph to my journey through Brazil and usefully occupy the mind on the long straight road in the heat to the Venezuelan border.

7

VENEZUELA

SANTA ELENA DE UAIRÉN
Thursday, 22 November

In crossing twenty-eight frontiers, I have been delayed only when entering Honduras where the Head of Customs insisted that I down a few beers and watch football on his office television. Passing from Brazil into Venezuela may be different. Guidebooks warn that a visa is obligatory together with a seventy-five-dollar banker's certificate and an International Driving Permit. I possess none of these.

The Venezuelan Immigration officer is a darkly beautiful woman. She briefly studies my application for a thirty-day visa. Her only query, *Why do I need crutches?*

Because a truck hit me the first day of this journey north from Tierra del Fuego; five weeks with a smashed ankle in plaster. No need to recount that I was pinned under the front fender while the truck slid forty metres.

'Thirty days is hardly sufficient if you get hit by another truck,' says the Immigration officer and writes *sixty days* in my passport.

A Customs officer issues a transit permit for the bike and I ride on into the border town of Santa Elena de Uairén. Santa Elena is raffish, low-rise, scruffy and a fun base for tourists exploring the vast plains of the Gran Sabana. Gold-panning, gemstone deposits and illegal logging along the border add spice.

Charming decay comes to mind when describing the Hotel Lucretia. However, the pool is clean and the owner is a splendidly flirtatious grandmother.

I have a thick wad of Brazilian reals. What is a Brazilian real worth in Venezuelan bolivars? Venezuelan banks don't change money; Grandma counsels checking the High Street money-changers.

High Street is a misnomer for a straggly lane with a few failed attempts at mid-market stores. For the rest, imagine mini-houses drawn freehand by a child at kindergarten. A blue-jeans and straw-Stetson dealer in gold and diamonds sits on an upright chair outside his office. His infant son, four at most, points to my baby Honda: 'Moto...'

'Moto,' I agree.

He leads me to the open door of the next house. 'Moto,' he repeats of a big Yamaha trail bike parked in the corridor.

A Honda 125 isn't a real bike: is that the message?

Maybe Brazilian reals aren't real money...

The dad fetches a wooden stool from indoors. We sit side by side on the sidewalk and enjoy the shade. I am cautious when changing money anywhere but a bank.

He gives me the rate in sterling and in euros for reals.

The dollar rate?

He is nervous of dollars.

And bolivars?

'Bolivars have no value. They are an illusion created by the government. We have a crazy government. Chavez is crazy.'

He fetches a couple of cold beers from the office and talks of the imminent referendum to permit Chavez to remain as president beyond two terms. 'Chavez wishes to be a dictator.'

I steer the conversation back to the value of the bolivar. My subliminal message finally connects. 'You wish to change money? How many reals?'

'One thousand...'

We go indoors and sit each side of a desk in a small office. He fingers my reals, checks a few against the light. 'Two million, seven hundred thousand bolivars.'

Two million, seven hundred thousand is too large a number on which to cast doubt. Congratulations are in order. I'm a millionaire – and joyful to be speaking Spanish again.

SANTA ELENA
Friday, 23 November

I am uncomfortable when writing in Venezuela. Venezuela has a feeling familiar from Cuba. The same Cubans are present. I refer not to the happy-go-lucky, *sleep with you for a bar of soap and a good meal* Cubans with whom most tourists become familiar. I refer to those from the Ministry of the Interior – the political cops.

'They're everywhere,' warns a young woman journalist. She has invited me home to tea at a shack on a dirt-road development on the outskirts of town. Two narrow bedrooms occupy three quarters of the house. The remaining quarter is a corridor with a lavatory at one end and a two-burner paraffin camper stove on a wooden shelf the other. Walls are thin concrete, unglazed windows with wood shutters; washing is a tap in the dirt yard. A bare-bottom infant crawls on the cement floor.

'There's a Cuban physical education teacher at the primary school,' the journalist says. 'And the new hospital is staffed entirely by Cubans. Chavez pays Cuban doctors double the salary of our doctors. The new hospital has everything. Venezuelan doctors in the old State hospital have nothing.'

The child makes a four-legged bolt for the exit. The journalist grabs him back. 'That's the message,' she says. 'Vote Chavez if you want to keep the new hospital.'

She is from Caracas where she wrote for a national paper. Her husband, an economist, couldn't find work. Santa Elena is a new life. They have been here a year. Her husband is trekking along the frontier attempting to buy gems, hoping for the Big Kill. The journalist doesn't believe in the Big Kill. She works part-time on the local paper and part-time for the Electricity Company.

'There's even a Cuban in our office. Why do we need a Cuban in the Electricity Company? He's reporting on what people say.'

Cubans are practiced in reporting what people say. They denounce each other once a week at the obligatory meeting of each city block's CDR – Committee for the Defence of the Revolution.

Friday evening and I am kidnapped and dragged up a mountain in a small jeep to celebrate the full moon. My ferocious kidnappers are employees in a Department of the Venezuelan Government committed to teaching indigenous people how to live where indigenous people have lived for a few thousand years and how to make genuine indigenous artefacts that are saleable to tourists.

The jeep-driving kidnapper, Fidel, is also a musician, a drummer. We collect Fidel's drums on the way to the mountain, two crates of beer and four bottles of rum. Our destination is a housing community of *marginales*. The road is suitable for athletic goats; homes are idiosyncratic self-build with help. The party is outdoors of a log and wattle house built by a painter and his wife. We sit in a circle round a log fire. Chucking wood on the fire fountains sparks up to join the stars and moon in a blue-black sky. A mediocre guitarist bellows songs in praise of President Chavez. I am reminded of the sixties and Ibiza full-moon parties on Mount Atalaya. Ibiza was booze and hallucinogenics. Santa Elena is booze and the Socialist Revolution.

The painter is slim forties with too little chin and a wife with long hair who talks and dances with other people – possibly because the painter is busy playing host. He is of a type treasured by political police: easily terrorised, ass-licker to the powerful and serial informer. He heads a government-financed community centre. I sit on the grass and watch as he attempts to persuade Fidel to join a committee. The Committee is doing great things, organising the people, cementing the achievements of the Revolution.

Fidel isn't a joiner and is too individualistic to fit the future pattern. In due course he will be denounced by the painter as an anti-social element. No jeep, no more fun job composing and teaching indigenous people indigenous music for tourists. None of the party guests are indigenous, surely odd amongst these protagonists of new-found equality.

One o'clock and the Chavez glee club leader launches into another pro-Chavez paean. Fidel is driving his drums on cruise control. Victoria, his partner in my kidnapping, is total energy, minimum direction. Her dance partners are a booze bottle and gourd rattle. She wears skin-tight leopard-spot pants and twitches her ample buttocks to the beat.

I sip rum and nod politely as a plump lady in her sixties guarantees that the Revolution will give Venezuelans the freedoms and equality enjoyed by Cubans for the past fifty years. Any minor difficulties in Cuba have been caused by the blockade.

Four o'clock and Victoria is the solitary whirling dervish. The bonfire is running out of wood and we remnants of jollity are a glaze-eyed half-dozen. Fidel asks whether I am ready to leave. I've been ready to leave since midnight. Corralling Victoria is a two-man task. We wedge her into the front passenger seat of the jeep. I sit in the back with the drums. Fidel drives. The wet mountain mist smears dust and grease on the windscreen. The wipers don't work. Visibility is near zero.

Fidel insists that I am a natural Santa Elenaite. 'We will find you a plot of land up here on the mountain,' he declares with an expansive gesture at whatever lies behind the mist. 'You must return. We will help build you a house.'

In a hugging mood, Victoria tries to join me on the back seat and gets stuck. Fidel drives one-handed while trying to unstick Victoria. The jeep bounces from boulder to boulder. I pray and cling to Fidel's drums while paying silent thanks for one more miracle of instant Hispanic-American friendship.

SANTA ELENA
Saturday, 24 November

Waking can be an adventure. In my youth I might worry whether I was where I ought to be: correct room, correct bed, correct companion? My present concerns are more mundane. Where did I leave my spectacles? My teeth? I swim sedately up and down the pool before strolling round the corner for breakfast at the Backpackers Hotel. Santa Elena lives off tourism. Tourists have been fleeing Venezuela ahead of the referendum and I am one of the very few left in town. A Venezuelan in the hotel business joins me. He has worked in Europe and the Caribbean, including the Cohiba in Havana. He has a *novia* back in Cuba, a doctor. She has been waiting for an exit permit for the past five years. So much for freedom…

I eat chilli prawns for dinner in a Chinese restaurant. A very fat black man chivvies a family of twelve to a long table. The man has Rasta hair and wears a wool hat knitted in the Ethiopian national colours. Yesterday I noticed two women with Rasta hair at the coach stop. The women were young and white and carried backpacks. Presumably they were tourists.

The copy-editor queried a paragraph on Rastafaris in my recent book. She was casting doubt as to whether readers would have sufficient information to understand what I had written. Rastafaris are a common sight and the web is at hand. Or am I stupid in presuming that people seek information?

Rastafaris believe that Haile Selassie is God Incarnate.

Haile Selassie was the Emperor of Ethiopia from 1930 to 1974.

He was a murderous autocrat.

He was also an Amhara, Ethiopia's ruling tribe.

One of the oddities of the Amharas is their belief that they are the only white race (Europeans are red). They consider and refer to those they consider black as either slaves or outcasts.

Jamaica is the birthplace of the Rastafari religion.

Haile Selassie seems an odd God for black Jamaicans. Perhaps marijuana helps?

GRAND SABANA
Sunday, 24 November

Today I enjoy one of the great bike rides. The road crosses the Grand Sabana National Park, a wonderful country of grassland and folded hills. Patches of woodland fill the hollows; Moriche palms edge the streams; villages are a sprinkling of thatched adobe huts amongst wispy grass. The road climbs to a cold, windswept moor blanketed by charcoal cloud.

The clouds lift to reveal a magic land of flat-topped mountains. What lies within the clinging mists and jungles of these small isolated plateaux? Imagine clambering the precipices, rocks kept slippery with spray from waterfalls, knotted tree roots, bright eyes of a dinosaur, ruined walls of a forgotten civilisation.

The road discovers a crack between mountains and plunges down to steamy rainforest. Glancing up, I catch glimpses of cloud spilling over jungle table-tops.

Serious soldiers man a check post – no small talk.

My passport is examined. Where have I come from? Where am I going? What is the purpose of my visit? Finally a stamp and signature are added to the back of the temporary import permit for the Honda. Other than at frontiers, this is the first time that I have been asked for my documents during my travels through the Americas. I am stopped three further times during the day by equally unfriendly Military.

I stop at a jumble of shacks huddled at the foot of a gorge. Cooking pots simmer on charcoal outside one of the shacks The cook is a buxom black woman, fifties, white apron over a flowered dress, spotless white cap. Soup served in a big bowl is chunks of beef and root vegetables in dark broth, deliciously rich and spicy.

'A perfection,' I tell the cook.

She replies, 'Have a good journey, my heart.'

How can so much happiness and companionship be gained in two short lines of conversation?

The road escapes from mountains and rainforest into open farmland. One week remains before the referendum. Cars, buses and villages are bedecked with red banners bearing Chavez's portrait and a simple message: 'Chavez Si'.

Dusk approaches as I turn off the highway into a small town and find a hotel across from the church on the central square. Applause for socialism booms from boom boxes on a slogan-draped truck. Cheerleaders on the truck urge support. Two pickups, three scooters and some thirty pedestrians complete the procession. Organisation is obvious, enthusiasm less so. Pizza is excellent at a pizza parlour the church side of the square. Sunday evening and the church is locked.

A car alarm screeches directly below my window. I fumble for spectacles, check my watch: four o'clock. Twenty minutes' peace then the alarm again and my bathroom door locks itself from the inside. The room key doesn't fit. I fumble my way downstairs and use the lavatory behind the bar. Back to bed and the car alarm shrieks again. Six o'clock and I give up on sleep and load the bike.

A smartly dressed organiser for Chavez is paying his bill. He has travelled widely through Europe, mostly in what was then the Eastern Bloc and resided for a while in Ulbricht's East Germany. He lives in Caracas now. Guidebooks and other travellers warn that the capital is dangerous. The politico says the people are good. They are poor not through their own fault. The rich are at fault. Stealing from the rich is justifiable. The poor can only feed their families by stealing.

I leave the hotel a few minutes before seven o'clock and head for Puerto Ortaz, an industrial city on the Orinoco. City traffic is scary and I don't handle it well. The bridge over the Orinoco is a great feat of engineering, five kilometres in length. Is feeding the poor of Venezuela so much more difficult?

This evening I am expected at an *estancia* owned by my Argentine cousins. I speed at ninety kilometres an hour on a good straight road across flat cattle country. Farms seem unplanned and unkempt, Zebu stock mostly bone. I lose the race against the setting sun. Murk is thick with dust and bugs. Manic drivers with headlights on full beam hurtle down the road. An oncoming car overtakes a truck and forces me off the road. Finally lights signal at the head of a dirt track. The track leads to modern farm buildings set amongst tall trees, farmhands hosing a cattle trailer. The manager's wife grills a vast steak before her husband drives me to the proprietor's house. My cousins are absent, visiting normally once a month. I shower and fall into bed where sleep eludes me. I overdosed on fear in the last half hour of today's journey. The experience has left me shattered.

First rule of biker survival:

NEVER, NEVER, NEVER RIDE AT NIGHT.

I inspect the house in the morning. Though spacious, it is simple in materials and decoration. Floors and benches are polished cement. Woodwork is carpentry rather than cabinet-making. Rough-cut beams support the roof. I ease tired joints outdoors to be blessed by sunshine and the clear waters of a pool. I slip naked into the water and paddle a couple of lengths. Sunlight, filtered by trees, dapples the water. I dry and stretch, waggle the bad ankle and do my squats. Bifocals in place, I admire emerald pasture spotted with white cattle.

Sixty-four thousand hectares is a big farm. At time of purchase, nineteen years ago, the land supported a small herd of Zebu. My cousins have invested massively. Now there are 10,000 beef cattle and 1,000 water buffalo, 450 kilometres of electric fencing. A dairy produces three tons of cheese each month from buffalo milk. Workers and managers are well housed. Machine shop and offices with air-conditioning have replaced the original shacks. Dirt roads dividing the paddocks are straight, well-drained and recently graded. Everything is neat and clean.

The Argentine cattle manager conducts me on an inspection. He is a tall handsome man, going grey, somewhat impatient and intolerant of Venezuelan inadequacy, very certain of Argentine (racial) superiority.

I know something of agriculture. I left school early to learn farm management in what is now Zimbabwe. That was nearly sixty years ago. The cattle manager is a reminder of those white farmers. The professionalism is similar, the hard work – and the occasional remark the cattle manager passes regarding the farmhands. And there is a connection with today's Zimbabwe: this *estancia* is under threat of expropriation.

I spend the afternoon and evening with the *estancia* manager. Though also Argentine, he differs in character from his cattle manager. He has no need of arrogance; his achievements are manifest. He has been here from the beginning, arriving in his early twenties. His commitment is absolute. He will work a fourteen-hour day until the sword of expropriation falls. He has a lover's feel for the soil. The eye for detail is Military. So are the planning and the precision and the delegation of responsibility down through the chain of command.

The vision may come from the owners. The overall planning is theirs, as is the allocation of resources and they are also lovers. I stalk the house and discover small details that tell of their love; and of their pride in creation. I am writing this beside the pool. I found a cold beer in the icebox and tuned the radio to a music station. The lowing of cattle melds with salsa and with the rumble of a grader working a farm road. An hour of sunlight remains. At this moment, this is close to Paradise. I think of myself as an old Lefty. Am I a closet Conservative? The truth is that I have never been against people being rich. I am against people being poor.

DEPARTURE
Wednesday, 28 November

Water buffalo prefer liquid mud to spring water. Only their eyes and nose and sometimes their tails show above the milk-chocolate surface as they wallow through the heat of the day and presumably philosophise.

Philosophising in a mud bath must be preferable to riding a small Honda in intense heat amongst homicidal maniacs. I load my bag on to the bike and have one last swim in the pool. Floating on my back, I peer myopically over my pink belly at the poolside oven and grill. Will a local Chavez politico inhabit the house next year? Sunday barbeques for loyalist beer bellies? Such is the way of Revolutions, Left, Right or Military coup.

Four days to the referendum and red pro-Chavez banners and posters decorate every lamp post and road sign in each town and village. Pickets in red shirts stop traffic to distribute pro-Chavez windscreen stickers. Refuse a sticker and the driver's car registration is noted.

Opposition is invisible in these small communities yet big-city protests by university students feature on CNN.

The road climbs through rainforest. Tin shacks lapped by rubbish rim the roadside. Tin roofs drip in light drizzle. Men shelter and drink beer amongst discarded bottles and plastic containers while women scrub clothes. A small netted vivarium advertises plants for sale in witness to one man's or one family's hope for a better future. The neighbours sit idle. Why don't they collect the rubbish?

Guidebooks describe Carupano as a splendid colonial coastal town, a World Heritage Site. The church has been ruined by restoration – imagine a tasteless B-movie tart-up. A few houses are good. The rest is a mess. I am in need of a bed and a cold beer. A road sign advertises a posada with pool and Internet. A German with tattoos, muscles and a ponytail tends bar. He has shipped a massive Suzuki trail bike from Germany and is heading for Chile to visit an uncle who fled Germany immediately after the Second World War. His geographic knowledge is a little vague and he doesn't carry maps but sort of knows that Chile is *down there*.

Excited at meeting a fellow biker, he suggests we ride a dirt road up a mountain in the morning. We will have fun bouncing off rocks and views from the peak are great.

Old men on pizza delivery bikes don't do fun dirt.

Preferable is an intelligent German woman reading a book in a hammock while her husband scuba-dives. Her husband is an expert on Central America. In Honduras he taught poor Central Americans to build cheap houses for themselves (out of adobe?). Now he oversees junior German aid workers who teach poor Central Americans to build cheap houses. He is a small man determined to be muscular. He showers and changes from one short-shorts sports outfit to another short-shorts sports outfit. His wife is an adult. He is a teenager. Both are in their mid-forties.

Later I talk with two Germans resident in Venezuela. They warn that Caracas is dangerous; Merida is dangerous; even Barcelona is dangerous. Barcelona is my next stop. It has a historic centre. Hopefully the centre will be less of a disappointment than Carupano.

TO BARCELONA
Thursday, 29 November

The winding coast road is blasted out of the flank of precipitous mountains. The coast is pierced with coves and inlets and gulfs; the sea is spread with rocky islands. I slow wherever possible to let trucks and cars pass. Don't let them pass and they overtake on the next blind curve. Why? Because this is Venezuela. Suicide behind the wheel is Venezuela's national sport. Every television channel carries a police advertisement featuring blood, guts, crumpled metal, shattered windscreens and this year's death toll: 36,211 and climbing.

Barcelona is draped in red posters and banners. A cop directs me to the historic district. 'After dark, it is dangerous,' he warns. 'Very dangerous. It is full of thieves, degenerates, drug addicts, homosexuals and prostitutes.'

Why are homosexuals numbered amongst the dangerous?

The accident in Tierra del Fuego has left me nervous. Add that everyone I meet warns that Venezuelan cities are dangerous and I have a strong desire to be somewhere else. I tour the historic quarter of Barcelona: no glorious churches, no glorious buildings, neither a cloister nor a beautiful square – and no sidewalk cafés. Disappointment is an understatement. On I ride…

Dusk approaches as I pull off the highway into a small town dominated by high-rise apartment blocks for oil workers. I find a modern mid-market hotel a block back from the beach. The manager recommends a restaurant on the beach that serves fresh fish; walking the block to the beach is safe if I am careful. A couple of beers and I feel less depressed. A young handsome couple sit at the next table. The husband will vote No in the referendum. He rates himself as middle class and works in the family business. He says that the super rich, with their greed and corruption and irresponsibility, have created Chavez.

'What will happen if Chavez wins the referendum?'

'We will resist. We are not like Cubans. Cubans are soft.'

Both he and his wife warn me not to ride through Caracas.

I find an Internet café. The Internet doesn't work. I chat with a Venezuelan civil engineer, mid-forties, short hair, heavyweight chinos, work-boots. He too claims that Chavez was created by the rich and their corruption of Venezuela. He is anti Chavez and anti the Cubans that he claims are flooding the country.

He says: 'Chavez surrounds himself with foreigners. If we must have a Revolution, let it be our Revolution.'

The engineer talks for half an hour on the telephone, giving detailed technical explanations and instructions. Later I fetch coffee and we talk of the US. He accuses US oil companies of arrogance and a colonial attitude – people in the US believe themselves superior and believe that only they are competent to run an oil field.

He is amused when I tell him that I have been advised to detour round Caracas.

His advice is to keep to the urban thruway.

I say that Colon, Panama, is the only city in which I have felt in danger while travelling through the Americas.

The engineer has worked in Panama. He says, 'In Colon they are blacks. Blacks are lazy and dangerous. Look at cities in the United States. All the blacks have guns.'

Pointless to mention an Afro-American secretary of state and an Afro-American candidate for president – as there was no point in asking the cop in Barcelona why he listed homosexuals as dangerous.

TO CARACAS
Friday, 30 November

The anti-Chavez vote mounted a huge demonstration in Caracas last night. Today the Yes vote mobilises. Every bus in the country is crammed with red shirts headed for the capital; banners wave, painted slogans gleam, klaxons screech a victory tattoo. Buses, old and new, collect at service stations; red shirts swirl in the forecourt and in cafeterias or clump forlornly beside a steaming radiator or a flat tyre with the tread worn smooth as an egg. Hills slow ancient buses to a crawl. Putative mechanics peer under a relic's hood. Bricks support an antique marooned by a broken spring. A shattered half-shaft strands another.

Six scarlet-draped chrome-and-polish monsters steamroll me off the hard shoulder. I hit soft dirt, skid as I break and nearly fall. Thanks, buddies, thanks for the brotherhood of man.

The urban thruway cuts straight through Caracas and out the far side. I stop once to check with a cop that I am on the right road. Approaching the city, I was too preoccupied by terror to notice that the road climbed. Now the highway plunges, twisting and turning towards the sea. Downhill drivers play fairground dodgem cars, swerving this way and that. Long convoys of Chavez buses climb towards the capital. An imaginative opposition would seek the bus park and puncture tyres. The referendum is on Sunday. Chavez supporters wouldn't get home in time to vote.

Beyond the hills, huge pipes snake across the littoral. Painted in giant red letters on a factory wall is that great motto of the Cuban Revolution: PATRIA, SOCIOLISMO O MUERTE. *Country, Socialism or Death…*

Finding a small beach-front hotel, I drink beer and eat fresh fish on the terrace with a young Venezuelan who runs launches for scuba-diving. No foreign tourists this season; the referendum or the subprime crisis has kept them away.

He relates a visit to Australian cousins. Strangers accosted him in bars: he presumed that they were either drug dealers or mistook him for a drug dealer (Latino). A week or two and he realised that Australians were simply friendly. A further week and he accepted that it was unnecessary to ask whether he would be safe taking a walk in the city. 'We Venezuelans need eyes in the back of our heads…'

He will vote No in the referendum though he sympathises with the Yes vote: for the poor, Chavez offers the only alternative to a continuation of the insupportable.

Sadly it is a false hope.

Supporters of Chavez are equally dishonest. A bigwig of the Revolution has built himself a mansion illegally on the peninsula here on National Parkland. The politico was penniless before Chavez came to power.

'It is how we are, we Venezuelans. We are all guilty. We think only of ourselves. Look at the way we drive…'

I assure him that Cubans are no different. Castro's long-term companion, the sainted Celia Sanchez, commandeered Havana mansions for all her family in the first weeks of the Triumph. How do I know? When first granted Cuban residency, we rented a mansion from Celia Sanchez's niece.

TO CORO
Saturday, 1 December

Centre for the oil industry, Maracay is a vast industrial sprawl of refineries and tower office blocks. It will be my last city in Venezuela. I am on a six-lane urban thruway. A truck pulling a trailer loaded with steel girders sits on my backside. I slow a second to check the overhead signs and he hits his klaxon. A small Chevrolet whips across from the outside lane to the hard shoulder, overtakes a truck on the inside, swerves back to the fast lane. A pickup shoots from the fast lane to an exit, missing me by inches.

I pull into a petrol station and walk to the toilets and confront myself in the mirror over the hand basin. I'm weeping and I can't stop. I don't want to be seen weeping so sit on the toilet bowl with the door locked. The longer I sit the more scared I become of continuing. A while passes before I kneel on the floor and vomit. I wash my hands and my face and go back outside with my face wet. The water hides the tears. The driver of a Nissan off-roader offers to show me the way out of town. I beg him not to go too fast and I ride as if in blinkers, shutting everything out except the rear of the Nissan. A sweet man, he drives at a steady sixty kilometres per hour to the city outskirts.

I have escaped the oil fields. Beyond Maracay lies a cool pleasant cattle country of rolling hills. Fewer trucks menace. Drivers of pickups and cars are more humane. Midday and I seek shelter from a rain shower in a small restaurant beside a petrol station. Colour lithographs of soulful saints and the Virgin Mary decorate the walls. A rosary hangs behind the bar. The owner is first generation Venezuelan. His parents emigrated from Portugal.

Why Venezuela rather than Brazil?

He grins and says, 'My parents weren't good at geography.'

Orange juice and a big bowl of mutton soup cost a dollar.

I stop again to take on petrol and coffee thirty kilometres short of Coro. A big *Yes for Chavez* poster is affixed to the wall of the service cafeteria. The man behind the bar doesn't like foreigners.

He isn't rude – merely stone-face resistant. I have ridden the length of Mexico, Hispanic America and Brazil. Stone-face is a reaction unique to Venezuela. It isn't common. But it happens. Foreigners are the enemy (unless Cuban). Chavez says so – particularly citizens of the US, and he condemns Britain as a US satellite.

Though a state capital, Santa Ana de Coro is manageable. Spaniards founded the town in 1527. Search here in vain for the splendours of Oaxaca, Cartagena or Popayán. Coro is on a humbler, more intimate scale. Even the cathedral is little bigger than a parish church. Yet if perfection is simplicity and immaculate proportions, then Coro is a jewel; safe, clean and joyful. No warnings here of robbers, muggers, drug addicts, homosexuals or degenerates. You can relax of an evening and walk the historic quarter.

The forecast is for Big City riots celebrating a Chavez victory. I want to witness the referendum, but from somewhere safe. Coro fits the bill. Firm negotiations at the Hotel Intercaribe lower the room rate for a mini-suite to the price of a poky single. I park, unload and head for a poolside table to sip cold beer. Music blares. A pretty young woman wears a pink T-shirt on which she has scrawled: I WILL LOVE YOU FOR ALL MY LIFE. I ask if this is true. She says it will be true – though she hasn't found the man yet.

A voluptuous black late-teen wears black net over an almost non-existent black bikini. A young man swings a rosary as if it were worry beads. The beads are pearl glass. His T-shirt bears two dice and the slogan: YOU CAN'T PLAY THE PLAYER. Children strew the poolside with crisp packets, candy wrappers and soda bottles. No one tells them to pick them up.

I finish my beer, dress and seek shelter in the sixteenth century.

Two guards sit on the steps to the Museum of Art. The museum is closed though the doors are open. One of the guards says, 'Take your time…' and shifts his backside so I can enter.

I don't ride at night. I take a cab to a Chinese restaurant. The cab driver is from Caracas. Violence made him flee the capital. He claims that Coro is a paradise.

Chavez monopolises television in my mini-suite at the Intercaribe. Chavez has been on all five channels for the past hour. He is attacking Western (US) media for a Fascist media monopoly dictatorship and for broadcasting nothing but Fascist lies and Fascist propaganda.

CORO
Sunday, 2 December

Referendum day and there is a heaviness to the air – that threatening stillness that precedes a thunderstorm. Streets are deserted, shops and restaurants closed. Two elderly men argue on the sidewalk. Are they arguing politics, football or ancient rivalry over a school-years sweetheart?

I attend Mass at the cathedral: pitched roof lined with timber, floor paved with unglazed tiles, white pillars, white walls. Does the congregation know that Chavez's hero, Fidel Castro, closed churches, banned religion? That wearing even a small crucifix became a criminal offence – as was celebrating Christmas?

The streets of Coro are already decorated with Christmas lights.

Coro claims to possess the first crucifix raised in South America. The crucifix is unadorned wood and stands in a domed shrine in the plaza between a convent, the cathedral and a church. Secret cellars lie below the buildings, sanctuaries against pirate attacks. Francis Drake and his associates were the pirates. I was taught at school in England that they were heroes.

The historians of Hollywood agree. Brits only become Hollywood villains with the American War of Independence.

Such is art.

All art is political, declared Fidel Castro shortly after the Triumph. Homosexuals and politically incorrect writers and performers were excluded from the Artists' Union and banned from publishing or performing. Homosexual painters were forbidden exhibitions.

In Coro, paintings by Elizabeth Ortiz are exhibited in the munic-ipal art centre across from the cathedral. Elizabeth's paintings are full of love and faith and colour. Her home is in La Vela, a fishing village midway between collapse and gentrification. Villagers wait in line at polling booths. Many men are already drunk and slouch in groups at street corners, caps reversed, sleeveless singlets, patched chinos, cheap trainers. Women hold hands and walk carefully in pairs.

Elizabeth Ortiz's home is newly built on a mud road. Elizabeth is a broad, dark, mature woman, comfortably overweight. She wears long multicoloured skirts and bright blouses. She has travelled through a Catholic upbringing to Buddhism and brown-rice medi-tation. Now she is born again as a Baptist Christian. She is quiet but determined in her faith: it shines through her paintings. She has two grown children, never bothered with a husband. She is dismissive of men; men are nothing but trouble.

She says, of the Chavez Revolution: 'The cure is worse than the illness. Write what I say.'

Late evening and Coro is closed tight. Fireworks celebrate Chavez's as-yet undeclared victory. I doze in front of the television – wake and discover that Chavez has lost by a couple of percentage points. Gov-ernment and Party machine worked for a *Yes* vote. Streets in every town were pasted and hung with posters and banners. Hundreds of buses carried supporters to Caracas. Yet, in tens of thousands, these same supporters of reform stayed away from the polls. The people of Coro must be in shock. I shall move on in the morning.

TO COLOMBIA
Monday, 3 December

The zone cither side of the Venezuela/Colombia border has an evil reputation. Drug cartel killers and right-wing paramilitary killers and moralist Colombian left-wing killers (the FARC so admired by

Chavez) fight over territory. Venezuelan police practice a low profile; Military keep to their barracks.

Two small towns separate Coro from the frontier. Late afternoon and a cop in the first advises me to book into the only hotel and stay in my room; outdoors after sundown is dangerous.

The hotel is a short-stop facility. Two guards pack massive handguns. Mosquitoes play Stuka dive-bombers in the bathroom. The showerhead is missing; so is the toilet seat. The tiny cotton towel might serve as a bandage for a pinprick. Take-out is beef leather and fries.

I lie in state on a smelly mattress, anti-bug incense spiralling at each corner, and flick channels on television. Choice is two men sharing one woman, two women in a homosexual tryst, or a moderately banal male/female one-on-one.

Football would be more interesting and I don't much care for football.

This is a fun way to spend my last night in Venezuela. I am out of bed and on the road by 6.30.

TO COLOMBIA
Tuesday, 4 December

Market day in the final town before the frontier and traffic is heavy. A yellow digger in the town centre backs across the road to load a dumpster truck. The first car breaks. A driver tries to squeeze through on the outside. A driver tries to squeeze through on the inside. These are Venezuelan drivers. Giving way is unthinkable. In minutes the road is blocked three vehicles wide in both directions. Klaxons and curses accompany me as I ease off the road, ride fifty metres in a dirt ditch and inch between market stalls. Circling through a couple of dirt lanes brings me back to the highway where two complacent cops watch the logjam build. By evening it should be one hundred kilometres deep. Maybe it will spread to Caracas. Venezuela will come to a halt.

Sixty kilometres to the frontier: poster after poster boasts of the the state governor's partnership with Chavez, thousands of houses built. Crammed on a patch of freshly spread gravel, no shade, stand a clutch of pale blue huts the size of garden sheds: unoccupied statistic houses – glories of the Revolution.

The highway divides a tidal lagoon and dams the flow of water. The lagoon inland of the highway is odoriferous. The seaward side is a shallow haven for water birds. A herdsman dressed in shorts and a baseball cap drives a few thin cows across the lagoon to graze sparse grass on a dune. I park and count bird species: two kinds of heron, waders, ibis, duck, oyster catchers, what appear to be moorhens, a small bird with long legs and a long, thin, curved beak...

Stretches of tar have crumbled on the narrow highway. Potholes are deep and dangerous. Scrub trees close in. Traffic is sparse and mostly indigenous inhabitants driving ancient rust-encrusted pickups with bent chassis and fenders lashed with wire. I am overtaken by two motorcycle cops. The cops don't wear helmets. They slow so that we can ride in company, turn back at the frontier and give a thumbs-up. Goodbye, Venezuela.

8

COLOMBIA

Frontiers demand patience and courtesy. I am first in the queue at Customs. A clerk issues a temporary import certificate for the bike. I require a signature from the Military and insurance. The Military commander hasn't arrived. I am directed to the army post the far end of Maicao town. I stop beside a biker at traffic lights. He points me to an insurance office on the next block. They issue certificates for a minimum of three months; a different company in the next town, Riohacha, issues monthly certificates.

I find the army post only to be told that the captain has left for the frontier. I ride back to the frontier and find ten drivers queuing outside Customs. The office will close for lunch in thirty minutes. The captain appears with the Customs clerk. The clerk spots me, speaks with the captain. The captain beckons me into the office, signs and stamps my papers. A sheepish smile is all I can offer those who had been ahead of me in the queue.

The highway cuts across the Guajira peninsula. This is indigenous territory, a dry land of sand dunes redolent with sea scent. Sun shines, a creeper spills pale blue flowers over thorn bushes. The Honda runs perfectly. We are freed from Venezuela and I am immensely happy.

The highway passes a state university and a private university side by side a few kilometres prior to the coastal town of Riohacha. The universities compete for students from Colombia's indigenous population. The ESCUELA BRITANICA is across from the universities on the right-hand side of the road. Bougainvillea and hibiscus cap a once-white wall. The wall encloses tree-shaded gardens, untidy buildings. The school nags as I ride on into Riohacha. A proper travel writer would investigate.

Our Brit hero, Drake, sacked Riohacha on a moral quest for pearls. Shade trees would improve the narrow concrete streets of low, whitewashed houses. The offices of the insurance company are closed for a two-hour lunch break. With an hour to wait, I sit on the steps beside a fruit cart, drink juice, eat a melon and chat with the cart's owner. He is a young man, married with two children. He scraped a living in Cartagena for a couple of years as a free-lance tourist guide before returning to Riohacha. The drop in violence brought him back. Guerrillas and paramilitaries are in retreat. Most of the country is safe. The economy has picked up and he can support his family – and he informs me that clocks in Colombia are an hour behind Venezuela. Offices won't open for a further hour. Motto: *When the going gets tough, men go for lunch.*

The fruit cart owner suggests the Gourmet Italiano – though he's never tried it. Fresh flowers, thick white-cotton tablecloths and napkins hint at a discovery. Stout matrons in tight dresses and fat men in suits occupy six of the ten tables – serious eaters. A waiter dismisses apologies for my appearance, seats me at a table against the wall and places my crash helmet and document bag on a vacant seat. I order lobster ravioli followed by a crème brûlée. The fresh pasta is perfect and perfectly cooked; the filling tastes of lobster as does the sauce. The crème is feather-light beneath brittle caramel. A lemon slice floats in the jug of iced water. A glass of a crisp white wine is perfectly chilled and coffee is memorable.

Colombia, Colombia, how I love you.

The offices of the insurance company are open: the computer system is down. Maybe tomorrow…

Tomorrow I will reach Cartagena where I won't ride the Honda; no need for insurance and the saving more than pays for lunch.

Guilt for gluttony hastens me back to the Escuela Britanica. A self-important indigenous gatekeeper, eight years old, directs me to park in the shade of a mango tree and conducts me to the principal's office. The principal is the owner, a Mrs Cohen. She is Colombian from Cartagena. Her mother is Catholic and she was raised a Catholic.

English is an essential of executive employment. English is a low priority of state schools and private lessons are beyond the financial reach of indigenous students. The Escuela Britanica is Mrs Cohen's attempt to fill the gap. It is a one-woman charity. It is admirable. Mrs Cohen is a warm intelligent woman. Her funds are limited and she needs a volunteer teacher. She can house and feed a volunteer and arrange part-time paying work at the universities. The job offers an opportunity to interact with the indigenous population. Riohacha is a safe town with good beaches and is a great base from which to explore the Guajira peninsula and the Ciudad Perdida high in the Sierra Nevada.

Readers, please pass the word…

SANTA MARTA
Tuesday, 4 December

Santa Marta is a major port and a popular tourist destination for Colombians. I enter Santa Marta at dusk and search for a hotel close to the seafront. School holidays and the first two hotels are full. My ankle gives way on the steps of a third where a room is vacant on the third floor – no elevator and the room is dank, dark and noisome. The receptionist kindly telephones a fourth hotel across the street – a clean room on the fourth floor is available. A boy offers to carry the small case that contains my books and diary. The elevator functions. I fetch the bike. Two men lift the bike into the lobby. I unstrap the bag from the rack and the concierge carries it to the elevator. I unpack, shower, change. I will write up my diary while eating dinner. Where is my dairy? Shit! The small case is missing.

I ask at the desk.

I ask across the road.

The case is gone.

The boy offered to carry it. Presumably he is still carrying it.

Frankly, I don't give a damn. I am too happy to be in Colombia – happy to be somewhere where eye contact earns a smile. I feel safe as I hobble on my crutches beneath Christmas lights on the seaside esplanade. I find an open-air café, drink cold beer and watch the holiday crowd.

TO CARTAGENA
Wednesday, 5 December

The small case carried off by the small boy fitted on the petrol tank. Turn the bike when parked and the klaxon button hit the case. Having only one case makes loading the bike easy. I stop at a bike mechanic on the way out of town and have the chain tightened. A bunch of bikers congregate, enquire how the trip has been – no charge for tightening and greasing the chain, or for a cup of good coffee. I love Colombia. I love Colombians. I wish that I were younger and able to clamber up the few thousand steps that thread the magical Ciudad Perdida in the nearby Sierra Nevada. Riding the coastal highway must suffice. Only in the last five years has this road been safe from FARC guerrillas and narco traffickers. Now army and police are in command and today's newspapers carry front-page photographs of a newly surrendered gang.

In places the sierra soars almost vertically from the coast. Other parts, there is a narrow coastal strip. The strip widens to harbour the most beautiful ranches anywhere on any continent. Shade trees are immense, rivers clean, magnificent views. Plump cattle and horses graze lush pasture; even the *vaqueros* appear well fed.

The highway divides, left to Bogota, ahead to Cartagena. I followed the Bogota road last year and stopped at Giron and Villa de

Leyva and Tunja, a wonderful journey – though piercingly cold over the passes at 4,000 metres in altitude. Now I follow the coast.

The highway crosses a vast lagoon. The lagoon was tidal prior to the building of the road. The water inland of the road is stagnant now and scum glistens on the surface. Fishermen's shacks on stilts huddle one against the other in the putrid water. Those who commissioned the road are responsible for both an ecological and a human disaster.

The historic quarter of Cartagena displays Hispanic colonial architecture at its best. The fortifications are immense. Churches and official buildings are superb. Houses range from humble and charming to magnificent. Medium magnificent describes the mansion where I stay. The mansion belongs to Anglo–Colombian friends of Anglo–Colombian friends back home. My room opens off a ground-floor patio where opulent breakfast is served by kindly maidservants.

Motorbikes are forbidden within the historic quarter; I have booked my Honda a night in the patio of a backpacker's hostel beyond the walls.

Evening and I wander the streets and admire the buildings and walk out through the gates to the Parque Centenario where I sit at a kiosk and order beer and a jumbo-size shrimp cocktail. The moon shines overhead. Arc lamps light the city walls. Shrimp are delicious; beer is chilled; so is the fat old Brit. Two elderly Colombians draw me into conversation.

'How are things?' I ask.

'Better, a little better.'

And, for me, infinitely satisfying…

I recall so many warnings of Colombia prior to my journey south; much of it based on media reports, Republican politicians, druggy American thrillers (Tom Clancy) and Hollywood. I rode south from Cartagena through Bogota, Cali, Armenia and Popayan to the Ecuadorian border at Ipiales. I climbed over passes and rode across lush cattle country and tropical wetlands, some two thousand miles. I met only with kindness and humour; not once did I feel in danger.

Surely the beauty is unrivalled and what magnificent architecture. Of all South America's cities, Popayan, abustle with university students and with wonderful views of the two cordilleras, is perhaps my favourite. The entire centre is Hispanic colonial: churches, monasteries, mansions of the Cauca Valley sugar barons, more modest homes of the bourgeoisie, simple cottages of clerk and artisan, all remain pristine and of perfect proportions.

And here, in Cartagena, forget for a moment the tourist hordes; wander moonlit streets within the walls, sit at an open-air café and people-watch or join my hostess and listen to tales of family and how it was in the bad years, friends ambushed and murdered by those FARC guerrillas so much admired by Chavez.

This glorious city was my starting point for the circumnavigation of South America: Colombia, Ecuador, Peru, Bolivia, Argentina, Chile, Argentina again, Uruguay, Brazil, Venezuela and back to Colombia. A painful ankle is a cheap price for the joys of so many new friendships and so much beauty. Tomorrow I will seek a yacht for passage to Panama.

9

SAN BLAS ARCHIPELAGO

CARTAGENA
Sunday, 9 December

Seventy-five is late in life to try proving something about myself. At best I am a cowardly lion. Fifty miles per hour in a Ferrari is too fast. Skiing black runs is for masochists or adrenalin addicts. The Road of Death in Bolivia is to be avoided. So is the Darién Gap…

The Gap is a ninety-mile stretch of swamp, jungle and mountain at the Colombian end of Panama. The indigenous population is unfriendly; as are a ragbag of paramilitary, guerrillas, narco traffickers and nameless nasties. Add snakes, alligators and billions of bugs and one fears for the sanity of those travellers who attempt the traverse.

A few bikers have succeeded by canoe and mud trail. So have a few backpackers. Others have been kidnapped, murdered or merely beaten. A few simply disappeared.

The alternatives are to fly or travel by boat.

A Chinese-American and I found passage on a banana boat when travelling south. Unbeknown to us, the crew were smugglers, not of drugs but of goods ranging from Chivas Regal to outboard motors bought in Panama's tax-free zone. They unloaded their cargo at night into launches off the Colombian coast. We were dumped on a beach thirty miles from the nearest police post.

Given my age, the Head of Immigration in Cartagena wondered at my lack of wisdom. Hadn't I recognised the smugglers for what they were? That they would have been safer cutting our throats and dumping us overboard?

Chinese-American Ming, now a monk in a Buddhist monastery, merely murmured the mantra, 'Simon, we wanted an adventure.'

Yes, but a pleasant one. A gentle cruise through the islands...

The San Blas Archipelago spreads along Panama's Caribbean coast from the Colombian border. Of the near 400 islands of the archipelago, at most fifty are inhabited. The indigenous Kuna run the islands as an autonomous province with little interference from central government and have maintained their language and unique social culture. Tourism is limited and strictly controlled. For yachtsmen, the islands offer a much-treasured cruising ground protected by one of the world's most ancient barrier reefs.

A few impecunious yacht owners based in Panama run a haphazard ferry service for backpackers through the islands to and from Cartagena. A message signed *Jean Paul* awaits me at the hostel where I've parked the Honda. Jean Paul will sail within the next few days. We meet at the Club Naútico. He is a dark, friendly, optimistic French-Canadian, mid-forties, worldly-wise (or unwise), certainly somewhat life-battered. His forty-foot steel sloop is equally battered. He is accompanied by a slim, balding, forty-something Bostonian with trustees. I will be the fifth paying passenger in company with two Brazilian brothers (one a student), a German college-graduate backpacker and a late-teenage Australian girl with blue eyes, golden curls and determination to pack ten years of experience into a single pre-university gap year.

Dyslexia (then unrecognised) ended my own schooling early; teachers graded spelling rather than content and term reports routinely warned that I could do better. Learned on the school lakes and on seaside holidays, sailing was my single skill, experience I bartered later into a career as yacht skipper in the Mediterranean. A wiser man with my expertise would have inspected Jean Paul's yacht before agreeing to take passage. On first view, poor paintwork hints at lack of maintenance. The coach-roof doors are flimsy ply, mangled mortise lock replaced by a small brass padlock. A two-burner household hotplate is lashed on top of the yacht's broken marine cooker;

the gas bottle is lashed to the rails. Not good – however I am short of time. I must be in New York for Christmas with my beloved daughter, Anya, who is due to give birth the first week in January.

CARTAGENA
Tuesday, 11 December

Jean Paul and Trustees Boston ferry the bike out in the inflatable dinghy, hoist it on board on the main halyard, wrap it in plastic sheet and lash it upright against the ratlines on the side deck. We motor across the harbour to a refuelling dock manned by a dark woman in short shorts. I pay with plastic as part of the fare. The lady produces a cold beer in commission and adds a couple of kisses to my ancient cheeks. Colombians are such hopelessly happy people … Heaven!

Late afternoon and my fellow passengers crowd the cockpit as we clear the harbour under motor. The bows lift to a light swell. Jean Paul asks me to take the wheel while he and Boston hoist the sails. The mainsail is obviously borrowed from a bigger yacht. The genoa has two holes in the canvas and one of the sheets is missing; the sail must be lowered when we tack, the sheet transferred to the other side. The swell builds as the coast fades. The yacht rolls and corkscrews. The Brazilian brothers and the German merely feel sick while Emma vomits over the side. Jean Paul and Boston drink beer.

My English accent irritates Boston and he is enraged when Jean Paul and I speak French. His own conversation is a litany of complaints: his ex-wife (a bitch) took his money; so did every other woman with whom he has had a relationship. His trustees are incompetents and thieves and refuse to up his monthly stipend.

The swell increases. This is the German's first time on a boat. Nervous, he asks if the waves are dangerous. Boston jokes of an impending storm and looks to Emma for admiration.

Wrong girl, even if she wasn't throwing up.

Neither Jean Paul nor Boston shows much understanding of sails. I suggest loosening the mainsail to balance the boat. The boat moves a little easier. Jean Paul goes below and collapses on a bunk. Boston opens another beer. Dressed in yellow oilskins, I act the Old Seadog at the wheel. Only Boston, maudlin drunk, keeps me company in the cockpit. Three hours and I am an exhausted Mr Reliable. The young German pokes his head out of the saloon. Could he make me a sandwich? Yes, indeed…

AT SEA
Wednesday, 12 December

I have forgotten (or choose to forget) the lesson of my sailing days: that the high seas come in a combination of three moods: boring, uncomfortable or scary. Coffee or soup would be comforting at night; however the household hotplate has no fiddles to keep a pot in place. Emma remains sick as does the younger of the two Brazilians. The German and the elder Brazilian learn to steer. Boston is a steady sipper. Jean Paul is good company; his yachting prowess is in doubt. He may have detailed charts; he never checks them. An admiralty pilot book would give information on the currents. Listening to the radio would be useful for weather reports. Jean Paul makes do with a hand-held GPS and doesn't own a hand compass to confirm his GPS position. Perhaps he is sensible in keeping out to sea rather than thread the archipelago.

Ming and I were fortunate last year with our horrible smugglers. They sailed inside the reef and anchored each night at a different island. They chose islands that had jetties and a telephone (perhaps all inhabited San Blas islands have telephones), rather than a small, uninhabited island out on the barrier reef – islands where yachts swing to anchor in glass-smooth water against a background of crashing surf.

Boston insists that none of the yachts making the ferry run cruise the islands; the voyage would take an extra couple of days; the owner would lose money; that sailing inside the reef is too dangerous in a sailboat.

Jean Paul's yacht draws four feet; the smuggler's boat was heavily laden and drew six.

According to Boston, chartering a catamaran is the only way to see the islands. Or sail with an owner who enjoys sailing and is confident in his navigation…

We passengers would have learned something of each other had we cruised in peace amongst the islands. At sea we are too tired for conversation, too isolated by our anxieties, too uncomfortable.

SAN BLAS ISLANDS
Thursday, 13 December

Thursday we creep inside the reef and anchor off Porvenir. At the western end of the San Blas Islands, Porvenir is little more than a sandbank topped with wispy grass and a few coconut palms, low-built Customs and Immigration offices and a police post. We have sailed outside and out of sight of one of the most beautiful and anthropologically interesting archipelagos in the Americas.

Jean Paul and Boston paddle ashore in the inflatable dinghy with the ship's papers and passports. The younger Brazilian is throwing up. His elder brother, Emma, the German and I swim to the beach. The Brazilian is a researcher for an Eco NGO and a freelance journalist covering environment and labour. His English is fluent, though guttural. A supporter of President Lulu, he believes that endemic corruption will defeat Lulu's efforts to benefit Brazil's underclass.

Emma's intelligence betrays her ambition to be a party girl. I suggest that ignorance of history causes the greatest errors in foreign policy.

Emma argues that all history is false; that her generation ignores history; history is written by the victors.

I suggest that historians gather sufficient facts for her to interpret according to her own prejudices and intellectual judgement. And I hear my youngest son chiding, 'Boring, Dad, boring…'

Jean Paul believes that he has a tame Indian on the adjoining island. The Indian knows that he has a tame yacht captain. The village is grass huts, sand streets, a concrete school building and no vehicles. Coconuts scent the air. I sit on the steps of the only store and watch cheerful children race each other round the huts. Given a week on the island without companions and I might learn something of the people, perhaps make friends. As a group, we interact with each other – and with a parrot that Boston abandoned here on a previous voyage. Villagers interact with our clicking cameras.

Nightfall and we sit round a fire and watch Jean Paul direct his tame Indian grilling fish, lobster tails and crab over the coals. Then back in the dinghy to the yacht, clouds beginning to cover the stars…

I have been sleeping in the cockpit and wake to rain and the wind rising. Thirty years since I last sailed; the reaction to the wind remains automatic and I sit hunched up and watch the lights ashore on Porvenir as the yacht swings, worrying whether we have sufficient chain out, whether the anchor will drag.

Finally Jean Paul surfaces and I go below. The screw fasteners on the port above the quarter bunk are missing. Rain has leaked in; my bunk is soaked. I switch to the saloon berth Jean Paul vacated and imagine a following sea breaking over the cockpit, water pouring in through the port and smashing the flimsy doors of the saloon companionway. This yacht is not ready for sea and should not be at sea. Jean Paul is irresponsible in carrying passengers and fortunate in their ignorance. Why do I enjoy his company? Primarily because he is a doer, an enthusiast, continually optimistic, and a giver of himself.

AT SEA
Friday, 14 December

We weigh anchor at dawn and sail into heavy rain clouds. The gap between two small reefs ahead should be easily navigated with charts, a reliable ship's compass, hand-bearing compass and GPS. Take the inshore course and we will anchor this evening in the bay of Mirimar where Jean Paul has parked his truck. Jean Paul chooses to sail out to sea. We head into the swell, a head wind and current of 1.5 to 2 knots. Tacking is hard work, dropping the genoa each time to lead the sheet across. The mainsail is baggy as a balloon and acts as a brake as opposed to generating power. At best we are gaining a couple of miles an hour. Passengers are depressed, the young Brazilian sick. His elder brother, the German and I take turns on the wheel. Emma, in the corner of the cockpit, huddles in jumpers and a windbreaker. Boston has switched from beer to rum.

Heavy rain-squalls drive the elder Brazilian and Emma below to wet berths. The genoa halyard jams – impossible to raise the sail. The mainsail rips. We struggle to bring the mainsail down and stowed and transfer the main halyard to the genoa. A squall rips the genoa cleat off its mounting. Jean Paul brings the yacht up into the wind so that we can capture the genoa sheet and make it fast to the main winch. Jean Paul goes below leaving the German, Boston and me in the cockpit.

The yacht is unbalanced without mainsail, genoa continually pushing the bows. I am at the helm and unable to keep the yacht on course. I call Jean Paul who starts the engine and we motor in towards the coast. The rain lifts and the sparse lights of a few villages show. I hand over the helm to the German and go below.

The furious slap of wet canvas wakes me. The yacht rolls violently. Jean Paul is yelling at Boston who has switched off the engine and lost the key. I clamber back on deck to persuade Boston that he go to his bunk before Jean Paul murders him. The German helps haul in the genoa so that Jean Paul can bring the yacht back on course.

Even the sick younger Brazilian is on deck now crowding the cockpit. Our greatest fear – that the engine key is lost overboard. Hopefully it has fallen amongst the wet blankets and wet clothes on the cockpit grating or has slipped under the grating. Jean Paul persuades the others to return to the saloon. He keeps the helm while I search fruitlessly through wet shoes and wet bits of clothing. Finally I lift the grating. There lies the key. The motor starts. Jean Paul won't approach Mirimar in the dark. We motor on west, rounding the northern cape at dawn to drop anchor inside Isla Grande.

ISLA GRANDE
Saturday, 15 December

Wealthy Panamanians have made Isla Grande their playground. The island is a steep jungle-clad rock a few hundred metres off the coast. A boutique hotel and luxury holiday homes face inward to the mainland village where we go ashore for breakfast. Boston drinks beer. The heavyweight black restaurateur jokes with Jean Paul about exchanging Emma for a better dinghy. Emma and the other passengers have had enough of the sea, faulty equipment, damp bunks, sliced-bread sandwiches and Boston's drinking. Better a bus from Isla Grande to Colon and onward to Panama City. I prefer to keep company with my bike…

Jean Paul is familiar with this last stretch of coast and we motor close in to shore. Mountains draped with jungle rise one behind the other. The sea is almost black below charcoal cloud; the coast is jagged cliffs with a few small curls of sand – one with two fisherman's huts huddled against the trees on the protected side of a creek. I no longer care that our progress is slow. I am content to gaze at the coast, enjoy its majestic beauty … And realise that I am freed of anxiety now that the others are ashore. Though only subconsciously, I have felt responsible for them. I was the eldest of the passengers and alone in having sailing experience; I knew that the yacht was unseaworthy and without necessary navigational instruments or sufficient lifejackets. What could I have done? Insisted that Jean Paul turn back to Cartagena? If he refused, threaten to denounce him to the Colombian and Panamanian authorities? My shame would have been the shame Cubans must surely feel when they denounce their neighbours. Why do I feel guilty? Both for failing in my responsibility that wasn't my responsibility and at the same time feeling disloyal to Jean Paul to whom I owe no loyalty.

Crazy? Unbalanced? Yes, but at least attempting to be honest…

My first cruise was on a double-ended Greek fishing boat bought on the Ionian island of Ithaka for eighty pounds. The boat had a single cylinder semi-diesel, a lateen sail and oars. I had rented a couple of rooms in an old house in the village of Assos on Cephalonia and was writing my first novel, *Even With The Shutters Closed*.

I sailed up through the islands to Corfu to be best man at an American's marriage to a Corfiot schoolteacher and returned to Assos with two English girls on holiday from Oxford University.

Compass? None.

Lifejackets? An inflatable mattress.

My chart? A sheet of brown wrapping paper on which a fisherman from Lefkada had drawn the Ionian Islands.

Now I criticise Jean Paul. Such is the hypocrisy or wisdom of old age…

Two rocky islets mark the turning south of the mainland coast. A deep passage lies between the headland and the inner islet. A shallow reef projects from the outer islet. A US registered yacht has driven on to the reef in the night. The yacht lies awash on the coral. The masts are clearly visible, the hull a white line in the surf. The crew has been rescued by the coastguard. Jean Paul takes the inner channel. One more hour and we drop anchor off the small town of Portobelo. The voyage is done…

10
PANAMA

The Spanish founded Portobelo in the last decade of the sixteenth century on the south coast of a deep inlet. It is a large village rather than a town and has been on a downward curve for the past few hundred years. Relics of Spain are three ruined forts, the Customs House (now a museum), a walled graveyard and three churches, one of which is famous for the statue of the black Jesus. Forested hills rise steeply immediately behind the village. Peaks are draped in black shrouds. Coconut palms mope, drooping fronds dripping. Inhabitants are mostly Afro-Caribbean.

When heading south, I waited a week in Portobelo in hope of a yacht. Memories are of rain and a damp mosquito-infested room and narrow bed with a thin nylon sheet that slipped off the damp spiky mattress each time I moved. The room overlooked the square where local drunks congregated. This visit I am Jean Paul's guest at his house on the hill. Jean Paul designed the house: he is not an architect. The best part of the house is a top-floor covered terrace. A male Nicaraguan house-sitter with an arm in a cast opens the door. He was cleaning the monkey cage yesterday. The cage was balanced on the corner of the terrace with a single wooden prop. The prop snapped. The cage fell fifteen feet to the hillside. Both the Nicaraguan and the monkey were inside the cage. The monkey is small and black. It survived the crash and now lies on the terrace curled against Jean Paul's Rottweiler. Neither dog nor monkey shows interest in our arrival; the cage incident has lowered their faith in man.

I travelled with Jean Paul to give Portobelo a second chance. He has promised prawns at the local yachties' bar. The bar is closed (wouldn't you know?). We eat fried chicken and chips in an empty restaurant beside a slot machine that burps tuneless music.

PORTOBELO
Sunday, 16 December

Up at dawn, I shower and follow a black lady in a pink nightdress downhill towards the village crossroads. Rain has left the tar wet and the earth verge dark brown. The corner restaurant at the intersection is closed. The restaurant is open-sided with a raggedy palm-thatch roof; steel shutters secure the concrete kitchen and store. I wait with the elderly cook on a bench outside and watch the night-dress woman cross the street to the Chinese store. The gutter outside the store overflows with abandoned fast food containers and plastic bags. A pair of vultures flaps at each other as they peck for titbits. Four men and a woman lean against a double-cab silver truck. The woman is marginally less drunk than the men.

The yearly Spanish treasure fleet gathered where Jean Paul's ghastly yacht swings to anchor. The treasure of the Americas crossed the small cobbled bridge to the right of the restaurant and was assessed and stored in the Customs House at the head of the village square. Imagine sentries armed with pikes and muskets where now a pack of skinny dogs sniff through a rubbish heap.

The restaurant owner crosses the square. On my first visit to Portobelo, she said of the local men, 'They are cold. They have no heart.' I responded by buying her a rose in Colon. Now she greets me with, 'The writer, you back?' and offers me her cheek for a kiss.

Two small boys drag chairs out from the store and arrange them round the plastic-top tables. The four drunks and the woman fall into the double-cab truck. The driver sucks on a quart bottle of rum and spits on the road (for luck?) before starting the engine. He stalls on the first attempt then speeds off towards Mirimar.

The small boys sit with me and we exchange family information. A passing drunk in a black leather hat interrupts from the road. I nod in agreement to whatever he says and mumble 'Yes,' a few times. He takes *Yes* for an invitation, sits at the next table, shouts for coffee and attempts conversation in staccato sentences. The sentences are unconnected. He is disconnected.

The village is wakening. Overweight men and overweight women head for the Chinese to buy marginally mould-free sliced bread. The restaurant owner summons the boys to help sell lottery tickets in the street. Two small optimistic chickens peck at nothing beneath my table. Vultures and a black ibis inspect the stream from the parapet of the Spanish bridge. Rubbish litters the stream.

A plain-yellow US school bus squeaks to a halt. The bus must be a newcomer to the bus community. Established buses are painted with pop stars and movie stars, Jesus Christ and a variety of Christian saints together with spiritual exhortations.

A Toyota double-cab stops outside the Chinese; the on-side rear door has taken a hit, front and rear fenders buckled and tied with wire. The driver gets down and yanks the passenger door open. An elderly man gets out, no thanks for the ride, no 'Good morning'. The driver climbs back behind the wheel and drives off. A fat lady, hair tied in a white-and-scarlet bandana and wearing a scarlet top and tight white knee pants greets me with, 'Good morning, uncle.'

A response of 'Good morning, my heart' earns a flirtatious smile.

My eggs come served with two slices of ready-sliced white bread spread with bottom-end margarine together with a third cup of the cheapest brand of instant coffee.

Jean Paul arrives and declines coffee in favour of a bus leaving for Mirimar. At the far end of the coastal road, Mirimar's inhabitants are mostly Afro-Caribbean. The hamlet is the supply point for Kuna Indians shipping supplies out to the San Blas islands in their canoes. Offshore mangrove shelters the wooden quay at the end of a yellow clay street. Recent rain has left the street wheel-grooved and puddled. The Customs House is the only two-floor building in the hamlet; the remainder are two-window tin-roof concrete bungalows. A couple of huts serve fried fish. Three open-front bars the primitive side of primitive provide social life for local alkies. Jean Paul's truck is parked beside an abandoned fibreglass skiff in a fenced lot. The gate has a broken padlock. We drive to the cleanest of the three bars and are midway into the first beer when a Suzuki jeep skids to a halt. Out scrambles a diminutive, skinny, grey-haired Frenchman waving a small-bore rifle. He is screaming abuse at Jean Paul. The abuse is less impressive than the rifle.

A falsetto giggle from a large black alkie at the bar adds fuel to the Frenchman's fury.

The barman shouts at the alkie to shut his mouth.

Jean Paul begs the Frenchman to be reasonable.

'Reasonable!' screeches the Frenchman. He is the owner of the vacant lot where Jean Paul had parked his truck – his rage that Jean Paul hasn't told him that he was taking the truck.

'My fault,' I interpose, explaining that I had insisted on a cold beer.

The Frenchman is pleasantly surprised at finding an Englishman who speaks French. His rage subsides from fast boil to slow simmer. Jean Paul both apologises for his thoughtlessness and sounds apologetic.

Forgiven, we drive back towards Portobelo. Potholes in the thin tarmac are more prevalent than last year. The rest is the same, rain clouds shrouding the hills, a few dairy farms, a few hamlets. We stop for a beer at a foreign-owned pizzeria where the road divides. Jean Paul talks with the owner while I join two couples in their thirties and an older woman at a table. The men are brothers, white and Texan. The younger lives here in Panama and runs an eagle protection program. His partner is Mumbai Parsee via the US. The elder brother is a crew-cut Bruce Willis lookalike. His wife is Afro-American – as is the older woman who is immediately outgoing, sharing her pizza as we laugh and talk politics. How did this happen? Wonderful! I need days, not hours. Sadly, we only have minutes. Or I could visit her in Manhattan.

Boston, the Nicaraguan and Jean Paul are on the yacht unloading the Honda. I sit on the end of the dock with the American whose yacht we saw yesterday smashed on the reef. A thin man in his late thirties, he has run out of tears and weeps dry-eyed as he tells of the wreck. His life has sunk with the yacht. His wife, children and his father are due this evening from the US. They were to cruise through the islands. Skipper was his chance to prove himself. He had imagined his children's admiration, his father and wife having to re-evaluate their contempt earned by past failures. Or am I arrogant in imagining relationships of which I know nothing?

Jean Paul, Boston and the Nicaraguan unload the bike from the dinghy. Boston attempts to be masterful by calling me Christopher, a name he apparently associates with Woosterish Brits. He then goofs by begging to borrow twenty dollars, assuring me that Jean Paul will repay the loan.

A dirt track climbs from the dock to the highway. A man shouts at me from the bar at the intersection, trying to scare me into falling. Such is Portobelo – and I recall on my last visit kids shouting and pretending to throw stones as I rode by. Of all the Americas, only on this short stretch of coast eastward from Portobelo has this happened.

Jean Paul introduces me to the mulato mayor in the evening. I wonder that the town's inhabitants show so little respect for the beauty of their surroundings; strewing the streets with rubbish is unlikely to attract tourists.

The mayor replies that improving Portobelo is a work in progress. 'We must first change the people's mentality.'

A *mestiza* masseuse visiting Jean Paul's house says of Portobelo's men, 'They are animals. They have no education. They don't want education. They are arrogant, so arrogant. For them women are nothing, only to be used…'

And later, sitting on Jean Paul's terrace, Jean Paul talks of the owner of the restaurant where we ate breakfast at Isla Grande as having raped at least four women.

Why did Jean Paul greet him with such apparent friendship? Yet I recall the restaurateur offering Jean Paul a good dinghy in exchange for Australian Emma. A joke? Yes, but is this someone you joke with?

Jean Paul answers that this is what it takes to be part of the coastal society. He tells me of other rapes. Rape apparently is the Portobelo equivalent of a mixed-sex croquet match.

I shall be out of here in the morning.

COLON
Monday, 17 December

The port of Colon marks the Caribbean end of the Panama Canal. Downtown Colon is dangerous. Beware!

On my first visit, I asked two policemen for directions to a bank; they wirelessed for an armed escort to lead me sixty metres round the next corner. Three teenage thugs jumped my travelling companion, Ming, ten metres from the entrance to his downtown hotel. One of them held a knife to Ming's throat. I stayed out in what was the Canal Zone during the US occupation. The hospital had been converted recently into a hotel, the Harbour Inn. I stayed there a week or more, one of their first guests. On this visit they comp me a room in gratitude for the publicity I've spawned.

A true US hero lives across the street from the Harbour Inn. Junior was a top sergeant in the US marines. He was running a parachute jump when a cord caught round his left arm. The cord plucked him out of the plane. He was midway down before he realised that he'd lost all but a couple of inches of his left forearm. Now he fishes from a dugout canoe, wrapping the line round his stump. A big fish will mark his stump with red burn lines. Puerto Rican, he is married to a Panamanian and they have a young daughter.

Of the local men, Junior says, 'About every man I know here has a wife and three women on the side, all with kids. The men sit around in new shirts and pants and trainers. The kids go hungry…'

When writing of Panama's coastal Caribbean, I quote Junior and Jean Paul, the masseuse, Portobelo's mayor and the owner of the restaurant in Portobelo. My own opinion: the landscape is beautiful; so is the sea; the San Blas archipelago is a glorious cruising ground…

11

TO NEW YORK

Poverty is the Master. The cheapest airfare to New York is with Taka from San José, Costa Rica, via Guatemala City. Landing time at Kennedy is eleven o'clock at night. I store the bike in Junior's carport and travel with Junior to Panama City and catch a bus up the Pan-American Highway to the Costa Rica frontier. This side of Panama's mountain spine is less humid and less tropical than the Caribbean coast. Horse paddocks and cattle ranches come decorated with billboards advertising golf courses and choice of beachfront or mountainside retirement communities directed at North American tax exiles.

A scruffy gentleman from Michigan (let's call him Mich) and his Panamanian Hispanic wife share the adjoining seat on the coach. Mich is in his early sixties with a small pension; she is twenty years younger and plainly dotes on him. Mich has bought a few acres on the slopes of the Cordillera Central where they aim to be self-supporting. A son by his first marriage stayed a month helping to build their house; a spare bedroom and bathroom for paying guests will follow when funds permit. They grow organic vegetables and soft fruit, keep chickens and have planted apple and pear trees.

Mich was a biker, Harleys of course. A broken back (four years on disability) and a broken leg (two years on disability) enforced his graduation to four wheels. Now he needs heart surgery. A Vietnam vet, he is entitled to free hospitalisation in the US. He won't go north without his wife and she has been refused a visa. Yesterday they waited three hours to be interviewed at the US Consulate. The interviewer was a young Chinese-American wedded to bourgeois respectability. Mich is an old gringo; his wife is a younger Panamanian – defined by prejudice as a Latina whore. That they might love each other is immaterial – or ridiculous.

The visa is refused, no reason given, no apology, no sympathy. One more enemy made, as if the US doesn't have sufficient enemies in Latin America.

Mich was already an enemy of the present Bush Administration and of corporate America.

He refers to the Iraq War as Dick Cheney's Great War for Oil and claims that the Bush family's best friends are the Saudi Royals.

Halliburton successfully lobbying for tax-free status for petrol-guzzling SUVs weighing in excess of 6,000 kilos (is this true?) induces further rage.

Ex-Military himself, he is most infuriated by water-boarding and US Military ill-treatment of prisoners.

The bus driver drops them off at the junction with a country road leading towards the cordillera; Mich's truck is parked up the road on a local's farm. I watch them set off, Mich with a slight limp. They walk hand in hand, both a little overweight, so obviously devoted to each other, so obviously a couple. Mich has given me directions to their home and a neighbour's telephone number – they don't have a telephone.

What will happen to them?

Mich can't afford surgery here in Panama and he won't go north on his own.

Damn the consular official for the nationalistic arrogance that makes him certain that all she wants in the relationship is to get into the United States. Living in the US isn't a universal dream. Would watching them, as I do now, alter his presumption?

And why am I damp-eyed over a couple of whom I know next to nothing and, despite the invitation, will probably never meet again

The border town of Paso Canoas is 400 kilometres from Panama

City and a little less from Costa Rica's capital, San José. No fence or wall separates Canoas Panama from Canoas Costa Rica. The backbone of the town is a six-lane highway with 200 metres separating the two sets of Immigration offices and Customs sheds. Trucks and coaches crowd all six lanes in each direction. Fatalistic truck drivers accustomed to waiting hours mooch from queue to queue. Short-stop hotels and stores cram the side streets. Many stores are Chinese-owned; stock packed roof-high in no discernible order makes shopping a treasure hunt. I was here last year in a successful search for mirrors and a headlamp for the Honda; I'd been daydreaming on a country road, missed the signs for a T-junction and hit a fence: *No fool like an old fool.* An arm cut on barbed wire, scraped knee and a few bruises were a lucky escape and I was fortunate in doing so little damage to the bike. Thick, hip-high grass on the verge acted as both brake and cushion. Today I'm on crutches and travelling by bus. Enough of that…

Costa Rican Immigration is on the night shift. The kid on duty wants to make a name for himself. Where is my yellow fever certificate? Lost in Tierra del Fuego.

No entry…

The kid's going to be on all night so I find a hotel.

TO SAN JOSÉ
Wednesday, 19 December

A Mrs Crawford posted on Amazon UK that her husband had binned my previous book, *Old Man on a Bike*, in disgust at it being nothing but a list of breakfasts (others binned it in fury at the politics). I am attempting to be a travel writer: breakfast is a major part of travelling, particularly for an old man who has to get up three or four times in the night; it is my fuelling-up time; time to gather my strength; prepare my head for the road.

Six o'clock this morning finds me seated at a table in Paso Canoas outside a shed with a sign claiming it to be a bar/restaurant. It is the only place open this early. Half a dozen slot machines line one wall opposite a bar that only a slot machine addict would frequent. The lack of background music blaring from radios is delightful. Ham and eggs are near perfect. Even the coffee tastes of coffee.

There is something pleasantly haphazard in strolling back and forth between countries without bureaucracy interfering. I am breakfasting in Costa Rica despite being forbidden entry. My hotel was in Costa Rica. The waitress at the restaurant where I ate last night thought that we were in Panama – though she wasn't certain. She was about to ask the manager. I told her not to bother; being off the map adds spice to a dish of prawns.

A triple line of trucks face south on the Costa Rican side of the frontier. Look towards Panama and the trucks face north. Mammoth Ford freightliners predominate. A few trees spaced haphazardly and not in line offer minimal shade to the dirt central division. Dwarfed by the trucks, the trees seem out of place and a little surprised by their surroundings; one is a small coconut palm.

Two tousle-haired truck drivers clamber down from their cabs, wander over, order breakfast and drag chairs and a second table out of the bar. A second cup of coffee and I am ready for CR Immigration. The Immigration kid's replacement is a young woman. I hand her my passport and she does the computer thing, stamps the passport with a ninety-day visa and wishes me good day.

Four coaches stand outside the CR Customs hall. Passengers have lugged their luggage to the search counter: kids with backpacks, Hispanics, a few indigenous. A Customs officer suggests I check for a seat with the conductor who holds the passengers' passports. The rear three rows are empty on the third coach.

The highway north through the mountains from Paso Canoas is narrow and serpentine. San José is in a valley at an altitude of over 1,000 metres. Razor wire for San José is what crinolines were for Victorian ladies, no butt unbuttressed, no wall unrazor-wired. I check the guidebook for a hostel. The hostel is vile and full. I walk a couple of blocks and find a small hotel not in the guidebook. The hotel began life as a private home. A wrought-iron gate protects the wooden entrance door, two sets of locks. The owner is a suspicious Costa Rican widow in her fifties, nicely plump, pinked lips, grey silk dress with a lace collar, beads.

Door ajar, she asks my nationality.

'Britanico.'

Not American?

'Britanico, Ingles,' I assure her.

The door opens fully. Only the gate separates us. How many nights?

Just the one.

The gate is unlocked. I am shown a small bedroom and bathroom off the entrance hall and invited to take tea in the rear conservatory: lace tablecloth, lace doilies on the chair backs, bone-china teapot and cups on a painted tray together with matching side plates and a seed cake. The tea is made with loose leaves rather than a sachet and the widow pours through a silver strainer. Truly respectable…

She tells me that she won't accept guests from the US, however old. Gringos (her word) only come to San José for the whores and bring whores into the hotel. The whores wait until everyone's asleep then open the door to robbers waiting outside.

Her husband was a gringo. He wanted her to sell up and move to Ecuador where he had business. He argued that Ecuadorians were nice people, good people, good workers. She argued that she was familiar with Costa Rica, knew the dangers and recognised the dangerous.

'Don't go out after dark, even on this street,' she warns as she cuts a second slice of seed cake. She was robbed last year not even twenty metres from the door.

'Young robbers. Always the young. They have respect for no one.' A small despairing shake of her head and she reaches for the teapot.

'More tea?'

'With pleasure…'

Where do I live?

A country village where a drunk caught urinating against a hedge would be a crime wave…

'You are fortunate, señor. Here also it was safe when I was young. Now…' She sighs. 'You cannot imagine how it has become. All is drugs and whores. The gringos have done this to us.'

As to her gringo husband, he has been dead eighteen months, shot in the head in Ecuador over a business deal. She receives letters from her husband's lawyer in Ecuador insisting that she come to settle his affairs. She has inherited money there – not much. A few thousand dollars. They can keep the money. She won't go. This sweet widow with neatly fluffed hair relates the tale with great calmness over the tea tray – as if we were discussing a small but slightly distasteful incident at the church fete.

To enquire as to her dead husband's business would be indelicate.

As for me, 'Be certain, señor, to call a taxi if you are going out. And remember to lock both locks on the iron gates and on the door…'

Seed cake is insufficient sustenance – shower and head for dinner. A couple of restaurants are on the same street as the backpackers' vile hostel – two blocks, surely no need for a cab. The widow is in the kitchen. Out I venture with the stealth of a teenager off to an illicit date. One of the restaurants is expensive. The other serves steaks and hamburgers at a dozen tables in the semi-dark. A posse of late middle-aged North Americans are at the bar. Two are resident and over-generous with local knowledge. A third is plainly infamous for never buying a drink. Subjects of conversation are which bar in town has the most girls and competitive boasting as to how drunk they were last night. The steak is OK; so are the fries. I don't risk the salad; suffering from dysentery on a long flight would be embarrassing. The waitress assures me that walking back to the hotel is safe – though not after ten o'clock.

SAN JOSÉ
Thursday, 20 December

A yellow fever inoculation seems sensible. The corner pharmacy opens at ten o'clock: steel shutters with three padlocks each and steel outer and inner doors with security locks top, bottom and midway are a reminder of my Russian agent's office in Moscow. The pharmacy manageress advises that I should take a cab to the Clinica Biblia.

The cab driver was a biker; the driver and a friend rode most weekends until the friend was killed by a hit-and-run on the way south to Panama for a Biker Fest. The driver hasn't got around to selling his bike, though he seldom rides. 'Too dangerous,' he says. 'Too many drunks on the road.'

And the streets round the clinic are dangerous. 'Drug addicts,' he says. 'They all carry knives…'

As to the inoculation, those over sixty-five must produce a letter from a doctor – so what to do in San José in the few hours left before leaving for the airport? Avoid drug addicts with knives. Better yet, avoid all robbers, junkies or otherwise.

The Metropolitan Cathedral on Calle Central is almost certainly safe. The exterior is tombstone grey. Inside, painted pillars support a glorious vaulted ceiling that runs the full length of the nave and leads to a half cupola beyond the high altar. I visited dozens of churches on the ride south. Churches have the right atmosphere in which to practice dying. I imagine death as a rosebud opening to release the spirit. Cling to life and the rosebud shrivels and becomes a prison. Hence the need to practice letting go. Getting hit by the truck in Tierra del Fuego was a true practice run and wasn't joyful – reason enough for my having avoided further practice until now.

So here I go, seated on a wooden bench, eyes closed, hands lightly clasped and concentrating on being thankful for a full life. Not giving thanks to anyone or to any God – simply being thankful, appreciative. And reminding myself that the body is a jail, that death is release and should be welcomed joyously as the route to being reabsorbed into the Oneness from which we come.

I am keen on the Oneness and balk at the God word...

To which our local priest back home remarked one evening that God doesn't mind what I call him or what route I take to reach him, merely that I arrive...

Getting in the mood for a practice run can take a while. Keeping one's eyes closed is essential to avoid distraction. I recall an indigenous woman in the cathedral at Cusco, Peru, short dress sprouting outward above muscled mountaineer's legs; or ballerina's legs below a multi-coloured tutu; Toulouse-Lautrec; late nineteenth-century Parisian debauchery – an unfortunate image to dwell on in a cathedral, especially when attempting a practice death run.

However keeping one's eyed closed for too long can disturb others in search of spiritual sustenance as in, *Is he dead*? Or, *Is he a Charismatic*?

In San José I am part of an unusually large congregation for mid-morning Thursday: prayer and razor wire are the twin defences in a city of robbers, murderous drug addicts, whores and gringos.

My attention is caught by two North American couples dressed in shorts chatting and giggling as they photograph statues. Would they act with similar disrespect in the Baptist church in Dallas?

I am not anti the United States. I am anti the present administration and feel sullied by our alliance. Is water-boarding torture? Yes, of course.

Local newspapers report that the tapes of torture have been destroyed by the CIA – not from shame at what was done but to hide the evidence from the law. So, yes, sullied seems a suitable word and is how we Brits are perceived now south of the Rio Grande...

12

NEW YORK

Thursday, 20 December

Pepe Gonzales, one-legged orthopaedic surgeon (retired), promised to get me back on my feet and riding. A promise of pain-free progress wasn't on the menu. Walk any distance and a spike pierces my ankle. I freeze and carefully turn my foot this way and that while waiting for the pain to ease. Aged gentlemen easily break a hip and slipping is my greatest fear. My balance is unsteady when first getting out of bed. Nocturnal bladder calls see me fumbling for light switches and crossing bathrooms with trepidation and I am travelling with crutches to trek through airports.

European travellers complain of rudeness suffered at the hands of US Immigration and Customs officials (US travellers are equally irritated when entering Europe). Near midnight at Kennedy and passengers wait hangdog in long queues to offer eyeball and passport for computer interrogation. A kindly officer waves me to the kiosk for diplomats. I have saved my pennies by travelling at an unsocial hour. Anya, dearest daughter, doubts my ability to cross a street and has ordered a limo to bring me out to Duchess County, New York. The limo surely costs her twice the price of my Taca Airlines ticket.

The limo driver is accustomed to Kennedy and has allowed an hour for officialdom. I am through in twenty minutes and wait his arrival. Snow deepens on the roads as we approach the farm. My daughter, belly proud, waits at the door. Love slices me open as would a scalpel. Joyously eviscerated, I disguise my tears behind an inanely sheepish and very British grin. 'Hi, Anya. You look great. Thanks for the limo…'

DUCHESS COUNTY, NEW YORK

I have been on the road three and a half months since leaving Rio Grande. This is recuperation time, crisp snow underfoot, views to the Adirondacks. My daughter's husband, Michael, explaining the intricacies of the racehorse business at midnight outside a mare's loosebox; his horse farm is what we Brits call a stud. I have never been a horse enthusiast; horses demand too much attention.

My brother is the horseman.

In Peru last year, I was proud at successfully riding my Honda on a viciously bad mountain road. Descending to the coast, I found an Internet café and was about to send a boastful email to Bernadette only to learn that my elder brother had won a cross-country jumping event; his fellow competitors were mostly teenagers!

The writer, Robert Sheckley, was Anya's genetic father. I am honoured to have been one of Bob's friends. English-language critics pigeonholed Bob as a writer of science fiction. He was judged differently in mainland Europe and in the Soviet Bloc where he was read for his ideas and admired as a master craftsman of the short story.

He is buried in the artists' corner of Woodstock cemetery. Anya and I visited his grave at Christmas. Snow covered the cemetery. We parked and watched as two deer broke out of the trees and bounded uphill across the gravestones. We will visit again when I've completed my ride; we will have Anya's son with us, Bob's and my grandson.

Anya…

I have one brother and four sons by two marriages, three grandsons, no sisters, no granddaughters and no daughter of shared blood. Anya adopted me when she was a young girl. I can imagine no greater honour than being adopted as Dad – Dad by love rather than Dad by blood. I wish that I was more deserving.

So there you have it, a love story when you expected travel.

Love is private and boring to the outsider so I leave blank the Christmas and New Year vacation and recommence confronted by a beautiful Taca Airlines clerk at Kennedy. Hispanic, she is young and small with short black hair and almost mauve eyes.

Why, she asks, am I flying to San José via Guatemala City?

I confess to being ruled by poverty.

The direct flight has vacant seats, she says, and issues a fresh ticket and boarding pass.

'Don't be silly,' she chides as I beg for permission to kneel and kiss her toes. Old whore that I am, I'm upgraded from cattle class to first. The bus south from San José to Panama City will return me to reality.

How do I feel?

Sad at leaving; sad that my grandson will arrive after my departure; sad not to have been home to see Bernadette and my sons and daughters in and out-of-law and my grandson and my brother and his wife; yes, and sad not to have visited Herefordshire with its villages and green hills and ancient woods and white-faced cattle. I have been away five months. Part of me is desperately homesick.

And I am nervous of the road ahead. I am also excited by thoughts of the road ahead. I will visit friends, meet new people, cross stupendous country. Finally I will ride north from the Mexican border through the United States. I understand Hispanic America. I know how it functions. I share thoughts and opinions and language with Latin Americans.

Small-town USA is unknown and unpredictable territory.

13
BACK ON THE ROAD

SAN JOSÉ
Thursday, 17 January

Nothing has changed over the holiday season; San José remains the razor-wire capital of the world. Ask if the city is dangerous and you are told, 'Very dangerous…'

So why visit?

God knows. Sex tourism is high on the list. Immature mature visitors from the US balance on bar stools and suck on beer bottles. Over-painted women a third their age cling to their arms and laugh at jokes made in a language that they don't understand.

A cab is the safe way into town. I am in good grace for not attempting to smuggle a whore into Hotel Posada Amon and am greeted with a kiss on both cheeks by the fluffy-lace widow. *My* room is ready, the room I occupied on my previous visit.

'And the grandchild?' the widow asks.

'No grandchild.'

Immediate sympathy for my daughter: 'Boys are always late.'

I am fortunate in finding an Iranian Frenchman for company over dinner. Producer of educational films, he has lived in Los Angeles, California. He is an optimist. He believes that the voters of the US have recognised Bush Administration politics as the dead end of the wrong road; that the US will change, recover its liberal roots.

I doubt that the US has liberal roots. The founding fathers were my fellow Brits and deeply conservative as were the leaders in the war for Independence; most were racist and religiously intolerant; many were slave-owners.

A Costa Rican gentleman buys me a couple of beers later in the evening in a bar owned by a US citizen. The Costa Rican complains of gringos owning so many of the hotels and bars in San José – those frequented by tourists. 'Even the beaches are owned by foreigners,' he says. 'They build walls to keep us out. Resentment is natural. Violence is natural.'

It is also natural for me to nod commiseration and continue listening to his complaints (he's buying). Such is life.

A retired Irish-American New York cop joins us. He is a New York cop type made familiar by movies: square jaw, short hair (in his case, grey) and the closed-shoulders stance of a boxer in the ring – though I have never watched a boxing match, so this also is opinion gained from Hollywood. The cop is a property developer. He began with run-down buildings on South Beach, Miami. Now he invests in San José. He owns a nine-bedroom town house that was a small hotel and two commercial buildings. He plans opening a bar in one of the commercial buildings. He says that every New York cop dreams of owning a bar; that the dream is a rebellion against the regulation that prohibits serving cops from owning a bar or dealing in booze.

The ex-cop is a Richard, which I find curious in a Catholic Irishman. He enjoys San José.

'You don't find it dangerous?'

'Nah,' Richard says.

We sip our beers while he considers.

Then, 'Yeah, maybe a little.' He tilts his head back to display a long white scar on the underside of his chin. A local kid knifed him, a real mess. A cosmetic surgeon worked magic.

We drink a few more beers and briefly discuss US politics. Were he to vote, Richard would vote Democrat – though all the presidential candidates are full of shit.

The gringo bar owner buys a final round. Then Richard escorts me to my hotel. His nine-bedroom home is on the next block. He walks with a slight swagger. At first glance I had presumed that he was in his mid-forties. Sixty is correct. His father is back in Florida.

Richard has taken him on eighteen cruises on cruise ships over the past few years.

Richard strikes me as a good man and unusual. However, I have known him barely an hour and have no proof that he was ever a cop or that he has a father. He may be a paedophile orphan crack-head gangster on the run from a triple murder charge; all that I can write with certainty is that I enjoyed his company. Such are the joys of travel…

ADVICE FOR BUS PASSENGERS
Friday, 18 January

I rode down the east coast Nicoya Peninsula on the journey south to Tierra del Fuego, then crossed over to the Caribbean coast, entering Panama over the infamous Bridge of the Americas. Why infamous? See pictures on the Web.

The Pan-American Highway follows the eastern littoral. The road from San José follows the eastern flank of the cordillera. Panaline coaches depart the bus terminal at one p.m. and are scheduled to arrive in Panama City at five o'clock in the morning. Heading north on the bus, we were on the inside lane. Heading south, we are on the outside. Don't look out of the windows unless you have a head for heights – and never watch the road: oncoming traffic will scare the hell out of you. I hide in a book until a truck sideswipes us and removes the side mirror. The truck doesn't stop.

Our driver halts on the soft shoulder. My idiot fellow passengers crowd that side of the bus to scope the drop; what they see is clouds. The bus tilts a little and I resist a desire to curl into a foetal ball.

Eight-thirty of a typical evening on a Costa Rican highway: our driver swerves. Thump! We've killed a cyclist. No lights on the bike. An ambulance removes the corpse. Cops remove our driver. He will be held six days pending investigation.

We passengers wait for a replacement coach.

In England, passengers would be in shock. Central America, dead cyclists are standard. The small boy in the seat ahead drapes a sheet to make a play house. Even a pair of nuns smile. I keep thinking of the family of the deceased – do they know he's dead? Or are they waiting up for him? And the driver? Horror must be churning his belly. All these lives changed.

I was under a truck in Tierra del Fuego.

Terror almost did for me in Venezuela.

Giving up takes more courage than continuing – the shame factor.

Ten-thirty and finally a local town bus arrives to take us to the frontier to meet a coach sent from Panama City. I sit in the front seat and watch the new driver. He drives with one hand on the wheel while jabbering into his mobile phone. The bus shimmies on the soft shoulder as he overtakes a truck. Surely murdering him would be justified…

COLON
Saturday, 19 January

One night to recuperate, then on to Colon by bus. My bike gleams in Junior's yard. Junior's brother-in-law opens the gates. Junior lies under the surgeon's knife in Panama City (hasn't Junior suffered enough?). I dawdle, sorting clothes and loading the bike while waiting in hope of news from Junior's wife. The operation is successful. Junior is in recovery and I can visit him on Monday.

I ride out along the coast to spend the night at Jean Paul's house on the hill above Portobelo (Jean Paul, on whose yacht I sailed from Cartagena). Jean Paul returned yesterday from visiting his family in Canada over the holidays. He sails with passengers for Cartagena on Wednesday. He has much to do; thieves have stolen all the copper wiring from his yacht. This is the village Jean Paul professes to love. Good luck to him – and good luck to his passengers. Two are young French women on vacation from a year at university in Cali,

Colombia – part of a five-year degree course at Lille. A third is Sicilian, perhaps in his late thirties, a tailor of men's and women's suits. He was a master diver with the Italian marines and has a disability pension – small reward for an embolism in the brain.

PANAMA CITY
21/23 January

President Noriega nationalised Panama's banks. The US invaded Panama and arrested Noriega for drug trafficking and money laundering (and concurrently slaughtered a thousand or so Panamanians – too bad).

Noriega was evil. He was a graduate *summa com laude* of the School of the Americas. Freed of his dictatorship, Panama has become an international financial centre. Restaurants serve excellent seafood. Waterfront condos are spectacular; so is the resulting traffic and pollution. Meanwhile property prices have quadrupled in five years. So have the number of banks. Many are US subsidiaries.

What do the banks do?

Launder drug money?

Surely not…

As for me, I've survived being Nigelled. Nigel is a burly Brit more or less resident in Panama and someone whom I shall remember fondly for years to come. He is a producer for Fox Sport, a fixer, and happiest when speaking on two mobile phones simultaneously – preferably whilst sneaking his car through an invisible rush-hour gap (he carries a reserve of Argentine Malbec on the rear seat and steers with his knees).

Nigel is friendly with a large portion of Panama's finance, real estate and hotel community. People enjoy his enthusiasm and his generosity. Visit Panama, he is the man to call. I called and have been wined and dined and lunched and breakfasted for three days. I have met people I hope to meet again, learnt statistics of Panama's property boom and joined with three of the city's foremost tourism experts on a live Spanish-language radio broadcast.

TO PUERTO ARMUELLES
Thursday, 24 January

I had either to flee Panama City or book into a sanatorium – such is Nigel's munificent hospitality. He took me for shrimp breakfast this morning on the waterfront before despatching me north to a sports fishing operation close to the frontier with Costa Rica. The Pan-American Highway crosses hill country with magnificent panoramas of Panama's mountain spine. I descend to the western plains and cruise at ninety kilometres per hour. The rear tyre blows. I am on a section of dual carriageway. Klaxons blare as the bike skitters side to side. Tip at this speed, end of journey – yet I don't dare brake and require a good fifty metres to halt the bike. Already breathless from fright, I push the bike up a gradient to a petrol station where a boy helps dismount the wheel. A three-inch nail has shredded the inner tube; fortunately I carry a spare; equally useful would be a spare leg and renewed nerves…

PUERTO ARMUELLES
Friday, 25 January

Puerto Armuelles began as a United Fruit company town. Texas Rex, his wife and daughter are establishing a sports fishing operation and run the Company's old guesthouse as a hotel. This is a splendidly romantic building with spacious air-conditioned rooms where I sleep in luxury – recompense for fear.

Rex landed an 800-pound marlin last week. Today he is boat-building in an old United Fruit warehouse. His daughter, Maria, runs the hotel and paperwork. His wife landscapes twenty kilometres along the shore, where the fishing lodge is nearing completion. The name of the fishing business is *Hookedonpanama*.

I have never recommended anything in which I didn't believe. I believe in Hookedonpanama. The new lodge has ten cabins and a clubhouse. The site is superb. Rex has five boats in the water. Young captains from the US are fanatic fishermen. Marlin fishing is the best in the world. The Puerto Armuelles guesthouse will remain open for casual guests.

The one downside (for a nervous biker) is a track of loose gravel to the lodge. I hate gravel. A truck pushes me wide and the bike slides into scrub. I struggle out from under and heave the bike back on to the track. My leg hurts…

Cameron is a Scot born in the Caribbean where his father was an agronomist with United Fruit. The Company have owned Cameron from birth. Now he is in his late fifties. He is big and florid and imposing as befits a king and he has been king in half a dozen countries. OK, Regent. The Company was king.

Cameron worked first at United Fruit's operation in Almirante on Panama's Caribbean coast from where United Fruit began shipping fruit at the turn of the nineteenth century. The road connecting Almirante to the rest of Panama was completed in 1995. Drive from Almirante to Panama City, you had to travel via San José, Costa Rica – a four-day journey even in modern times. The bridges into Costa Rica were built by and belonged to United Fruit: same for the road and railway and the port and the schools and hospital and ninety per cent of the houses in town.

Though less imposing than Almirante, Puerto Armuelles is typical of United Fruit towns. Housing is according to Company status: three small bedrooms and a small yard for clerks and mechanics; three medium bedrooms in a large garden for engineers and accountants. Offices and the guesthouse are zoned at the foot of a small hill that overlooks the town and wharf. Management houses are on the hill. The Regent's house is on the crest where I slump in an easy chair, drink cold beer and talk Company history with the good-natured Cameron.

Throughout the first half of the twentieth century, United Fruit had a near monopoly of the world's banana trade. They produced for seven cents and sold for seven dollars and enjoyed the wealth and power now wielded by narco-traffickers.

At best they were paternalistic.

At worst, they chose and deposed presidents and fermented civil wars: the clandestine war that crucified Guatemala for thirty-six years was a United Fruit Company creation supported by the CIA. The war began under the presidency of Dwight D. Eisenhower.

John Foster Dulles was Eisenhowser's secretary of state; Dulles' law firm represented United Fruit.

John Foster Dulles' brother Allen was on the United Fruit board before being appointed head of the CIA.

President Eisenhower's private secretary, Ann Whitan, was married to United Fruit's director of public relations.

I disagree with those political commentators who have drawn comparisons with Halliburton and the George W. Bush presidency. United Fruit was never tawdry. Good or bad, United Fruit had presence…

Here, in Puerto Armuelles, the plantation workers came out on strike in 2006. The operation was losing money: the King abdicated.

Cameron persuaded the Company directors to go the workers cooperative route; the cooperative is subsidised by the Panamanian government and Cameron's job is done. He and his wife are packing. Next stop is Mozambique where Cameron will oversee a multi-crop agricultural venture financed by Brits. This will be Cameron's first visit to Africa. He is in his late fifties and has made a ten-year commitment to the financiers. His enthusiasm is that of a twenty-year-old. He runs me back to the hotel at two in the morning. I have been moved in with one of the young boat captains from the US who snores gently. I snore loudly. He retreats to a couch in the lounge.

***

FRIDAY, 25 JANUARY

A DAY TO REMEMBER

ANYA AND MICHAEL ARE THE PARENTS OF AN EXTRAORDINARILY HANDSOME

AND INTELLIGENT SON,

SHANE RAVI.

I AM A DELIRIOUSLY HAPPY GRANDPA.

***

COSTA RICA BORDER
Saturday, 26 January

Entering Panama from Colombia, I was issued a thirty-day visa. Customs gave me a thirty-day permit for the bike. I received a fresh visa when returning from the US. Not so the bike. The bike has overstayed. Panamanians sympathise with such small irregularities. The Customs officer at Carpacho glances at the bike documents, stamps them and gives me a grin. The relevant clerk in Costa Rica is a small man, grey wiry hair, half-moon spectacles and a power complex. I watch as he revels in exercising his authority over bus and truck drivers; Danes call such an official a counter pope.

My bike documents are photocopies. I have crossed the length of South America on photocopies. I have a letter from the police in Ushuaia explaining the loss of the originals. The counter pope doesn't give a damn for South America. I produce originals or I don't enter Costa Rica.

I sit in an office and wait for the Head of Customs. A woman Customs clerk glances at me from behind the counter. She is plump and comely, wears a nose stud and frequently smiles. A while passes before she enquires as to my problem. She disappears for a few minutes, returns and escorts me outside. 'Get a lawyer's stamp on an affidavit,' she instructs and grabs one of the touts who seek tips for aiding travellers transit the border.

The tout conducts me to a kiosk where a young Chinese Panama-nian woman types my affidavit and complains that Costa Ricans are a pain in the butt.

A lawyer´s mother runs a dress shop. Learning that I am a writer, she charges me a poem for taking the affidavit to her daughter´s office in David.

The daughter charges twenty dollars for a stamp (less stressful payment than the poem).

The Costa Rican counter pope accepts the affidavit with ill humour.

The comely Customs woman accepts a kiss on both cheeks.

Finally I am on my way.

Caribbean Costa Rica was banana plantations and almost tourist free. West coast Costa Rica is for sale. The Pan-American Highway follows the littoral. Flat land is given over to oil palms and billboards advertising subdivisions and condominiums, spas and country clubs, serpent farms and butterfly farms, horse riding, surfing and canopy trails – plus every other type of crap that might gull a tourist into an investment

I take a side road into the hills. Thirty years ago this would have been virgin forest. Now billboards tower over the road and holiday villas squat on cleared lawns amongst the trees. Glimpses of the ocean are small compensation for such desecration. Worse is a piercing screech from the motor as we climb. Please God, not a bearing. This is a Honda 125: Honda 125s never ever break down.

I pull on to the verge and switch off the engine. The screeching is even louder.

The screeching is cicadas protesting at billboard encroachment.

Quepes is my destination. The final forty-seven kilometres are dirt. Massive trucks drag dust clouds. Grit fills my eyes. Construc-tion machinery looms out of the dust. Rocks kick the front wheel and the rear wheel; my butt is numb and my thighs cramp. More dust. A sign looms out of the dust. The sign warns of a bypass round an uncompleted bridge. Miss the sign and plunge twenty feet down a dead drop. This is not fun…

Dusk as I enter Quepes. I peer through eyes bunged up with dust and spot a small hotel with a courtyard protected by iron gates. The receptionist hails from the US and resembles a late middle-aged undersized frog in a straw hat. He supplies information while entering my details in the guest book: gringos frequent the bar one block to the left on the sea front; the working girls are safe. Best fish restaurant is across the bridge and a further two blocks. The fish interests me.

My room is clean. Towels are big. The shower has hot water. I rinse off sufficient dirt to construct a beach in the shower tray.

Down in the courtyard a woman dismounts from a 650 KTM trail bike. The KTM dwarfs the Honda. It has aluminium side panniers and a proper biker bag on top of the petrol tank. The rider is fair, late thirties, my height, green eyes, long hair. She wears a proper full-face helmet and is dressed in a proper biker suit with a spinal support.

I feel somewhat inadequate.

'Hi,' I say.

She says, 'Hi…' A real biker conversation.

She took a fall yesterday and limps a little. She declines my offer of help in carrying her bag. Maybe she will catch me later at the fish restaurant two blocks up from the bridge. Or maybe not…

QUEPES, COSTA RICA
Sunday, 27 January

Quepes by day is OK. I load the bike, visit the ATM machine, eat breakfast. Eight-thirty and my fellow biker remains in bed. She joined me for dinner last night. She is from Denver, Colorado, and deals in eco power such as commercial wind farms. She is a sportswoman. Too many falls on mountain bikes and skis and whatever have turned her into a physical wreck. She and my mountainboarder son, Jed, could compare scars. Probably her knee played up and kept her awake. Now she needs a lie-in. Whatever, I can't wait; sad, as I want to wish her well and hope to learn whether she takes the Limon/Almirante road out of Costa Rica into Panama. If so, how did she find the United Fruit rail bridges, particularly the Bridge of the Americas?

I loathe having trucks on my butt. The wind strengthens all day, finally threatening to shove me off the road, or, worse, under the wheels of oncoming traffic. I stop for coffee in Liberia. A posse of Panamanian bikers on Harleys pulls in. The bikers say *Hi* in that distant manner rich guys on Harleys reserve for old men riding pizza delivery bikes.

I ride on into the wind.

The wind becomes a gale.

Tomorrow will be better. So why am I persecuting myself? Sensible to turn off prior to the Nicaraguan border at La Cruz.

A Dutchman owns the hotel at the top of the hill in La Cruz. The hotel is down-market and old-fashioned, much of it built in timber. The Dutch are friendly. This Dutchman is exceedingly fat and is watching television out on the terrace. I am invited for a beer by a gentleman blessed with a long straggly beard. This gentleman owns a cabin in South Carolina where he fishes, and a cabin in West Virginia where he distils moonshine. He claims that his moonshine has cachet in West Virginia circles and fetches double the price paid for legal bourbon. He gives me his address and his telephone numbers and invites me to stay on my journey north through the US. The Dutchman is watching television on the terrace.

I walk over the crest of the hill. The gale shoves me towards the edge. The view is spectacular. I watch the sunset and walk back to the Dutchman´s hotel. The Dutchman is watching television on the terrace.

The hotel is without a liquor licence; the Moonshine Oldie keeps a private ice chest behind the bar. We drink a couple more of his beers while the Dutchman watches television. We switch to bourbon and lime while the Dutchman watches television. The Dutchman doesn't strike me as particularly friendly. But how would I know? I am at the bar. He never speaks and never takes his eyes off the television. Weird…

Sunday and the restaurant is closed: all restaurants are closed; I find a bakery open near the church and eat cake. Thus passes my last night in Costa Rica. This traverse has been very different from the journey south. Reading my notes, I find few moments of real joy, possibly because I have been on the road so long and am homesick – more importantly, because I haven't connected with Costa Ricans, perhaps because of the route I've taken; those using the Pan-American Highway seldom have time for conversation and the entire coast is under development for tourism; foreigners are either seen as exploiters or marks to be exploited.

Heading south I stayed a few days in a small hill village on the Nicoya Peninsula. San Francisco Coyote. I had fallen off the bike for the first time. Touching the front brake did it. I was almost at a standstill and looking back over my shoulder to wave down two locals for directions to a hotel. The fall shattered the right-side mirror and a shard sliced open the back of my right hand. A doctor stitched the cuts on a table in a local restaurant. Saturday and he and his wife were on their way to a party. The wife sat beside me. She wore a short dress that exposed her thighs. My looking at the thighs might have irritated the doctor so I watched television, a gangster movie starring Al Pacino. The restaurant's clientele were more interested in the doctor's needlework. The doctor told me to rest a few days. I rented a room behind the general store and sat in the shade out front and chatted with locals of every age. Fun…

And crossing Costa Rica, west to east was a good experience.

I am not complaining. All journeys have their good times and bad. This hasn't been bad – merely somewhat tedious.

14

NICARAGUA

The gale forced me off the road into La Cruz yesterday evening. This morning I suffer both gale and continual rain and arrive soaked at the frontier. A queue of trucks a kilometre long waits for clearance into Costa Rica. A driver tells me that transiting a truck across the border on a good day wastes twelve hours; bad can be as much as three days. Costa Rican officials are self-important and understaffed. Nicaraguan officials are pleasant and understaffed. The rain becomes a downpour – no shelter for the bike.

I chat with a US biker on a 650 trail bike. He and a band of biker brothers took the wrong road yesterday, more of a riverbed than a track. He dropped his bike seven times. Heartening, this further confirmation that I am not the only biker who falls on his butt.

A Nicaraguan official issuing vehicle import permits passes my photocopies to his boss. I explain the loss of the originals in Argentina. Lunch hour and two of the boss's juniors take a break. The boss is of generous nature and processes my paperwork himself, moving from desk to desk, searching through drawers for the necessary stamps and ink pads. Meanwhile, a thirteen-year-old boy carries my briefcase and laptop and crash helmet. An elderly cop teases the boy in a kindly manner. Ninety minutes and my papers are suitably emblazoned and I am free to ride on through the rain.

The Pacific Ocean lies a few miles to the west. The littoral is a flat, lush land of neatly fenced cattle paddocks. The road to Granada follows the shore of Lake Nicaragua. Low black cloud blankets the lake and I crouch over the petrol tank as squalls chase each other across the water.

GRANADA
Tuesday, 29 January

The Conquistador, Francisco Fernandez de Cordoba, established Spanish sovereignty over Nicaragua in 1524. The beautiful colonial city of Granada is sited on the west shore of the immense Lake Nicaragua. I am staying a few days in luxury. I met with Gillian and Joe on my ride south. Gillian is a Brit. Joe is Texan. More than Texan. Joe *is* Texas – the Texas we Brits know from Hollywood. Six-six, blue-eyed, rangy, and both an oil man and a rancher: what more could a Brit maiden desire? As for the oil, Joe's father would remark that even a blind hog could find an acorn in an oak forest – thus Joe's *Blind Hog Oil Company*.

Gillian and Joe have resurrected a seventeenth-century colonial house a block from the cathedral square. The house has two patios. The rear patio has a pool bordered by tropical shrubs and climbers. I swim sedate lengths between sipping gin and tonic – a very, very, very, privileged guest.

The house has no need for air-conditioning. All rooms open to patios or the road. Through-drafts keep the air moving and cooled by water in the patios. A big room on the first floor between the two patios is open both to the front and rear with stupendous views of the cathedral and volcano. That New World meld of Islamic and Hispanic architecture has never been equalled, let alone surpassed. What joy to sip coffee of a morning at a café across from the cathedral on the square and people-watch; eat fresh lake fish at a restaurant in the shore-side park; wander the streets in the cool of an evening amongst so much architectural beauty.

GRANADA
Wednesday, 30 January

Today I glut on a different beauty: Gillian and Joe drive me down a dirt track to the perfect Pacific beach. The beach lies at the head of a small bay below a wooded hill. The beach is protected on each side by reefs and from the front by a small island. The sand is soft, the sea is clear. A fishing skiff floating to moorings would be to the beach as an olive is to a dry martini – delightful but not truly necessary. We walk the sands and swim and drive later to a small fishing village, drink beer and eat freshly caught snapper at a wooden table overlooking the sea.

Joe has been dipping into my diary and finds my retelling of Latin American opinion of the United States a little rough. He doesn't disagree – merely finds the reading uncomfortable. Joe, rancher and oil man, is a Republican. He finds President George W. an embarrassment. I suggest that the father was wiser, more intelligent, better informed. Joe disagrees: he has known the family all his life, loathes them. A bunch of thieves…

There is a natural prejudice to Joe's opinion. Joe is true Texas. His grandfather settled the family ranch in the late nineteenth century. The Bush family are late twentieth-century carpet baggers.

Nor is Joe a regular Republican. Rather than fearing Latino immigration, he fears the birth of a Texan Latino underclass and would be content to pay even higher property taxes were the tax dollars ring-fenced for education.

Staying with Gillian and Joe forever isn't an option. The bike waits. Joe is jealous of the bike. He has ridden an ancient Vespa round Europe and the Middle East. He would garage the Vespa for years where so ever his journeying took him, return to reclaim it when the travel bug next struck.

Aged fifty, Joe discovered hot air balloons and forsook all other interests. Gaining a pilot licence, he crossed to Europe, won a bunch of prizes. Kenya came next where Gillian discovered Joe flying tourists over the game reserve. Joe retired from Kenya and professional ballooning aged sixty-five and moved with Gillian to Granada. A couple of years ago he canoed down Nicaragua's San Juan River. Now he seeks a new adventure. He is younger than me by six months and great company. However I prefer to travel alone. Travel with a companion and you talk with the companion rather than with natives of the country through which you pass.

GRANADA
Thursday, 31 January

My hosts held an expat dinner party this evening for two wealthy couples owning vacation homes here in Granada. One of the couples founded and funds a school in Granada for mentally handicapped children. She is Dutch; he from the US. His conversation centres on people he knows – rich or powerful people. It is a conversation of which I have been free for the past eight months and a game I don't wish to play.

The other couple are also from the US. She collects historic mansions and sculptures. We talk of Mexico. I recall spending a day with students at a private school in Oaxaca. She seems annoyed that I found the students less racist than their parents. Or perhaps she finds me arrogant in having an opinion. How could I know? I reply that I spied on the students during break. She remains dissatisfied – or irritated.

I am a Brit, of course, and have no rights – an old Brit on a small bike. Mexico is a US preserve: so affirms the Monroe Doctrine.

Now I head for Honduras…

GOODBYE GRANADA
1 February

A good road skirts Lake Nicaragua and turns east through the out-skirts of the capital city, Managua, then north through dry hills reminiscent of the Horn of Africa. Shacks by the roadside give evidence of poverty – though the people are decently dressed. How do they survive on a minimum daily wage of under two dollars?

I am aware that I have lost contact with Central America. I have become a tourist. The voyage to Panama marked the change. I sailed with fellow travellers from Colombia to Panama, followed by Christmas and New Year in the States. Back in Panama City I enjoyed Nigel's company before heading onward to stay with the Texan owners of the fishing camp. In Granada I have stayed with Gillian and Joe. I have been travelling for so many months. Mental exhaustion is in command. Entering into conversation with strangers demands so much effort.

On my first ride, I took a back road to Nicaragua's other great colonial city, Leon. The road bisected vast ranches. The horses were better fed than the people, stables superior to village hovels. The same was true of Cuba; I recall weekending with Guillermo Garcia Frias' eldest son at a horse ranch controlled by his father. Who is Guillermo Garcia Frias? Saviour of Fidel Castro at the landing from the yacht *Granma* on the second of December, 1956; Commander of a brigade in the Sierra Maestra; Deputy First Minister; Minister of Transport; Founder and Director of the Empressa Nacional for the Protection of Flora and Fauna (and avid collector of horses and fighting cocks).

The farm is in the west in the province of Pinar del Rio. At the time of our visit, the monthly meat ration for Cubans was a few grams of minced gristle. Guillermo's farm manager slaughtered a sheep or pig for us each day.

Garcia's son, Willie, owns a large modern house in the Havana suburb inhabited by diplomats. Furniture is new, big television and HiFi, electric generator capable of powering the air-conditioning. Such are Latin American oligarchies – Left or Right.

On a lighter note, our youngest son, Jed, aged five at the time, was infuriated to be mounted on what he considered a slow plodder. The horse, bored with being whacked by a brat, lay down in a river and floated Jed out of the saddle. A gaucho scooped him up…

The road between San Isidro and Estell crosses a vast flat valley of emerald-bright rice paddy. The surrounding hills are dry dust and rock. The road climbs again, twisting through mountains to the frontier. Clouds cover the sun. I stop and put on my leather jacket for the first time since leaving Patagonia.

15

HONDURAS

The border between Nicaragua and Honduras is a few buildings and a few shacks on a two-lane country road in the hills. Leaving Nicaragua is quick. Entering Honduras takes a couple of hours. None of the officials are obstructive. They are simply understaffed to deal with a slew of regulations. Transiting a truck takes a day. Truck drivers waste a further day passing from Nicaragua to Costa Rica and a day at the Costa Rica-Panama frontier. Central America industry must compete with China yet the cost of these delays is critical to Central America's economy. Damn-fool governments…

Lushly wooded hills cradle Dali, the first town into Honduras. The market is central to the town's existence. Trees shade a pretty square of simple colonial houses blessed by a pretty church – nothing grand. I was warned on my way south of bandits. I didn't meet them. I did meet a woman and her daughter selling stationery and herbal medicines, surely an odd combination for a small shop? The woman was leaving for Spain to work for three or four years and save to buy that dream of every Latin-American peasant – a double cab pickup.

My guidebook recommends a budget hotel behind the Esso station. The guidebook mentions cleanliness, television, hot water, parking. The parking is accurate. I find an Internet café; the connection is painfully slow. The owner recommends a Mexican restaurant – beans, rice and three small squares of leather. My friend of the herbal remedies and stationery has departed for Spain with her daughter. I retire to a damp bed and listen to pop music blaring from a neighbouring discotheque.

A mechanic serviced my bike here on my ride south. He came highly recommended by Danli's bikers. They referred to him as the Kikuyu; I expected a man with African features. Wrecked and semi-disassembled bikes bordered the sidewalk each side of the street outside of a corrugated-tin shack behind the market. A pale *mestizo* dressed in old oil appeared out of the murk and worked on my bike for an hour, adjusting this and that. He refused payment, assuring me that being part of my trip was ample reward.

My editor asked why I wrote of him as the Kikuyu. I knew him by no other name. I rise early this morning and ride to his shop. He embraces me, checks my bike, tightens the chain an unnecessary millimetre.

Brave, I ask, 'Why do people call you the Kikuyu?'

He shrugs: 'It is an unpleasant habit people have.'

A pickup arrives towing a trailer loaded with trail bikes. The Kikuyu is the team's support. He and I embrace again, wish each other good fortune and head our separate ways.

Back home, our garden gate opens on to the Colwall Cricket Club's upper cricket field. The groundsman, Derek Brimmel, is a dear man, younger than me by a few years. He is called Brim by all and sundry. We moved to the cottage eleven years ago. Bernadette and I asked if he preferred Brim to Derek.

He said, 'No – my name's Derek…'

Fellow bikers visiting Danli, ask for the Kikuyu. Remember to address him as Francisco…

TO COPAN RUINAS
Saturday, 2 February

I have emailed Eugenio at Hacienda Tijax on Guatemala's Rio Dulce that I will arrive on the fifth. Now I head direct to Copan where I can work for two days and explore the great Maya ruins. I stop for lunch at a restaurant on Lake Yojoa – fish from the lake grilled on charcoal. The restaurateur is a woman. We talk of this and that, her tiresome husband of whom she is delighted to be rid, our children, the cost of living, my journey. She refuses payment. I ride onward, happy to have made contact with someone from the country through which I am travelling. I am so happy that I become overconfident and head on through the hills to Copan with dusk already falling. I stop at a police post and ask whether there is a hotel before Copan.

'No, but the road is safe.'

'No bandits?'

'No bandits, but don't stop.'

Don't stop is hardly a confidence booster…

My Honda is kick-start, no battery; drop the engine revs and the headlight dims. The road twists through mountains. On a climb I follow a slow-moving truck with good lights. The driver knows the road and speeds downhill. I lose touch on the curves and crawl onward alone and somewhat scared. I pull into the curb when cars overtake. I am not having fun. Two more hours of purgatory as punishment for breaking the most vital of my safety laws for Latin America: *Never Ride at Night*.

I made the same damn-fool mistake in Venzuela. As for riding on ice…!

COPAN
Sunday, 3 February

Copan is a tourist town dependent on the Maya ruins. Every other building is a hostel, hotel, restaurant or shop selling tourist tat. Architecture is humble Hispanic colonial. Mini boulders pave the streets, though my guidebook refers to cobblestones – the guidebook writer should ride a small Honda. Hotel Patti is on the first block. Rooms surround a courtyard on three sides. My bike is safely parked. Water is hot day and night, cable television. I shower, change into clean clothes and sit with the owner by the gates, chat and people-watch. What more could a traveller desire?

The Copan archaeological site is small when compared with Tikal in Guatemala. Tikal is the lost jungle city of myth and magic. Copan is a Maya parkland of trim lawns shaded by huge deciduous trees and protected by a ring of hills. I require permission to photograph inside the museum and reproduce photographs. Oscar Cruz is the professor of archaeology at the ruins. Certainly I can photograph. 'Please mention the source in your book.'

I imagine the difficulties in obtaining a similar permission in the British Museum.

I head first for the ball court. English sports coaches urge players to *Put your heart into it.* Maya sportsmen did put their heart in – chop chop with the sacrificial knife.

An emigré Honduran family visiting from the US shares with me seats on fifth-century stone benches. We chat a while. The grandmother hugs me; a small daughter adds her own hug and clasps my hand for a group photograph.

A Maya gardener rakes fallen leaves from the lawns. He earns five dollars a day and is the father of four children of school age. Can he live on five dollars? Barely. He longs for a better future for his children and bewails his children's lack of interest in education.

A bilingual notice at the foot of a pyramid typifies the difference in Hispanic and Anglo cultures. The Spanish version is an apology for prohibiting tourists from mounting the pyramid: *DESCULPE NO HAY PASO.* The English version is a stark NO TRESPASSING.

I am part of a small group seated in the shade. The wife of a Puerto Rican architect is exhausted after climbing halfway up another pyramid. She is a small woman; as with all Maya pyramids, the steps have tall risers and narrow treads; hard work to climb but pitch a dead body down from the temple top and it wouldn't stick midway. Her husband and I wonder if the designers used a dead body or a sack of straw to work out the angle. I remark, as always, on how many flies there would have been on the pyramid in the days of human sacrifice. A middle-aged Englishman from Leeds argues that I am wrong to judge the Maya according to modern standards. I ask why the Spanish Conquistadors are condemned according to modern standards.

The centrepiece of the museum is a huge replica of the temple built on the summit of one of Copan's pyramids. The temple is painted in the original gory red: God as Blood Lust, Temples designed to terrorise…

Sculpture in the museum raises a fresh chain of thought. Pre-Colombian artists worked within a box. Break out of the box and you risked being next up the pyramid for a little knife work. Yet sculptors did break out. The humanity of the artist escapes in the minor works and in tiny details: the hint of a smile on a stone face, the line of arm and belly, humour in the portrayal of a plump frog.

If sculpture is universal and timeless, why not the simplest strictures of good and evil?

In Christendom, the doctrine of universal human rights was expounded first in the late sixteenth century by a Franciscan mendicant in Hispanic America. Others must have had the same belief. To express such beliefs was dangerous. To express anything outside the box is dangerous – or, at least, uncomfortable. Heretics are burnt or marched up the pyramid for heart surgery. Or gassed or merely jailed.

Silence is safe – thus acceptance of Hitler or McCarthyism, Fundamentalist Islam, Fundamentalist Christianity, Fundamentalist Hinduism and Buddhism, parts of the Patriot Act. People recognise the evil. They are frightened to speak. Fear is the constant. People are always frightened.

Hilary Clinton voted for the Iraq War. Why? She was frightened of endangering her political career.

I will visit the ruins again tomorrow and bring my writing up to date. Meanwhile I spend the evening with a young Irishwoman, Nikki. She is the product of Trinity, Dublin. Trinity should be proud. They have aided the development of an enquiring mind.

16

GUATEMALA

INTO GUATEMALA
Tuesday, 5 February

This is the friendliest of all borders. Honduran and Guatemalan Immigration share the same low building. Riding south, I drank beer and watched Mexico play France on television in the office of the Head of Honduran Customs. Today officials ask about my journey. Which country was most beautiful? The kindest people? What difficulties did I overcome? Is it true that food is scarce in Venezuela? What do I think of Chavez? And the habitual, and almost obligatory, condemnation of US President Bush…

The Guatemalan Customs officer is in his late twenties. He rides a 200cc Honda. He leaves tomorrow to holiday in Nicaragua and will sleep a night at San Pedro Sula. Can he reach Granada the following day? We are into a typical biker's conversation. A border guard brings coffee…

Beyond the frontier, I ride through hills on a fine twisting highway. Trees spill pink blossom beside the road and on the lower slopes. Bougainvillea tumbles over a cottage; a vine with pale blue flowers trails amongst the tree tops; scarlet berries, splashes of fierce yellow. I catch the sour-sweet scent of molasses, pine tar, pungent odour of a pigsty, coffee beans raked to dry on concrete. A rock peak pierces the pine forest. The river below flashes shards of sun reflection. Green is brilliant in the irrigated fields along the riverbanks. Beyond the valley rise dry, pleated hills, summits pillowed in white cumulus. New construction in small towns and villages suggest a cash flow absent in Honduras and Nicaragua.

The past month much of the travel has been distance to cross; no fun in it; a chore to be undertaken; drudgery. Today I rediscover the joy of earlier months. Why? Because I will reach Hacienda Tijax this afternoon, sit with Monica and Eugenio on the terrace in the evening, absorb the view? Or because Tijax is one of the final way stations on this journey? The end is in sight. Or was the friendliness of the frontier officials a catalyst for happiness?

Or did yesterday in Copan Ruinas reawaken my enthusiasms? That sign at the base of the pyramid? Professor Cruz? Nikki? The owner of the hotel? The gardener raking leaves? Somewhere in there I recaptured a sense of being more than a passer-by, of being in contact, of caring.

Hacienda Tijax has been seventeen years in the making. I visited first from Cuba in 1992. What is now the town of Fronteras was tin shacks and a few unpainted concrete-block buildings either side of a dirt track. Eugenio had completed a bar, bunkroom and half-a-dozen thatched huts and was planting rubber, teak and mahogany. Now sailboats moor at the Tijax marina; luxury cabins surround a five-star restaurant; a ten-person Jacuzzi bubbles beside a pool. Fronteras has developed a tar main street stretching north one and a half kilometres towards El Peten. Latino machismo blocks the traffic. Klaxons and curses are weapons of first recourse. Between the trucks whiz lunatic un-helmeted young on motor scooters. All five of Guatemala's major banks have branches. Hotels, restaurants, pharmacies – all are new. Only the whorehouse remains the same, unpainted (unlike the women) – and that Fronteras is a dump with few redeeming features. Why do I feel such affection for a dump?

The lands of Hacienda Tijax swoop up from the Rio Dulce. The resort lies on the riverbank. A raised walkway leads inland through mangrove to horse and dairy paddocks. Eugenio has built his home midway up the ridge. Rubber, teak and mahogany plantations share the highland with primary and secondary jungle. A stone meditation tower stands on the crest. I burnt my leg last time I visited. I was wearing shorts and tried riding to the tower. The first rut in the track did for me – and self-delusion: that I was back in my twenties in Ibiza and riding a 350 Bultaco trail bike, *Brrmmm Brrmmm*. The exhaust tube did the burning. Ah, well…

This evening Eugenio drives me to the tower in the pickup. Below glistens the river and Lago Izabal. Turn and we gaze out over tree canopy. In the distance stand mauve mountains; layers of gold float behind the western peaks.

We dine down at the resort. The restaurant is full and we eat at a table in the marina-side bar. I order shrimp. Light reflections spike the river between wooden docks; sailboats stir in the wake of a passing taxi launch. We talk of mutual friends and of our various children and of Eugenio's latest victories in protecting the ecology.

HACIENDA TIJAX
Wednesday, 6 February

Eugenio leads me on a hike this morning. Two and a half kilometres of gravelled paths and cable bridges thread primary jungle. One bridge, seventy-five metres in length, spans a ravine. Look down through tree tops to ferns and water and spits of reflected sunlight; stay at Tijax resort and walk the trails in the company of knowledgeable guides. A visitor from the US complained on Lonely Planet's Thorn Tree forum that Eugenio charges for access to the jungle and mangrove. Perhaps she believes that paths and cable bridges and stone towers are created and maintained by God. Or is she one of those backpackers from the First World who consider the Third World their playground and resent having to contribute more than a minimum per diem? The kind of tourist who proudly boasts of having beaten down the price of a piece of woven cloth without caring that hunger in the weaver's family is the tourist's bludgeon? How dare I be so cross on such a glorious afternoon…?

I am writing at a table on the front terrace of Eugenio's home; forest protects us from the town and the resort; cows and horses graze the paddocks; cloud softens the distant mountains, humming-birds dart and whir along the hibiscus hedge. This morning we saw blue Morpheus in the jungle, admired wild orchids, sniffed crushed leaves from the allspice tree, hunted for vanilla pods, listened to bird calls. Perhaps I am envious of Eugenio's achievements – and admiring of his bravery. He is a survivor of the thirty-six-year clandestine war: though deeply scarred by the horrors, he remains an optimist and believer in a better future for his nation.

HACIENDA TIJAX
Thursday, 7 February

Casa Guatemala is an orphanage. Doña Angie founded the orphanage. She owns the Backpackers Hotel on the riverbank south of the road bridge. The hotel supports the orphanage. So do charitable donations. Local people complain that confusion or lack of clarity exists in the twin finances. Doña Angie is Honduran: foreigners are suspect always.

A launch delivers me from the hotel to the orphanage. I sit in a classroom built out over the river. The teacher is female, young, Spanish, charming, sincere, dedicated. Her students range from twelve to fifteen and are remarkably well behaved. They are reading children's books translated from North American English. Characters in the books have Anglo names: Jack, Jill, Annie, Mollie, Robert.

Is this important?

Yes.

The message is clear: Books are foreign. Education is foreign. Children with Maya names are unworthy of being characters in a book.

The teacher agrees and shows me the library. Books in English fill the shelves. The books are donations. The donors should consider what they give. Guatemala has its own writers. Guatemala has publishers and printers.

Donors, please: Guatemalan books for Guatemalan orphans…

Break time, and I sit on a low stone wall. Boys play football; girls gather in groups and giggle. Two girls lead each other to me by the hair – play pulling rather than painful pulling. I ask which of them is the most vicious. The smaller of the two. She is a witch. A real witch? Yes, yes, a real witch … They collapse with laughter.

A smaller girl sits on my lap while I am interrogated by the real witch and her friend. A small boy squats behind me and rests his chin on my shoulder.

A young Nordic woman with blonde-blonde hair sits on the same wall and is happy for small girls to use her as a climbing frame.

Happiness appears abundant.

So does dedication.

Staff are volunteers. Of the teachers, ten are Guatemalan, four are Spanish. Other volunteers build or work on the orphanage farm. Two are Israeli. The blonde-blonde is Finnish. An eighteen-year-old of Danish and Asian-Indian parentage conducts me on a tour. The farm has excellent pigs. It has a non-functioning bio gas plant that requires cleaning and rows of non-functioning hydroponics beds built recently by volunteers from the US. The farm has chickens in chicken houses, cows, grows vegetables and beans and fruit; fish abound in the river.

Two hundred and fifty children are fed at the orphanage each day. This is an achievement.

Many of the children are not true orphans. Poverty has forced their parents to leave their children at the orphanage. The orphanage clothes and educates them.

A miniscule few from the orphanage go to university. One is studying medicine, another is an economist. A minuscule few is way better than none. Well done, Doña Angie.

Volunteers at the orphanage contribute 180 dollars. This is a one-off payment. They can stay as long as they wish and return as often as they wish. Food is free and they occupy the volunteers' house. OK, shack. Why has no volunteer bothered to build a little comfort into the place? Work is over for the day. Two volunteers sit on the small terrace. A third lolls in a hammock. They shouldn't smoke. They absolutely should not smoke where children see them. They should be particularly careful as to what they smoke…

Yes, I know. I am carping again.

I chat briefly with an elderly worker on the farm. The land is poor; rains leach all goodness out of the soil. A couple of kids hoe beans. They should hoe natural fertiliser into the soil. Chicken shit, pig shit, kitchen compost.

A boy leans against a wall to ease the weight of freshly laundered sheets from his shoulders. I carry the laundry for him upstairs to the boys' dormitory. I barely manage the climb and am twice the size of the boy.

I will carp again: the orphanage lacks direction, lacks planning, lacks management discipline. Perhaps this is partly reliance on volunteers who stay a month or six months or leave after a week.

The orphanage clinic is the exception. For coolness, it is built on stilts over the river. Everything is freshly painted white. Two lavatories are being installed. The pharmacy is well stocked and spotless. So is the doctor's office.

The doctor is Spanish and a recent arrival. He has spent the past year travelling through Hispanic America. He is imbued with endless energy and mental discipline. He is a rock thrown into a pool. His influence will spread each day.

How long will he stay?

He has no idea.

Pray, children. Pray…

I am unable to connect to the Internet up at the house. I am writing at the resort bar. Odd guests turn up looking for a room – or a nest in the case of a giant white egret strutting down the dock. I am almost up to date with my writing. The bar is a good studio. I wrote the Guatemala sections of a thriller, *Aftermath*, here in the early days of Eugenio's development.

HACIENDA TIJAX
Sunday, 10 February

Monica and Eugenio have offered a haven towards which I rode. This morning I am in kiddies' paradise. Eugenio has given me my birthday present: driving the bulldozer. The bulldozer is yellow, as are the butterflies and the blossoms and the breasts of small birds flitting amongst the red hibiscus. Tonight we dine at the resort *en famille*. Eugenio's daughter has baked me a birthday cake. Rather than a celebration, I suffer the sadness of one more parting. Such is this journey, seemingly endless separations – because of my age, probably final.

In the *Tijax Blog* on the web, Eugenio claims that I have been an inspiration.

If so, I am humbled.

Eugenio is my inspiration.

Tijax demanded vision and is an ongoing achievement.

TO ANTIGUA GUATEMALA
Monday, 11 February

A seventy-fifth birthday is a biggie. I leave this morning for Antigua, first capital of Guatemala. The day begins with incompetence: I leave my passport at Hacienda Tijax. I realise my error as I pass the police post at the south end of the bridge over the Rio Dulce. Back I go to the house, set off again and race a rain squall to a road-side shelter. A dozen men sit on wooden benches beneath a thatch roof. Two have pedal bikes; one owns a scooter; the remainder wait for a bus.

Sun strikes the rain curtain as it speeds towards us. Dry tar is grey. Wet tar is black. Trees bend and leaves point down beneath the rain. The shelter shudders as the squall hits.

'Five minutes,' comments a young man in jeans, red T-shirt and white trainers. A man wearing a white plastic Stetson asks whether I am from the US or am I German?

'Britanico,' I reply. 'More or less from the US. We have been sold by our government to President Bush.'

'Bush is an ignorant man,' says the Stetson. 'He has no education.'

'With much arrogance,' says an older man. 'Much arrogance.'

The others nod and murmur agreement. What do they know? They are country folk, *mestizo* Latinos, or Latino *mestizos*...

All Guatemala's trade to the Atlantic passes through the port of Barios. I recall the road up through the hills to Guatemala City as a suicide run. The road has been widened and Guatemala City is bisected by a six-lane highway. I am a survivor of Venezuela. Guatemala is easy. I left Rio Dulce shortly before midday, stopped midway for coffee and a bun, and am in Antigua soon after five o'clock.

Spanish conquistadors founded Antigua. It is a small compact town. Much of the architecture is sixteenth- and seventeenth-century. Streets are cobbled; bougainvillea spills over ochre and terracotta walls and climate is permanent spring.

Three volcanoes surround the town. Though spectacular, volcanoes make uncomfortable bedfellows. They erupt. Added to which, Antigua has been devastated by earthquakes. Though rebuilt and lovely, the town now suffers a fresh plague. It is the number-one tourist destination in Central America. In such quantity, locusts would be preferable.

My host in Antigua is a family connection. His house lies outside of town in a gated community. He meets me in the plaza and leads me home in his ancient Land Rover.

Lucia is a Guatemalan painter; her husband, Eric, is French. We are friends of long standing and they are perfect companions for a seventy-fifth birthday dinner. My host drives me to their Antigua home where we drink rum in front of an open fire before driving to a restaurant that boasts a French chef. Both food and wine are excellent (an Argentine Merlot Norton). We are served *pastis* on the house as an aperitif and *anejo* rum on the house to finish. Sadly, my host is a habitual early riser and likes to be in bed by ten. End of party...

I am to do a BBC broadcast live over the telephone at one-thirty in the morning: El Antiguo in La Antigua: *The Old One in the Old Place*.

I am in bed before eleven. Though mildly drunk, I am a responsible citizen and set the alarm before switching off the bedside lamp. The alarm wakes me at one-fifteen. I fumble for my spectacles and search for my dentures. I am still searching for the dentures when the telephone rings.

Ring, ring, ring … I have to answer.

Am I ready?

'Absolutely,' I mumble – though I am lying on the floor, head beneath the bed as I search.

Bernadette will be listening (so will half the village) and my diction is poor. The interviewer blames a poor connection and brings the interview to a premature closure. I finally discover the dentures beneath the pillow, drop them into their bath with a cleansing tablet and turn off the light. Seventy-five and a failure – I can't sleep.

ANTIGUA GUATEMALA
Tuesday, 12 February

I visited Monica Smith today in Antigua Guatemala. Monica is eighty-six and frail. Monica's husband and my uncle Mark were business partners (both men are dead). My uncle Mark married Helen Rolfe. Helen's sister, Lilian, was a radio operator attached to the French Resistance during the Second World War. She was caught and tortured by the Gestapo, sent to Ravensbrück and shot.

I find Monica seated on a bench in the patio of her colonial home. She has been rereading the Lilian Rolfe biography. We sit on the bench and peruse the photographs in the book. Lilian Rolfe was so young when caught, young and fresh and innocent and shared a remarkable beauty with her sister, Helen.

Monica spent a joyous period in Paris before the Second World

War and her French remains fluent. We sit together for an hour and admire the flowers, watch birds pick seeds from a bowl and the changing sky above the patio, and chat in French of this and that – memories, mostly – and that we will meet next on a heavenly cloud…

ANTIGUA GUATEMALA
Wednesday, 13 February

I have moved residence to Lucia's home in town. Eric is oversee-ing the building of a new house. Five pint-sized Maya workers mix concrete for a terrace. A studio apartment for Lucia's son, Manuel, is complete. Manuel is in residence. A passionate and expert rock climber, Manuel graduated from university in Colorado and now works as a mountain, white-water and nature guide. He is more qualified than most and has a good Toyota 4×4. He is also young and handsome which is no bad thing in a guide. Fluent in Spanish, English and French, he makes ideal company for an ascent of Anti-gua's volcanoes. He will also take clients to visit haciendas that are closed territory to the standard tourist.

ANTIGUA GUATEMALA
Thursday, 14 February

Eric and I visit the flower market early this morning: Valentine's Day roses for Monica Smith and for Lucia. My youngest son, Jed, has organised flowers for Bernadette. I wish I was home and holding Bernadette in my arms.

Back home in England, I don't do parties. I don't do rooms with more than eight people. In the Americas I am working and attending a party is only marginally more unpleasant than riding my Honda up a mountain in sleet.

We attend the opening of a painter's exhibition this evening. The gallery is small and pleasantly empty but for the paintings. The celebration is on a large roof terrace and crowded. Most of the crowd is retiree North American. Eric and I arrive late and the wine has run out. People talk a great deal – mostly of each other. And the paintings? Don't be silly…

Later we are seven for dinner at a Japanese restaurant. One of the seven is an early-teenaged boy wearing a baseball cap. I am of a generation that considers wearing a hat indoors to be ill-mannered. Wearing a hat indoors *is* ill-mannered unless you are a woman. Baseball caps are a disease anywhere other than on a baseball field. Baseball is a disease anywhere other than North America and Japan. I suspect that North Americans wear baseball caps to bed and with the peak reversed so that they can nuzzle.

Yes, I know. I am an aged Brit Blimp…

An intellectual Italian architect is attempting to design a cash-free sustainable living environment as an example to the rural population. He lives on the shores of Guatemala's most beautiful lake, Atitlan. He finds Atitlan deeply spiritual. He intends generating his electricity through solar panels. Solar panels are cash costly.

In his youth, Eugenio worked with a team that designed a clay stove that cost nothing and burnt a minimal amount of wood. Eugenio also spent years attempting to wean the rural population from subsistence agriculture. In distributing foreign aid, he financed peasant cooperatives producing cash crops. The cooperatives have been successful financially. Visit and you will see women and children in traditional dress bent double in fields of vegetables; the men drink and drive pickups and wear fancy shirts, cowboy boots and shiny plastic Stetsons.

Friday, 15 February

I haven't ridden for two days. I haven't written for a week. I want to plead mental exhaustion. Truth is that I am a coward. Writing fact, or my perception of fact, is uncomfortable. Safer to hide in a foxhole … Or stick to writing fiction – though the novel I have with my editor is anything but safe. And riding this wretched bike, am I courting danger? Or have I, in my seventies, finally become an adult? Adult writers don't whine. Adult writers write. Here goes:

My mother's brother, Mark, owned a plantation on the high slopes of the volcano that dominates Lake Atitlan. In my early twenties, Mark invited me to work on the plantation. A month later Mark changed his mind. I wasn't suitable. He was probably correct.

I have lived for fifty years with a *What if?*

What if has stopped me visiting Los Andes.

Eugenio has pressed me over the years. 'You need to free your head…'

I am seventy-five, an adult. I don't have much time. Eugenio is correct. I do need to free my head.

Mark sold the *finca* late in the clandestine war.

Jim and Olga Hazard are the owners. Jim has invited me to stay Friday night.

I ride down from Antigua to the coastal highway. Harvest time and smoke rises from vast tracts of sugar cane as landowners burn off the leaf.

The road up to Santa Barbara heads straight for the reverse side of volcano Atitlan. This was guerrilla territory. A swing barrier bars the road. An armed guard asks my destination and my licence number is recorded. Sugar gives way to brittle pasture. Boulders litter paddocks. Santa Barbara is one street, low houses, a few mini stores. The road is newly concreted beyond the village. The white central line weaves a little and giant bamboos form a tunnel. Concrete gives way to cobble where tyres kick and slither – dangerous to lose concentration.

Two locals riding a 250 trail bike ask my destination and beckon me to follow. We cross shallow fords and climb through rubber plantations. A loose feathery leaf-canopy softens the light. The air is cool and fresh with forest scent. Above towers the pyramid peak.

My guides pull in at a small modern house.

'Straight on,' they tell me. 'You will see the entrance.'

They would have been young during the clandestine war.

Which side did they support?

Was my uncle the enemy?

Would I have been the enemy?

A light breeze stirs the rubber trees and small spits of sunlight penetrate the canopy; trunks are pale grey; knife wounds scar the bark and white gum bleeds into tin cups.

The cobbled road climbs. A culvert cuts through pale red earth. Coffee bushes are dark green, multiple stems. Another memory opens: playing rummy at the Greek Club in Arusha, Tanganyika. The Korea War was over: no need for sandbags; the sisal boom had turned to bust. Coffee was king. Multiple stem pruning increased yield. I helped Charlie Zagaritis introduce multiple stem pruning to an Asian-owned coffee-plantation.

Why was I in East Africa?

Because I wasn't in Guatemala. That is the easy answer. Another would be that I had no education, no qualification, and was searching for my father. My father settled in Kenya prior to the First World War. He died when I was five. I have no memories of him. Searching for other people's memories? Risky thoughts when riding a small city bike on slippery cobbles up a mountain…

An old man slithers down the bank. He has one upper tooth; I have none. He has no lower teeth; I have six. My six are vaguely white; his one tooth is dark green at the gum fading to yellow at its peak.

Am I visiting Don Jim?

Yes, I am visiting Don Jim.

Had he known my uncle?

Certainly he knew my uncle. My uncle aided him during the time of the guerrillas.

The old man left the *finca* at the time of the guerrillas. He had to leave – I am uncertain why; lack of teeth impairs his diction and

I am moderately deaf; added to which I am astride a bike with the motor running. I nod in understanding of that which I don't understand and ask directions to the house. The old man points this old man uphill.

The house is white and overlooks an acre of lawn and trees and flowering shrubs. Look a little further (sixty kilometres) and the darker blue way below is the Pacific Ocean. A woodpecker pecks a rowdy tattoo.

A community of some 150 families have their homes on Finca Los Andes. Two full-time and a part-timer teach at the primary school. High school is down on the coastal plain and the *finca* funds university scholarships. The young woman who greets me and shows me to my room studies business management.

Jim Hazard is out on the *finca*. I sit in what was my uncle's sitting room and explain myself to Olga Hazard. Olga's bloodlines reach south from Mexico to Colombia. She is a warm woman, kind and gentle – yet steel must lie at her core. There is steel in any woman who survived the clandestine war and possesses the courage to create a life up here on a volcano that was guerrilla territory.

Guerrillas entered the house when Mark and Helen were here. The leader addressed Mark as Enginerio in recognition of the hydroelectric system Mark designed and installed. In describing the incident, Mark told me that Helen behaved very well. Though a Scot, Mark was schooled at Eton and was very much an Englishman. *Very well* was high praise indeed

My Aunt Helen created the garden that stretches beyond the window. Seed for the camellias came from the botanical gardens at Kew, London. My uncle built a relationship with Kew and sent orchids from the cloud forest to the orchid house.

The relationship was useful.

Mark was keen to plant tea at Los Andes (none was grown in Central America). I smuggled twenty kilos of seed from Kenya to England. I don't recall the name of the botanist at Kew whom my uncle told me to quote should I have difficulty at Heathrow airport.

Mention of Kew was sufficient. Mark had a connection at the Guatemalan Embassy in London and the seed was forwarded to Guatemala as diplomatic baggage.

Jim Hazard is a quiet, polite, thoughtful man, mid-seventies, slim, bearded, upright. Anglo-Guatemalan, he is a civil engineer by profession. By passion he is a husbander of land and of those who live on it. He has organised Los Andes as a workers' cooperative. The cooperative runs a savings bank and a store and owns a mini-van which, when required, the *finca* hires. The *finca* covers 1,500 hectares. Coffee and tea are the main harvest. Macadamia trees have reached their first fruiting and there is a quinine plantation. The top portion is cloud forest and borders a nature reserve that rises to the peak of Atitlan. This is great bird-watching territory (quetzals are common) and Los Andes supplies forest guides. Check the website for room rate and a bird list: www.andescloudforest.org

Jim drives me through the lower slopes of the *finca* and we walk a forest track to the hydroelectric plant my uncle installed. Mark harnessed two mountain brooks. The fall is some 300 feet and has generated 5 kilowatts with minimum maintenance for close on forty years. I recall lunching with Mark in London and his describing the installation. He had no training as an engineer. Jim describes it as a remarkable achievement.

We drive back to the house and swim in the pool before lunch. Small birds dart amongst the blossoms. Mid-sized birds are marginally more sedate. Butterflies drift on a light breeze.

Later we visit the school and the office and the health clinic. Jim introduces me always as Mark's nephew. I sense the atmosphere between Jim and the indigenous population as one of mutual respect and understanding. Jim is not a boss in the traditional sense, nor is he paternalistic. Imagine an elderly tutor in semi-retirement.

He is proud that one of the field foremen is a woman.

He is proud that the tea pickers are self-organised to be most productive.

I suggest that a workers' cooperative is vulnerable to expropriation.

Jim says, 'Surely that is a risk worth taking.'

I recall a discussion in London with my Uncle Mark's partner's brother many years ago. I had learned in Africa the near-impossibility on a large plantation of instilling into a workforce the value of each tree. Better divide a plantation into independent sections each with its own workers; sections in which workers could feel pride in accomplishment and compete both for awards and bonuses.

My interlocutor reasoned that such a system would open the plantation to a workers' takeover.

Which was my intention…

FINCA LOS ANDES
Friday, 15 February

The tea picked on Los Andes is certified organic. Coffee is sold to Starbucks: Starbucks insists on eco-production. In my uncle's day, water flowed through the coffee factory, washed the beans and flowed back to the stream. Now water is used again and again before being held in tanks where the sediment settles. The sediment is spread in long shaded trays and covered in black plastic. Worms are introduced into the sediment. Juice from the trays is a natural fungicide and the sediment becomes a powerful natural fertiliser.

Infected by Jim's enthusiasm, I dig my fingers into the sediment to sample density of worm population.

FINCA LOS ANDES
Saturday, 16 February

The house at Finca Los Andes is comfortable. I lie in bed and wonder. I wonder that I smuggled the tea seed out of Kenya. I had my instructions as to what I should say were the Customs to stop me at London's Heathrow. Except to the seed, Heathrow was never the danger point. At most, British Customs would have confiscated the seed. Kenya was critical. In Kenya I was committing a crime. What would my uncle have done had I been arrested?

The seed was important to him – hence the arrangements in London. My safety was a minor side issue.

Not a pleasant thought…

And I recall another time when my uncle used me. It was a more distasteful role and involved his youngest daughter. My uncle knew that I would never refuse what he asked, that I accepted his intellectual domination. He was a Renaissance man (perhaps the last): agronomist, engineer, widely read, possessor of an excellent palate, great collector and connoisseur of the arts with an astonishing eye. I never met with him without gaining a new and exciting line of thought or being told of a book that excited me – that is the facet that I treasure. He has been dead nearly thirty years…

I will leave before lunch. Jim drives me uphill in the early morning. He planted cypress for timber on one slope. Last year a freak gale felled every tree and blasted on down a narrow gorge to strike a planting of macadamia nuts.

Jim shows me the trees blown one on top of the other as if they were spillikins: Yes, he had wanted to weep.

We head back to the house for breakfast. Children play football on the field below the school. A woman tells Jim that the coffee harvest is complete.

More farewells, more pain of parting. Olga tells me that I am family: that I must return. Jim has honoured me by sharing his passions (and his worms). And I am joyful. *What if?* no longer occupies even the smallest corner of my head: it has been replaced with a *thank God.*

Thank God that Jim and Olga own Los Andes. No member of my family, certainly not I, could have achieved what Jim has achieved. Here, in a land ripped apart by a vicious internal war, he has created a place of hope and laughter and a shared pride in achievement.

Yet, as I ride slowly and carefully down the cobbled lane, I wonder that not one of Mark's five children wanted to make this their home, wanted to inherit their father's achievement and take it further.

As for me, Mark and Helen crocheted a rug together in the evenings at Los Andes. It is the one possession of theirs that I long to possess. It would keep good company with the small, treasured landscape painted by Mark that hangs above the mantle in my study.

17

MEXICO

TAPACHULA, MEXICO
Saturday, 16 February

Saturday afternoon and I am the sole traveller at Guatemalan Immigration and Customs. I cross the border, dismount and kiss the road: Mexico to Mexico via Tierra del Fuego. A Honduran tourist asks permission to photograph me astride the frontier. Kindly Mexican Customs officers invite me to rest awhile in their office, enjoy a celebratory Corona beer.

Tapachula is the closest town to the Guatemalan border. It is more sedate than most border towns (perhaps influenced by German immigrants). Saturday evening and a pair of portly middle-aged chess players sip water abstemiously at a sidewalk café on the cathedral plaza; short-sleeve synthetic summer-shirts, trousers shiny at the knees and worn trainers suggest minor bureaucrats. Observing is permitted; I draw up a chair.

Tapachula is celebrating the half-century stage and screen career of the city's favourite daughter. A juvenile lead in a television soap drones praise. Male songsters follow in Hollywood Mexican dress: big sombreros, embroidered jackets, gun belts, boots and breeches.

Readers inquire why I seldom mention music. Because Latin American pop is a crime against humanity. Salsa and meringue may be fun on a two-week holiday romance: be bombarded for four years, as we were in Cuba and the Dominican Republic, and you pray for silence. Romantically tragic Mexican weep music is a depressant; a bad book is preferable to the poetic schmaltz of Argentina's tango. In Brazil, four days of musical hell on the riverboat to

Manaus have left me scarred for life. Most vile is *rigaton*, Central American rap: the beat is offensively aggressive while lyrics glorify violence (particularly against women), and are homophobic and linguistically obscene.

A woman in a long white dress finishes her set in the plaza. The crowd claps. The chess game ends. A fellow onlooker passes me a newspaper; the lead story recounts daily arrests of small-town mayors on charges of corruption. We are joined by a dark-complexioned man who speaks passionately on whatever subject. That he is president of the small coffee growers' association is a strange coincidence given that I have arrived directly from Finca Los Andes. Instancing Nescafé and Starbucks, he rails at those who make fortunes from coffee and demands why small farmers must starve.

I don't have an answer. Fair Trade? Trade is seldom fair.

As to gaining organic certification, frequent inspections are beyond the peasant farmer's purse. Nor is a cooperative practical: growers distrust each other; inevitably one or other would use fertilisers; the cooperative would lose its certification – or so my companion insists.

He is keen for members of his association to supplement their incomes by making artisaneria from coffee prunings. He displays a photocopy of a vase made from shards of old tyres.

'Beautiful,' I encourage and hide my scepticism behind a fresh Corona.

TO TEHAUNTEPEC
Sunday, 17 February

Teenagers suffer from facial spots. Mexican roads have speed bumps; Sleeping Policeman is the traditional English term; the Mexican word is *topes*: some are painted yellow; others in yellow or white stripes; a majority have no paint at all. Drivers may be warned by a series of lines across the road prior to the *topes* or by road signs.

Inevitably the traveller either misses warnings or there is no warning. A long day in the saddle is a pain in the butt.

Today is a short stage on the Pacific coast. Neat fences segment the littoral into huge paddocks rich in grazing. Plump cattle are in delicious contrast to Brazil's scrawny zebu. Inland, the great wall of the Cordillera rises almost vertically; granite-scattered flanks glitter in the sun, peaks cocooned in soft cloud. Tehuantepec guards the west coast of the isthmus and is famous for strong-willed women. The women wear long skirts and ride standing up in the backs of motor-trikes: veritable Boadiceas.

In 2006 I dropped my false teeth in the bathroom at the Hotel Izmir. The plate shattered. I took it across the neighbouring plaza to an orthodontist and novice writer, Fernando Villalobos Peto. Fernando mended the plate while I read his furious denunciation of Mexican politics. Teeth repaired, we sat in his office and discussed writing, politics, travel, and compared racism in Mexico and England. He and his wife drove me home and introduced me to their two late-teenaged sons. The sons are contemporary with Bernadette's and my two sons. They dress similarly, listen to the same music, complain that their new computers don't work. Why? Because they download music from illegal sites infected with viruses.

No we don't.

Yes you do.

No we don't.

Yes you do.

Enough!

In 2006 I lunched as Fernando's guest at a restaurant on the banks of an irrigation canal. Fernando's eldest son accompanied us. Recently graduated from high school, he intended studying history. Food was outstanding; so was the conversation.

Sunday and Fernando's surgery is closed. I will meet him tomorrow. This evening I connect to the Internet in the Hotel Izmir patio and write a little before disturbing a man working on his laptop at the adjoining table, Boris Corredor.

Boris Corredor is a literature professor and married to a literature professor. He is Colombian; his wife, Adela, is Mexican and an Associate Professor of Romance Studies at Boston University. Adela's family originate in Tehuantepec and Adela has inherited a *huerto* (market garden) here on an irrigation canal. She flies in from Boston tomorrow.

Boris prefers working as an editor to teaching. He is a short square, vital man, hair thinning, eyes very much alive. We drink beer; discuss the race for the Democratic Presidential nomination; Cuba, Hollywood portrayal of Hispanic Americans; US publishers' choice of Hispanic American literature; the magic realism of such writers as Allende and Marquez so politically anodyne and safe.

I prefer Salman Rushdie. Rushdie has courage. He pierces his targets with an epée, slices them with a sabre and finishes them off with a cudgel. For superb political invective and imagery, read his denunciation of Iran's Khomeini in the *Satanic Verses*. No wonder the holy Ayatollah declared a fatwa.

Boris Corredor agrees: or is polite. Colombians are polite – though this isn't the Hollywood projection. Hollywood Colombians are slimy degenerate greaseballs who deal drugs and destroy America's oh so innocent youth.

TEHUANTEPEC
Monday, 18 February

Such a great day makes travel a delight. I have neither climbed a mountain, trekked through jungle, nor glissaded down a glacier; nor did I spot a whale blow or glimpse a rare bird. I lunched with Fernando Peto and dined with Boris and Adela Corredor. Perfect bliss…

Fernando is a kind man, thoughtful, and perhaps deprived of intellectual companionship beyond his immediate family. He drives me for lunch at a four-table shellfish stall outside town where he relates the dilemma of his eldest son's education. His son wishes to study history at Mexico City's university (Mexico's best). In Mexico, intelligent crooks enter politics: kidnapping is for the unintelligent. Fernando's son shares the same names and is the same age as one of Fernando's nephews. Fernando's brother, a successful businessman, lives in Mexico City and can afford bodyguards for his boy. Fernando fears that brain-dead kidnappers will mistake his own unguarded son for the protected nephew.

Such fears and quandaries are foreign to Herefordshire parents.

Boris Corredor criticises BBC coverage of world news. Why has it become so bland?

The easy answer: Prime Minister Blair and his supporters frightened the BBC hierarchy (Blair, in turn, lived in fear of Rupert Murdoch). In his emasculation of the BBC, Blair was aided by a judge. The judge presided over an inquiry into BBC reporting of the build-up to the Iraq war and the falsification of intelligence.

I suspect that the judge believed that he was serving the nation by protecting government: he furthered the distrust the nation has for its politicians and judiciary.

The judge was also parochial. He never considered the respect the BBC once earned for Britain. The BBC flew the flag of truth. BBC journalists were fearless. The BBC was a unique link to the wider world. In my youth, the terrorised in far countries crouched over radios to listen to BBC World Service broadcasts.

This is the service that Blair and his Director of Communications, Alastair Campbell, sacrificed for short-term political advantage.

Lord Hutton was the judge abetting them.

Does he sleep well?

And the journalists who worked for the BBC?

Some of the best now work for Al Jazeera.

Al Jazeera is financed by the government of Qatar – a small sheikdom in the Persian Gulf and a supporter of the United States of America. The Qatar government believes that financing a respected international news service earns them credit. Al Jazeera does what the BBC once did: report the news and both sides of any argument. President George W. Bush believes that there is only one side to an argument. He wanted to bomb Al Jazeera's studios in Qatar. The US Military slammed missiles into Al Jazeera's Baghdad and Kabul offices.

President George W. Bush claims that the US is the final bastion of freedom. To quote Kurt Vonnegut (a great philosopher of the absurd): *Ah, well...*

This journey has taken me through every Latin American country other than Paraguay and El Salvador. Texas is the next frontier. I am nearing the end. Riding through Mexico, I must commence writing my conclusions. Boris Corredor's criticism of the BBC keeps me awake in the night. I first visited Hispanic America some thirty years ago: we Brits were viewed as different from visitors from the US. We were quieter, less arrogant, better informed, more courteous. I write in generalisations. An individual North American might be treasured: a Brit could be a real pain in the butt.

A change has taken place; we have become indivisible. Any attempt at claiming a difference is countered with a reminder that the Founding Fathers were Brits, slave-owners and racist.

There is a commonality. Our cultural view of Latin America draws on the same cinematic sources. We speak the same language; watch the same movies; read the same magazines and books. A further self-censorship by market effects UK publishers: *Will it sell in the US?*

There is more, of course: US support for Britain during the Malvinas/Falklands War; Britain's subservience to the US in the invasion of Iraq; our present alliance in Afghanistan.

President George W. Bush is held in contempt throughout Latin America. We Brits share in the opprobrium.

TEHUANTEPEC
Tuesday, 19 February

Tehuantepec was a small Hispanic colonial town. Developers have destroyed or vandalised much of the original architecture. Fernando is fighting to protect what remains and is amassing a photographic history. The older photographs record the laying of the railway across the isthmus to the Caribbean. Inaugurated in 1894, the railway was built to compete with the Panama Canal. Brits were the engineers. The railway was never a success and was closed some ten years ago. Now it is being modernised to transport containers. Trains will run at 300 kilometres per hour and queues at the Panama Canal may make the railway finally profitable.

Boris and Adela are academics. They speak perfect English yet chose to converse with me in Spanish. My son, Joshua, criticises the errors I make in Spanish (many). However, writing the preceding diatribe on the BBC and Al Jazeera has made me uppity. Perhaps diatribes are good for the soul – or lower one's cholesterol level?

Adela hunts through albums of photographs with Fernando and his wife in search of family connections and is joyously successful. We visit Adela's *huerto,* which borders land owned by Fernando's in-laws. A dirt track follows one of Tehuantepec's pre-Hispanic irrigation canals. These man-created oases fed Tehuantepec for more than a thousand years and were treasured even in Fernando's childhood. Fernando points proudly to a nearby conical hill where the Teahuantepeca finally vanquished the Aztec invasion. Aztecs were softer foes than the national supermarkets that feed Tehuantepec now and the young scorn agriculture; lack of irrigation has laid waste a grove of coconut palms; adobe walls lie tumbled; old trucks rot.

Will Adela and Fernando resuscitate their inheritance?

Am I arrogant in delighting at having brought them together?

TAOS ON SEA
Thursday, 21 February

Salinas del Cruz is twenty kilometres west along the coast from Tehuantepec. An oil refinery brought investment and new construction borders broad streets of what was recently a village. Tehuantepec has charm because it is forgotten. A little of the old ways survive. People are open; they forge friendships. I want to stay a further week; watch Adela unearth her routes as she interacts with Fernando and his family; and I would enjoy talking with Adela and Boris in the evenings. I could test my thoughts on the Conquest. Instead I ride towards a community that I first visited on my way south; I think of it as Taos on Sea to acknowledge those many of its villagers who have worked in Taos, some as legal immigrants, most as illegals. Its true name is Barra de la Cruz.

Route National 200 climbs and plummets through scrub woodland with glimpses of sea and surf breaking on empty beaches. In May of 2006 I left Tehuantepec at sunrise. The rains had come; the air was fresh and clean; hills glowed emerald; white and yellow blossoms splashed the canopy as did cascades of blue and crimson climbers; vultures and hawks circled on dawn patrol.

Now I leave near midday. Heat is oppressive; hills are pale smoky grey, trees brittle and stripped of leaves. Rivers have shrunk to a few muddy pools. A lone white heron or greater egret stands frozen in green shade beside a puddle. I spot a second in the next riverbed, then a third; narrow heads and long spindly legs make for cartoon cavalry officers.

I pull in at a small restaurant. Venison stew is dish of the day. Is this the last remaining deer? Should I refuse? What difference would refusal make? I am a lone old man on a small bike: at most an eccentric. Influence? None.

The lane to Taos on Sea is on the left near the crest of a hill. In 2006 only the first fifty metres were concrete. Now the track is paved to the village perimeter, some two kilometres. The design of the village is open-unplanned. Trees shade the few dusty streets. Two Internet outlets are a surprise. A few homes are new; a few have gained an upper floor. Construction is concrete block.

I stop at the house opposite the school where I stopped first in 2006. The same man greets me. He had hoped to return to Taos where he had worked as an illegal for a few years roofing houses. Tighter border controls have dissuaded him. He presumes that I have come to meet the Korean.

Tales of a Korean who taught English at a village school were the original attraction. I learned later that the Korean had come to the US as an eleven-year-old on a scholarship to an elite private school in California. Berkeley and grad school followed. Further studies were interspersed by spells with Wall Street banks. He was respectable: did the right thing; wore respectable suits, city shoes, abstemious ties. And sometimes surfed…

Harvard Business School undid his desire for the American dream. His fellow students were amoral; profit governed their judgement of right and wrong. These were the future leaders of Corporate America. The Korean envisaged an endless parade of Enron executives, of small investors bankrupted or robbed of their pensions. Fearing infection, he loaded his surfboards on his truck and drove south in search of the perfect wave: he discovered a self-governing village community to which each member contributed a service. Teaching English to both children and adults is the Korean's contribution. Sadly, he is visiting California.

I turn in at a row of thatch cabanas with a shower block. An open-sided *palapa* has been added since my previous visit. Though simple food is served, it is essentially a lounging zone with hammocks and a colour television with satellite connection to the sports channels. Four young blond visitors are watching football.

The owner is now the mayor. A slow and thoughtful speaker, he is in his early forties, slender and bearded. He was first to head north from the village. Legal immigrant, he owned his own business in Taos. He and I sit under the *palapa*. He tells of the sponsored 2006 surfing competition. Many surfers came. There was no competition in 2007. However, the sponsors paid 20,000 dollars bringing champion surfers to the beach, not to compete, but to spread the word as to the dependability and quality of the waves. The sponsors intended building a major hotel and tourist complex. The community refused to sell them the land. The sponsors responded by paying people from a neighbouring village to invade the east end of the beach.

'We chased them with machetes,' the mayor says.

The beach is two kilometres from the village. The villagers constructed a good dirt road and visitors pay a two-dollar toll. A sanitary block and two *palapas* are the only buildings and belong to the community. One is a bar/restaurant where villagers take turns serving. Today they are trimming fresh palm thatch. A turtle protection squad patrols the beach, which ends at a rocky point. Waves build off the point; each wave forms a perfect barrel. A couple of tourist novices fall repeatedly in the white water close to the beach. A few locals are surfing off the point. I watch a while before riding back to the cabanas.

A young Canadian couple occupy the next cabana. He is a deep-water dive instructor and has worked the Caribbean, Asia and Australia as well as the US and Canada. He and his schoolteacher girlfriend played poker in Las Vegas. She broke even; he won the price of their people-carrier. The truck is packed with camping gear, surfboards and dive equipment.

We walk to the general store for dinner. An open-sided restaurant on the roof is new. We share a table with two New Zealanders. The man is a software engineer and describes a spell working in England as seven-a-side rugby, rock climbing and joyful gym sessions.

His wife is less sporting. She has spent the day dutifully tumbling off a surfboard, has skinned knees and has been vomiting – probably too much sun and insufficient liquids.

We eat stuffed tacos and drink a good few beers. I pick up the bill: eleven dollars.

PACIFIC HIGHWAY
Friday, 22 February

Last night's beer is extra weight as I head up the coastal highway. The first sixty kilometres twist through dry hills. Corners are sharp and badly cambered; stray goats and donkeys graze the verge and wander across the road. The country flattens. Beggarly village follows beggarly village, each scented with dry dung and sun-scorched earth. Inevitably I miss a *topes*: brakes screech, back tyre slithers, saddle slams my crotch.

Daylight is on the wane and I have ridden 500 kilometres. I don't spot *24 HOURS* painted on a sign outside a small-town hotel. *24 HOURS* denotes a house of assignation. The woman seated in the lobby balloons out of a low-cut blouse, short shorts fastened with a gold glitter belt, high heels. She strikes me as a nice woman, a little motherly. She asks why I travel alone; whether I am married; how many children we have; whether Bernadette minds my being away. She is here to meet an all-night client, a regular arrangement. He is due in half an hour. All night is one hundred dollars; short time is fifty.

I negotiate a twenty-dollar room down three dollars with a wizened male receptionist short on teeth. The only restaurant in town is closed. I buy two beers and a packet of biscuits for myself, and a carton of peach juice for the woman.

A short-time client drops by for a quickie and the lady apologises for leaving me alone. I take my provisions upstairs, shower and surf a soulless TV selection of football, soaps or preachers.

ZIHUATANEJO
23 February

Acapulco may stir romantic fantasies. Reality is a crescent of steep hills cupping a haze of blue petroleum fumes, the sea beyond hardly visible. Streets are designed to capture the unwary and signs deliberately bewilder. Hesitate and klaxons screech. Make the wrong choice and you ride down a near-precipice. A cab driver directs me to the harbour-front where cafés and restaurants are overpriced and gleaming yachts bob contempt for the poverty-stricken. Two hours of Acapulco suffice…

Onward to Zihuatanejo to meet with the last of my writing buddies of Ibiza days, Clifford Irving. Cliff has had his difficulties (haven't we all): witness the recent Richard Gere movie of Cliff's fake autobiography of Howard Hughes. However, Cliff is a fine and varied writer: read *Tom Mix and Pancho Villas*, his legal thrillers, or his investigation of a double murder, *Daddy's Girl*. He is also expert at making money from his work (I am a total failure) and has a home in Aspen, Colorado. Two months in Zihuatanejo is his yearly escape from the cold. He has warned me by email that room rates, even off the beach, run upward from forty-five dollars – not having to live cheap for some years, he may have forgotten how.

I ride into Zihuatanejo in mid-afternoon and spot a posada down a quiet side street in a middle-class residential zone convenient both to beach and downtown. An eccentric son of the owner shows me a large room with a double and a single bed (great for strewing clothes). The fan works and is silent, shower has a rose and the lavatory has a seat – such are the luxuries of down-market travel. The son suggests twenty dollars a night. I suggest ten. We settle for thirteen and I take the room for five days.

Cops direct me to the beach complex where Cliff shelters for the winter. Stunted palms and the standard tropical plants grow insecurely in damp dirt each side of a brick path leading towards the beach. The dirt separates two lines of concrete tourist hovels. The hovels are poorly painted with a chocolate wash; front porches boast a hammock in chemical colours and a couple of uncomfortable garden chairs. The damp and lack of sun create a mosquito heaven and the few resident tourists on display are overweight mosquito-yum-yum.

Cliff has a studio apartment on the upper floor of a two-level building right on the beach. Cliff is taller than me, older and harder of hearing – though readers should be aware that I am prejudiced as Cliff and I are competitors in the health stakes. He opens the door on a mini version of his work studio in Ibiza back in the early sixties: concrete couches with thin foam cushions; kitchenette in which a portly man (me) would barely fit. Cliff's Ibiza studio was light: this is dark. Cliff's Ibiza studio was damp: this is very damp. Cliff's Ibiza studio was cheap: Zihuatanejo is expensive – not by Palm Beach standards, but this is Mexico.

ZIHUATANEJO
25 February

Cliff does his yoga exercises in the mornings. We breakfast late at Patty's beach restaurant, Mar y Mar. Patty has Internet. Run out of battery, I recharge while seated at a corner of the bar where I struggle to complete my standard 1,000 words from ten a.m. to six p.m. each day. One thousand is amateur stuff. Cliff writes 5,000; he told me so way back in Ibiza. He was my writing guru. He read and edited my first manuscript, which a boutique imprint at Heinemann published without further alteration.

Cliff's 5,000 has been my yardstick for forty-five years. I have striven and striven and striven; yet here I am at Patty's producing the same paltry wordage.

I confess my amateur status to Cliff.

Cliff says that he would be more than satisfied with 1,000.

'Five,' I protest. 'That's what you said.'

'When?' counters Cliff.

'Ibiza – your studio.'

'Never,' says Cliff. 'I've never written 5,000 and I never claimed I did.'

I remonstrate. Cliff repeats his denial.

Back at the posada, I lie on my bed, watch the ceiling fan spin and replay the scene a dozen times. Ibiza is the set. My antidote to struggling with a second novel is to visit Cliff at his studio when he isn't there. Two girls are staying in the studio rent-free in exchange for typing a clean copy of Cliff's latest manuscript. Dark, good-looking and sexually sophisticated New York Jewish girls, they do everything as a team.

Cliff sets 5,000 words as punishment for my visits: a subconscious action, of course – and one that Cliff has forgotten. I accept the punishment (again subconsciously) as rightful penance for being wrongfully enamoured.

Here, in Zihuatanejo, Cliff has finally absolved me of my dalliance. My penance is served. No further guilt for having written too little and too slowly.

Does my relief seem manic?

And looking back, I believe that spelling was a greater handicap to my career. I was ashamed of submitting work. Better bin it than suffer editorial contempt.

Why didn't I use a dictionary?

Visit our home and you will find dictionaries in every room: English, French, Spanish…

Non-dyslexics consult a dictionary for meaning or to check whether a word ends in *ant* or *ent* or has a double or single *l* or *p*. I don't get that close. Spellcheck frequently fails to divine what word I intend. I try various versions and finally search the thesaurus for a synonym in which I have more confidence and am thus led to the word I originally intended. Yes, time consuming…

Three of my four sons are dyslexic. Mark is the eldest of the three. The same Catholic private school stigmatised us both for our spelling. I left without graduating while Mark was forced to study art as less academically challenging. He went to night school, converted to science, gained his degree in marine biology and now teaches graduation-year science at a Manchester grammar school. His perseverance and achievements are exemplary.

Joshua and Jed are a younger generation but were equally stigmatised at school by incompetent and prejudiced teachers.

ZIHUATANEJO
26 February

I have a love/hate relationship with Zihuatanejo.

Hate because Zihuatanejo is a Pacific beach resort for self-obsessed health-obsessed North American retirees. Regiments of beach parasols protect the cancer-wary. Conversation is dietary, medical or yoga; sport is a colonic irrigation and Spanish is the few words misspoken to waiters who speak English.

Love because I feel young (I'm the youngest visitor on the beach); and because Cliff has freed me and I'm working well.

We have taken Patty's daughter to dinner at a restaurant owned by an arrogant and impolite Algerian. Cliff goes to bed early. Patty's daughter and I head for a bar in company with a Brit Mexican, Joe. The bar owner is a stocky young woman with a sour expression. Company is a couple of North American jazz musicians. Conversation becomes tiresomely lurid around three in the morning. Joe drops me back at the posada shortly before dawn. I have drunk eight beers in ten hours; I am sober and my reasons for seldom frequenting bars or pubs are reaffirmed.

ZIHUATANEJO
27 February

Joe's father owns a furniture factory in Pueblo. Joe marketed the furniture in England while reading for his Master's at Manchester Business School. He has been playing the money market with imaginary funds for a month and has made a substantial paper profit. He will begin operating with real money on the first of March. He is a shrewd young man and may do well.

He drives me to a party at a Mexican friend's house close by my posada. We sit on green plastic chairs beside a pool. A middle-aged North American couple have ridden a Harley down from Montana where he works as a forester. The couple have blue eyes in common, grey longer-than-shoulder-length hair – no beads. He dreams of riding south to Tierra del Fuego. She touches him often: a sign of love or ownership or insecurity. I advise him to ride a lighter bike if he heads south. The party progresses slowly into a state of shared monosyllabic near-coma. I totter to my bed.

ZIHUATANEJO
28 February

Spring Break is here; I spotted a pair of kids in their sixties jogging (slowly) on the beach this morning. Cliff has friends staying. They are rabid ex-meat-eaters, rabid ex-smokers. He is a rabid ex-Wall Street profit glutton and rabidly political – a Democrat. They are fun people. Their conversation has care content.

Cliff doesn't do politics. He remarks on the futility of my being angered or concerned by things over which I have neither control nor influence. I counter that there is no point in writing if you don't care.

This is not a productive conversation.

Meanwhile Patty is hosting a yoga convention and is converting the flat roof above the bar into a permanent yoga floor. A workman bashing concrete directly overhead is no place for a writer. I have 6,000 satisfactory words to show for five days and am out of here in the morning.

TO MORELIA
Friday, 29 February

I am miserable amongst foreigners; they are reminders of Berna-dette and my sons and separation becomes almost unbearable. A shortcut to the east/west expressway is two hours of hills and villages and speed bumps. The expressway is a biker's delight, good surface, no *topes*. Climbing through pine-clad hills, I recall the outset of the ride south to Tierra del Fuego and the pass on the road to Oaxaca. I feared then that the journey would be too hard, that my heart would give out. The scent of pine tar was a comforting reminder of child-hood in the Scottish borders.

This journey has replaced such ancient recollections. Pine tar now is a reminder of Guatemala and one glorious morning swooping down from Coban to Rio Hondo; and of riding a full day on dirt through forests in Honduras, horsemen picking their way between the pines, and thinking of my brother and a horseback ride we talked of, but never took, across the Shandur Pass from Chitral to Gilgit in Pakistan.

The temperature drops. I pull on to the hard shoulder and strug-gle into my leather bomber jacket. Vending machines at tollgates swallow coins and don't deliver. I take the exit to a small town of cobbled lanes. Buildings are low; walls washed in white and red ochre and dusky pink; pan-tiled roofs on wooden pillars shade the sidewalks. Inquiring for a restaurant, I am directed to a house with a single long table in the front room. Lunch is bean soup and a slice of beef sweated with onions and chilli. Three policemen join me. Family men in middle age, they speak quietly and slowly. Perhaps they are corrupt – this is the Hollywood image. How would I know? I am merely passing through, grateful for company and grateful to inhabit a different reality from Zihuatanejo.

Forgive me, Morelia. I walk your grey pavé and try to admire your granite palaces and mansions. This is Spain of the Inquisition built to impress and subjugate. I feel no love.

I park the Honda in the splendour of the Hotel Colonial's sev-enteenth-century patio and find a restaurant opposite the cathedral. Downstairs is dimly (romantically?) lit. I must write and a waiter conducts me to an upstairs dining room where I sit in solitary command of windows that open to the cathedral's twin towers. Yes, they are impressive and beautifully illuminated. My pleasure lies in another Morelia high in Spain's Sierra Maestrazgo and memories of celebrating the bicentenary of my Spanish great-grandfather, Marshal Ramon Cabrera, who captured the city for the Carlists.

So onward westward towards Queretaro…

QUERETARO
1 March

The sun is fierce on hills of harsh rock and dry dirt. Emerald oases of rice paddy gleam in valleys patterned with narrow canals. Those first Spaniards came from a similar land, Extremadura, as did the Moors.

Water is the treasure that toil with hoe and mattock husbanded.

Men are redundant now. Machines accomplish a century's work in a few days. In doing so, they bury memories of how it was; yet how it was is the fascination: who those first Spaniards were and what they found.

Lakes fill much of a valley. Whitewashed cottages crown a conical island. A dyke carries the expressway. Two grey heron play at sentry amongst patches of tall reed; lines of white pelican form a right angle above a fish trap – or is it a breeding pen for tilapia? The Honda cruises at ninety kilometres an hour.

Where Morelia is harsh, Queretaro is joyous. Only the paving is grey; walls are deep rose, ochre and faded buttercup. The city is great for walking. People are courteous and sidewalks seldom crowded. Safely stroll the lovely parks on the periphery or wander the pedestrian streets and lanes that connect the four plazas in the historic quarter. Cloisters and clipped trees surround the plazas; water jets from every fountain. Late in the evening I share a wrought-iron bench on Independencia with two elderly men and listen to a guitarist and vocalist perform at a sidewalk restaurant. Guilt for freeloading soon threatens my tranquillity and forces me to a table where I sip a cold Corona.

Days as a proper tourist, I stand in wonder in the theatre that witnessed both Emperor Maximilian's 1867 trial and the drafting of the Mexican constitution; dawdle through museums and galleries; sneak looks into public and private patios; visit churches, not grand but immensely beautiful. What do I do in churches? I admire the architecture, yet long for fewer and better statues; and I run a couple of trial death trips and pray a little – or do what I think of as praying. I give thanks for the gift of life. I confess that I have abused the gift and abused my fellows. I determine to do better with my talents in the last few years of my life and be more generous both materially and in spirit.

I used to be most careful in avoiding the G word. Somewhere on this long journey, in some church up on the Alto Plano, I accepted that other peoples' God is my Oneness by another name. God is OK. The traditional over-egging with ego and id and super ego puts me off – the beard and crown and thunderbolts.

So there you have it: a personal view, probably pompous. Have no fear, this is a one-off. I won't go there again.

QUERETARO
4 March

A municipal art gallery is a magnificent modern space within ancient walls. A youthful professor discusses communication with his students. He stands in front of eight small, unframed oil paintings. The paintings hang in a horizontal line on a large white wall and equidistant one from the other. The paintings could be arranged as a narrative: sea monster, sinking ship, telephone, satellite dish…

The painter has arranged them haphazardly – perhaps because that is the manner in which we are offered information on the web

Haphazard offends a male student.

Submissive silence is the role of the female students. They have been silent throughout their education. Sad that they haven't learned to speak (other than by cellular).

A coffeehouse in the cloister facing across the Jardin de Armas makes a fine place for writing. A pack of cowboy Goths crosses the square, both sexes dressed identically: black Stetson, tight black sleeveless T-shirt, black stovepipe jeans, black knee-high boots festooning laces.

An oyster bar on Calle Corregidora offers a six-dollar set menu: prawn cocktail, a red snapper off the grill and a flan. What more could an old man desire?

I ride the bike uptown to the Honda outlet for a 3,000-kilometre service. If you don't speak Spanish, Rodrigo King is the man; he speaks perfect English. He calls me to collect the bike in the late afternoon. A couple of newspapers and a television channel wish to do a story. Is that OK?

It is certainly OK. I have become accustomed to speaking Spanish on camera. The questions don't change much. I wear my ancient Church's shoes and Alpinestars top. The service is free – nice people…

TEOTIHUACAN
6 March

Teotihuacan is one of those musts for visitors to Mexico City. The Pyramid of the Sun is the main attraction. The pyramid is sixty-four metres high and covers approximately the same area as the Great Pyramid in Egypt.

An expressway runs directly from Mexico City to the archaeological site. Take a bus and the excursion is painless. I am in Queretaro. Avenida Lopez connects with the expressway to Teotihuacan. Avenida Lopez is a ninety-minute ride. Truck drivers try using me as an ice-hockey puck. So why am I risking my life? Pyramids don't do it for me – particularly pyramids in Mexico and Central America.

I have become too close in my travels to the first Spaniards. I imagine the pyramids through their eyes: heaps of skulls at the base, steps a butcher's midden of blood and defecation. Or did a horde of scrubbers work the steps? Did the cleaner scrubbing the top level earn extra? Only a few hundred steps to the summit, great job…

Those first Spaniards are condemned for destroying a culture.

Perhaps a culture that vile merited destruction.

Yes, I know. I am politically incorrect. Please excuse me. I am an Old Brit Blimp. I can't feel the romance … Though I find it in Hispanic America's churches: I am a descendent of that culture.

A final evening in Queretaro, city of guitars: fountains cool the air; a gentle breeze barely whispers in the trees. Elderly musical pensioners sit on benches or chat on the sidewalk, all with their instruments. A joyously throaty blues vocalist at a café in Jardin de Armas is accompanied by two musicians. Two small children, mum and dad, sit listening beside me on a bench. Mum is a plump mum; kids are well behaved and cradle baby guitars; Dad is a tall thin schoolteacher wanting to be a writer. He and I talk US politics. He is pro Obama. All his friends are pro Obama. Obama is proof that the US can change.

SIERRA GORDA
7 March

Five Franciscan missions in the valleys of the Sierra Gorda date from the 1730s. Fray Junipero de la Serra designed the churches and presented the façades as canvasses for indigenous sculptors. The baroque façades they created are unique and give the missions their artistic importance.

The mission at Jalpan, north-east of Queretaro, will be a good base for exploring. A gale swirls dust across the Queretaro plains. Tequisquiapan is hot-spring spa hotels and restaurants with pools. I halt at a hardware store and buy plastic safety glasses. The storekeeper warns of dangerous winds in the sierra. I take nourishment for the climb in the next town, Cadereyta, at a butchery serving delicious tacos.

The road rises from irrigated fields into a barren land of sparse scrub. A massive rock escarpment towers ahead. The road winds through a ravine to the right of the escarpment only to face a higher barrier. Now begins the true climb famous (or infamous) for 700 hairpin curves. The road is cut into the mountain. Drops are vertiginous. Ahead towers a yet higher wall. Ravines funnel the gale: total calm in the lee of the mountain is transformed at a corner into a tempest that blasts the bike sideways.

Is this fun?

No, terrifying.

I near the summit and expect to look down on Jalpan. I look up at yet higher mountains. On and up the road clambers into a frontier land of sparse pine forest. Turn a corner and ahead rise yet higher mountains. The forest thickens. Sun bakes out the familiar scent of pines. I wear two jumpers beneath a leather bomber jacket; a chill wind discovers cracks and I shiver as I park the bike and look back down at a Martian landscape of creased rock ridges. How far to the final pass: La Puerto del Cielo, Doorway to the Sky…?

The pine forest thickens and trees hide the fearsome falls. The road crosses the final pass at an altitude of nearly 8,000 feet. Paving was completed in 1968. The dirt road would have been impassable in the rains. A mule trail predated the dirt – a ten-day trek from Queretaro to Jalpan. Imagine attempting to govern a country where provinces were so isolated one from another and from the capital; and even provinces were divided within themselves by sierra and river. The miracle of Mexico is its survival (though, as Mexicans protest, the United States stole a vast swathe).

Trees shade the road as it turns and twists down through the forest. Two dark shaggy-coated donkeys, mother and daughter, graze a small patch of almost invisible grass. Pines give way to broad leaf. Music at a comfort break is a stream splashing over rocks way below. I have ridden from near desert up into the chill of a pine cloud forest and am now descending into watered valleys. Such continual changes are the fascination of Mexico.

With a population slightly exceeding 5,000, Jalpan is more a village than a town. Central is the Franciscan mission. The church is cruciform. Two small side chapels form the arms while a dome rises above the altar; to the left of the sculpted façade stands a tower, to the right, a simple cloister surrounds a small garden.

I have hit on Easter week and the seventh year of a seven-year cycle, the year of painting and renovation. Scaffolding shutters the façade; purple drapes of Easter mourning hide statues and paintings within the interior. The scaffolding is a disappointment – not so the drapes. The interior of the church gains in a simplicity that contrasts wondrously with the exterior exuberance. The mission square is beautiful; the town has charm; pace is leisurely; the few streets are narrow and lined with painted houses. Posada Los Angeles is one block back from the square on Calle Mariano Matamoros. The hotel is new and the owners are new to the hotel business. The wife and late-teenaged daughter designed the decor. The result is pretty and quirky with painted tiles and water pouring from painted pitchers into matching hand basins. Best of all is the friendliness of atmosphere.

SIERRA GORDA
8 March

I leave to explore the missions at a reasonable hour. Landa de Matamoros is my first target, eighteen kilometres. The BMW Bike Club of Queretaro is breakfasting at a restaurant on the outskirts of town. I present myself and am seated at the head of the table. The bikers are successful businessmen in their middle years indulging an unfulfilled fantasy of their youth. They are good companions, cheerful, funny, generous and intelligent and range from Germanic pale to dark mahogany.

Landa Matamoros is on what passes for a main road here in the sierra. The church is simple in architecture: the façade is an explosion, every centimetre basted in sculpture by artists ecstatic as they worked unbound from dogma or tradition – *freed from the box* – even the prison bars of scaffolding defeated. So on into the tranquil interior – from which I exit to confront a coach load of photography students from Mexico University. One aims her camera at me. I return the compliment.

Mission Tilaco is a further fourteen kilometres down a side road that twists up over a pass. A lake gleams down in the valley, a sprinkle of white houses and a church tower amongst freshly ploughed fields; the tower is too plain to be a mission. Onward I ride to find Tilaco low on the flank of the next valley. The valley channels the wind, cooling in summer, now chill. A line of skinny cypress trees twitch beneath the wind: whipped all in the same direction, gleaming palm fronds suggest poster-art Valkyries of Hitler's Germany or Soviet Union.

Two painters are at work at the mission. I ask why redecoration is undertaken every seven years. I am a foreigner so must be speaking an unknown language. I repeat my question slowly. Two young women are taking photographs. The painter asks them to translate; thus commences an odd conversation. I speak in Spanish to the young women. They speak to the painter in Spanish. He answers them in Spanish. They relay his answer in Spanish. The crux of the conversation? They paint the church every seven years because they paint the church every seven years.

The interior is tranquil. I sit a while, pray a little.

Riding back up the pass, the village by the lake is too tempting to ignore. A side road snakes down through the hills. The village is small, houses scattered. I ride slowly and am greeted by each person as I pass. The small church lies at the far end of the village. It was built by villagers and completed in 1904 and is as unadorned as a Methodist chapel. Trees shade the façade. A pickup is parked outside. The driver sports a diamond ear-stud. I ask if he has worked in the North. Yes, for five years. Will he return to the North? There is no reason to return. He saved well. He bought the pickup and is building a house. He accompanies me into the church where four men are panelling the wall behind the altar in cedar. A woman serves fresh lemonade before I remount. All those I pass bid me good evening and goodbye as I leave the village. I am having a very good day.

Back in Jalpan I share a table for supper at a taco restaurant with a salesman of gifts from Queretaro. He has four grown children. One is a law student in Queretaro; the other three are engineering graduates and have emigrated to the US.

He is away from home much of the month. His work paid for his children's education. Now he has lost them.

It must be hard.

Yes, it is hard. They change. Even when they visit, it is not the same. 'Perhaps it is the travelling,' he says. 'I was away too often.'

SIERRA GORDA
9 March

Sunday morning and another day of exploration: I stop for coffee at a non-mission village on the road to Mission Conca. Parents and grandparents wait for Sunday Mass on benches in the tree-shaded plaza. Children in clean Sunday clothes chase each other round the shade trees. Mothers call to them to stay clean; men inhale a last cigarette until the bells toll their summons. The church is late nineteenth-century and bigger than the mission churches. The exterior is plain. Inside, a multitude of statues hide behind purple drapes. Floor tiles are laid in patterns; gold paint is garish. The priest is young, his server old. A girl in her early teens reads the epistle. I creep out midway through the sermon.

The village seems deserted.

Trees shade every street in Mission Conca. Breeze wafts citrus scent, doors glow in fresh paint, geraniums tumble from clay pots.

Wondrous to imagine indigenous sculptors at work on the mission's façade, every centimetre patterned, saints quarrelling with goblins for space. Such vibrancy serves to accentuate the calm simplicity of the domed interior. Only the scaffolding is a disappointment. A Mexican family on holiday has seen me on television; we pose for a photograph before going our separate ways.

The bridge a few kilometres short of Mission Conca crosses a gorge below the junction of two rivers. One river is fed by thermal springs. Thick-trunked trees shade the beaches on the far bank. A shed shared by half a dozen entrepreneurs serves barbequed meats and chicken. I park the bike the near end of a line of double-cab trucks and order chicken and cold Corona.

Three black on white geese waddle by, followed by two laggards. Canned Mexican weep-music wails from speakers. Two families unload from Texas-registered used cars. Men roll their pants; women hike their skirts; children are stripped to swimsuits; the current draws patterns in the water as they wade.

A man in his mid-thirties fetches my beer and sits at the table. He wears an embroidered denim shirt, jeans and cowboy boots. He says, Yes, the money for the new construction I've noticed in all the villages comes from El Norte (the United States). Many men from the Sierra Gorda work in El Norte. Every one of them returns home with a car or truck: *US politicos beware – halt illegal immigration and the US market in used cars will collapse.*

The riverbank cowboy brings my barbequed chicken and seats himself again. I remark that donkeys and mules were the sole transport prior to the road. They are now where there are no roads, he tells me: modern animals, they travel by truck to the foot of the trail.

One of the geese takes flight and lands midstream. Two more geese take to the water; a white butterfly zigzags on the breeze. Chicken is tasty; beer is chilled, enjoyable conversation, another good day…

Few North Americans visit the sierra. Perhaps the roads scare them – or meeting bandits. This evening a married couple in their late fifties occupy the next table at a taco place round the corner from my hotel. They have flown direct from a New York winter and seem very pale. He is a university professor. Though they visit Europe frequently, this is their first trip to Mexico. The wealth of architecture surprises them. I am surprised by their surprise. The professor immediately questions me on Mexican racial attitudes. Such is the US obsession...

SIERRA GORDA
10 March

Today is a rest from riding; time to write at a table in the hotel restaurant. The table faces the open doors to the street. It is a quiet cobbled street with few passers-by. Coffee is unlimited, the occasional salesman of vegetables or fruit the main distraction. I have walked the streets in so many towns on this journey, imagined how life would be, what street to live on, which house closest to perfection. Jalpan would be a fine place. It is the right size in which to become accepted, enjoys a benign climate, charming architecture, exciting country, excellent fishing.

So why am I so tired? Tired is a misnomer. Even exhausted is an understatement. I have been away from home and on the road eight months, always vulnerable – such was the first day's lesson when the truck struck and made fear my travel companion.

Seemingly endless series of packing and unpacking; trying to recall in each new hotel room which direction the bathroom is and where the light switches are. Country to country, monstrous poverty; endless tales of corruption; belief so many have that the system is too entrenched; that there is nothing to be done; even trying is to waste one's life.

Such is the reality of Hispanic America. How does the traveller hold to his optimism? And, by nature, I am an optimist (aged seventy-five, only an optimist would attempt this ride).

Now my bag is packed. The bike is loaded. I must bid farewell to Spanish and return to my native tongue, yet in a different land. This in my thoughts, I lie in bed tearful with longing to be cradled in Bernadette's arms. Seventy-five and a baby! Where is your shame, old man? Stop whining. Kick yourself up a gear. Dwell on the milliard joys of the past months and reflect with gratitude on your immense good fortune…

NORTHWARD
11 March

The road north winds through the sierra. A dry stone wall divides a small paddock of coarse grass. The wall ends at a fast-flowing burn. Broad-leaf trees grow on the banks. Pines grow further up the slope. Wall, burn, trees, quality of hill pasture: all are reminders of the Scottish Borders – even the wet mist. I look down on clouds one last time south of the Rio Grande. The US lies ahead. The US frightens me. It is foreign territory in all but language. I long to be home…

From Ciudad Victoria to the border at Brownsville is one vast flat field of sorghum. The field is 200 miles long; God knows how many miles wide. Rains are late and a television news presenter speaks of farmers in panic.

I am invited to lunch by the middle-aged owner/editor of the local newspaper. We discuss politics and the erecting of the fence along the frontier to keep Mexicans out of a land that once was part of Mexico. US Border Patrol catches an illegal, the illegal is returned to Mexico. Smugglers of illegals are called coyotes. The coyote takes the client across the border again and again until successful. The present-day fee is 1,500 dollars.

Lunch with the editor takes a while. I reach the frontier town of Matamoros in early evening. I had expected streets of strip clubs and massage parlours as in Tijuana. Budget sex has been supplanted by budget medical treatment; strip clubs and massage parlours have given way to hospitals and doctors' surgeries. Medical costs are half those across the border. Doctors and surgeons are equally qualified.

My medication is a final dish of grilled chilli prawns with garlic and a good bed at a price that doesn't make me flinch. I shall cross into the US in the morning. Goodbye, Mexico. You have been kind to an old man, protected me, shown me glorious architecture, beautiful scenery, fuelled me with delicious food. Most precious has been new friends made, old friendships renewed. Yes, thank you, Mexico, thank you indeed…

18

USA

TEXAS
Thursday, 13 March

I expected to wait in line at the Brownsville border. I was through to a Customs bay in minutes and through to Immigration with equal speed. Immigration takes a while. Back home I understand computer delay: our sons download viruses. I don't like to ask the female official what Homeland Security downloads.

I want to ride with an agent from Border Patrol on a night hunt for illegals. The head office for this sector is in Edinburg. The public relations officer is young and made uncomfortable by my questioning. Illegal immigration is a forbidden subject as is progress in erecting the border fence – major points of discussion amongst Washington politicians, candidates for the presidency and ordinary citizens of Texas, New Mexico, Arizona and California – and 99.99 per cent of Mexicans.

Accompanying a border patrol is also illegal (I might get shot). A poster of a Nascar saloon car decorates the office. The car is sponsored by Homeland Security. Racing cars are cool with the type of kid Homeland Security hopes to recruit. Has the car won races? PR doesn't know – or is that another forbidden subject?

A patrolman recommends Motel 6 in Edinburg for a cheap clean room. Motel 6 began life as a Holiday Inn and I have a room the size of a South American small-town hotel; towels would bandage an army. I am due Sunday in Galveston, Texas. I am way behind with writing. I book in for three nights; drag out the waterproof purse that hangs round my neck on a steel wire. Where in hell is my credit card? Have you suffered the same disaster?

You hunt through every pocket.

Then you hunt through every pocket.

Finally you hunt through every pocket.

The receptionist comes to my aid with a bright suggestion: Have you checked your pockets?'

Don't snarl – the clerk means well.

'Where did you last use it?' the clerk asks.

How would I remember? Aged seventy-five? Close to the end of my journey and I was careless. Stupid, stupid, stupid…

I pay cash for the room, dump my bag on the bed and cool my brain in a shower. Then I call the bank to cancel the card and call Bernadette to wire me money through Western Union.

I ask directions to Edinburg town centre. Edinburg doesn't have a centre. Edinburg has malls. Drive enough miles in any direction and you are in the next town, which is also malls. I ride seven kilometres to a Starbucks. Starbucks considers itself superior. So do its staff. In need of black coffee, I am faced with an incomprehensible menu. Bewilderment merits a sneer and half an inch of black liquid in a ceramic cup. Wi-Fi is an extra.

A woman whispers that Internet is free at MoonBean. Moon-Bean is in a neighbouring mall. Staff are friendly and relaxed. Coffee comes in a beaker. Other customers talk to me. I am happy.

A Chinese restaurant serves a buffet: all you can eat for 6.95. The buffet contains four different shrimp dishes, stuffed crab, calamari and every kind of meat. A notice hangs above the buffet: PLEASE TAKE ONLY WHAT YOU CAN EAT

Customers serve themselves mountains.

I eat there both days that I am in Edinburg. One meal is sufficient intake for the day. The Chinese lady who runs the restaurant has a sweet smile and is happy to sit with me and chat. And, joy of joy, I feel slim. People here waddle rather than walk. Obese is an understatement.

Edinburg is a good place to write. The alternative is visiting a couple of malls (no great temptation) – or making the coffee run to

MoonBean. Our home is in a small Herefordshire village. Ledbury is our local market town. The route to Ledbury from our cottage runs through country lanes and over hills and through ancient woods and glorious green pastures. My wife, Bernadette, tailors hand and travel luggage and numbers movie stars and Royals amongst her clientele. Her work is exhibited at Ledbury Market House. The Market House was built in the thirteenth century. Bernadette and I were married there. This is not a digression. I am writing of coffee. An Italian café serves great coffee upstairs at the delicatessen on Ledbury's Main Street. The café is the same distance from our cottage as MoonBean is from my Edinburg motel. Ledbury is a pleasant drive from our cottage. Riding to MoonBean is six-lane urban highway, innumerable intersections with other six-lane urban highways and innumerable malls.

Between writing I watch television news. Commentators on FOX and CNN are delirious with joy. They have grabbed an opportunity to destroy Senator Barack Obama. Obama's pastor is the weapon. FOX and CNN broadcast endless repeats of the pastor bouncing up and down while fuelled with rage at the suffering of Afro-Americans. 'God damn America,' the pastor yells.

God has saved McCain, breathe Republicans.

God be blessed for passionate Afro-American Christianity, whispers Hillary Clinton to herself.

TO GALVESTON
Sunday, 16 March

Three days of Homeland Security PR, coffee, malls, obesity and politics: here is a return to travel. Galveston, Texas, is 650 kilometres of flat. A highway flyover rates as a hill. Cloud hides the sun – fortunately no rain. Other dangers lurk: primarily an Old Man's stupidity. I take on petrol midway. Three Harleys cruise into the petrol station. I ask permission to touch the big, broad, leather seats.

Heaven! Excitement makes me forgetful. I run short of fuel 150 kilometres from Galveston and discover that I left my billfold and address book on the petrol pump at the last halt.

This is bad.

Actually, this is very bad.

I am almost out of petrol. In Galveston I am visiting Carol and Peter Davies. Turn back a few chapters to the Panama section and find a description of our meeting at a roadside pizza joint on the Caribbean coast. Carol and I talked politics and publishing for thirty minutes. We have exchanged emails on politics. Carol teaches at Texas A & M. Peter is head man at Galveston's Beach Patrol: Mister Baywatch. I am invited to speak with Carol's students and be the Oldie at a seventieth birthday party for Peter's mother. I have Carol's telephone number. I don't have fifty cents for a phone call.

Very bad…

The gentleman manning the cash register at the petrol station is an 'evil' Muslim immigrant from Karachi, Pakistan. He is a small man, grey-haired, mid-fifties. I relate my predicament and offer my camera for a gallon and a half of petrol. He is unimpressed by the camera.

He says, 'This is a misfortune that happens to everyone some time in their lives,' and takes six dollars from his billfold. 'Is this sufficient?'

'More than sufficient.'

I ask for his address.

He tells me not to be silly.

This is my *thank you* to a dear kind sweet man.

Galveston is a small city built on a sandbar a couple of miles out from the Texas coast, to which it is connected by a causeway. By nature of being a sand bar, Galveston has beaches. The seaward beach is forty miles long and has reasonable surf on a good day. The landward side is protected and has excellent wind surfing, good fishing and dinghy sailing. Five million tourists visit Galveston during the summer months. Two hundred thousand students visit for Spring Break.

This is Spring Break.

I ride into Galveston in early evening and head for the city centre. Four good-natured Afro-American men in a Lexus pull alongside at each red light intersection. A man on the rear seat is filming me. The others attempt conversation. The lights turn green and drivers behind immediately hit their klaxons. So it goes, so it goes, all the way down Broad Street. I make a U-turn at the Catholic cathedral and halt beside a Latino family taking photographs.

Would doing a Sunday good deed make them happy? Do they have a mobile phone? Could they call Carol Davies for me? I have the number.

The mother calls Carol and tries to hand me the phone.

I plead that I can never hear over a mobile phone; that I need Carol's address and directions.

The mother writes directions on the back of a hymn sheet. More gratitude!

Early evening and a chill wind blows across the beach-front promenade. A few crazies are in the surf. A few throw balls on the beach. Thousands spill out of a rap concert. Cars and bikes crowd the beach road. Kids sit out of car windows; on seat backs in their convertibles; on car roofs, feet dangling through sun roofs. The vast majority are Afro-American. Age is unity. High on mirth, they shout joyfully in a foreign language: US student-speak.

A kid throws dollar bills. The breeze grabs the bills. Kids give chase. Chaos!

I sneak through gaps.

Galveston beach is a thirty-mile housing development. Bermuda Beach is unpretentious houses on pillars. A hurricane removed thirty metres of sand and most of the front line of homes a few years back; at high tide, survivors have their feet in the sea.

Carol and Peter live two rows back from the shore. Carol is waiting at the gate beside an antique Volkswagen camper home-sprayed bright green with red-and-black shell borders. For company Carol has two dogs and a fit white ponytail in his fifties. One dog is a pug; the other is questionable. The ponytail is sucking on a cold Corona beer. Carol introduces him as Ed.

Carol has beer in multiple-choice for the Brit. Choice in beer is less stressful than a Starbucks coffee menu.

Late Sunday evening of Spring Break weekend and Peter is searching the sea for a missing girl down the far end of the island. Carol has had no news for the past two hours. No news is bad news. The Davies' two-year-old daughter, Kai, is asleep. Carol and Ed and I drink beer and speak quietly.

Years ago (the year France withdrew from Algeria) I went spear fishing with a Frenchman in his inflatable. The Frenchman was a hard-right ex-colonial. Had he known my politics, he might have speared me in the gut. This was a cold morning and I wasn't comfortable.

I am equally uncomfortable in Texas. Mostly I am way off message. In Bermuda Beach, I have hit on a clandestine cell of Democrats. Peter, Carol and Ed are for Obama. Ed's wife, Terry, backs Hillary Clinton. Ed and Terry own a house on the shore. I am to stay in their ground-floor studio apartment. Meanwhile we drink another beer.

Peter Davies drives up in canary-yellow Baywatch pickup with a pair of rescue surfboards on a roof rack. He has been sitting the past two hours with a dead sixteen-year-old. The girl was spotted from a helicopter. Peter picked her up on the Beach Patrol's Honda aqua-scooter and tried revival – too late. The girl was declared dead on the beach and the ambulance driver refused the body. The rap concert crowd were in riot mode and blocked the sea road so the funeral parlour's van couldn't get through. Now Peter is home and he needs peace. I cross to Ed and Terry's studio apartment and watch politics on television.

GALVESTON
Monday, 17 March

Peter Davies drives me to Beach Patrol HQ where I sit in on a meeting of Peter and his crew. Peter relates diving for the missing girl in the last of yesterday's daylight; the helicopter pilot spotting the body; Peter's attempts at revival; waiting with the body. The drowning took place outside the Patrol's zone of responsibility. No blame is attached to the Patrol, yet a young girl died and these men feel responsible. Humour is the antidote to tragedy and Peter works to lighten the mood.

He and I eat at a Vietnamese noodle bar. The strain is noticeable in his eyes and around his eyes. I try to normalise this one tragedy through a maze of statistics. How many lifeguards does he employ in the summer season? Five hundred. How many drownings? Maybe half a dozen. How many children get lost? In the height of summer they have a tent on the beach manned by two lifeguards; ten or fifteen lost children in the tent at any one time is normal.

Mid-afternoon and Peter patrols the beach in his truck. A few hundred holidaymakers make sparse covering for a four-mile stretch of sand. Peter copes fluently with a Spanish speaker who has lost his mobile phone and with a young dad whose son has been stung by a jellyfish. Next he calls a warning over the loudhailer to a couple of bathers prancing in the sea between two DANGER signs.

A rip current surges off a stone jetty where two families with young children watch the waves: slip and Peter would face another tragedy.

Teenyboppers don't mob us – so much for *Baywatch*…

GALVESTON
Tuesday, 18 March

The ice cap would melt were Terry and Ed to live at the North Pole.

They possess that intensity of warmth. They care. They care for the underprivileged, for those who suffer. They are enraged by the shenanigans of Washington. Terry is conversant with the shenanigans. She worked in Washington for Texas' State Government.

A spiral staircase leads up from the studio apartment to their living room. Ed doesn't sleep much. He has a bubble in one eye; the bubble should be absorbed over the next weeks; meanwhile he is restricted to peripheral vision. I climb the stairs and find Ed reading the newspaper through a magnifying glass. He pours coffee and we watch morning news. Meanwhile Terry is working on other people's tax returns. Returns are designed to be incomprehensible to those on low incomes who should benefit from rebates and tax credits. Terry is a certificated public accountant and member of a team giving free advice to those who can't afford advice.

Galveston is a sandbar. Locals call it an island. Real locals wear BOI buttons: *Born On Island*. Peter's mother is sixth-generation BOI. In company, she demands attention by speaking barely above a whisper. She is a schoolteacher by profession. Surely she must speak in a normal pitch to her students. Peter is the eldest of four sons. His three brothers have arrived to celebrate their mother's seventieth birthday. Carol is Afro-American; Son Two is married to a Japanese; Son Three is in company with a Parsee (Mumbai via the US) while Son Four has a companion from East Germany. Does Mrs Davies feel rejected?

In their student days all four Davies brothers studied drums with a Cuban exile. The youngest brother, Chris, is excellent; the other three are good. The brothers play together on Easter Sunday in Peter and Carol's garden. Ostensibly they are celebrating their mother's birthday. Son Two is a philosophy professor at Loyola University. Son Three is employed in a Central American eagle protection programme. Son Four teaches school in Colombia. The brothers have kept the birthday party secret from their mother. The brothers appear one by one. Their mother is truly surprised (or acts surprised)

and touched by their thoughtfulness. Many cousins are present –
and three grandchildren. Kai is part Afro-American. The other
two grandchildren are half Japanese. The half-Japanese grandson is
already a keen drummer.

GALVESTON
Wednesday, 19 March

Carol, Kai and I drive to town for breakfast. Carol parks and Kai
takes my hand as we walk from the car. I am proud at being chosen.

For the past week and more, television channels here have been
broadcasting the twenty-second loop of Reverend Wright bouncing up and down in apparently insensate rage at the wickedness of
the United States. Barack Obama made a speech yesterday. I lay in
bed in the studio apartment and watched on television as Obama
addressed the most divisive aspect of the United States: Race.

Race is dangerous ground. Politicians avoid the subject. Obama
wasn't speaking as a politician. He was asking people to confront
the truth and think outside the proscribed box. The speech was the
finest and most relevant I have heard by an American. Much has
happened during the Bush presidency to shame Americans. For this
speech alone, Obama should make them proud.

GALVESTON
Friday, 21 March

Carol is Afro-American. Black is part of her beauty. It is also integral
to an upbringing different from my own. We interest each other. We
map who we are by exploring our recollections. Carol is a PhD: she
has a disciplined mind. I am a secondary-school dropout: I have an
untidy mind.

Nervous, I sit in an upright chair with my back to a blackboard.

Thirty students face me. This is an Afro-American literature course at Texas A & M. I waffle about Latin America.

Carol interrupts, 'Simon believes that Americans are obsessed by race. Do you agree?'

A brave blond student in the first row raises her hand tentatively to shoulder height. Others follow. Finally all agree. A medium-brown student in his mid-twenties tells of a white co-worker asking what black people were like.

'Like me,' he said.

'Normal black people.'

'I'm a normal black person.'

You're not a proper black person. You're educated, was the unspoken rebuttal.

A Latino student talks of feeling that she came from a different planet when an Anglo boy asked how her family lived and what they ate. 'You know – like sleep in hammocks and eat beans and rice… '

A black student from a family tells of switching from a majority white high school to a largely Afro-American high school. Her fellow students accused her of talking white – to which she retorted, 'I'm talking English.'

None of the students had listened to Barack Obama's speech. Weird…! Yet this is the conversation Barack Obama requested: sharing attitudes and experiences of race.

Have any of the students read James Baldwin?

A mature student in the far back corner gives me a grin as he raises his hand. One student, yet Baldwin was obligatory reading in my twenties and admired for a surgical precision of language. My favourite quotation comes from *Notes of a Native Son*:

Havens are high-priced. The price exacted of the haven-dweller is that he contrive to delude himself into believing that he has found a haven.

I tell of the Hollywood image Herefordshire high school students gave of Mexicans: fat, sweaty, big moustaches, big hats, comic accents. A student relates his surprise at being shown photographs of upland meadows by his Ecuadorian girlfriend. Hollywood Ecuador is sweat, bugs and jungle. The class has run thirty minutes over time. Kai's babysitter will be impatient.

GALVESTON
Tuesday, 25 March

My replacement credit card arrived yesterday. This morning I drink coffee upstairs at Ed and Terry's for the last time. We dined together last night at Terry's favourite restaurant. Now Terry presents me with a Rockets sweatshirt on which she has written: *Ya'll come back now, ya hear!*

For the ignorant, the Rockets are Houston's basketball team. I shall sport the shirt with pride – and I would dearly love to return. Galvestonians share with folk from other islands that sense of being different, somewhat off the wall.

Memories of Terry and Ed will warm me through bad patches, as will memories of the Davies family.

On the road again and I have reclaimed my travelling persona: a weird old bearded Brit with crutches riding a small bike. The American character possesses a warming openness and generosity. A tangled grey beard in a hooded yellow rain-slicker approaches while I wait for the ferry east from Galveston to the Bolivar Peninsula. Where have I come from? Where am I going? My replies are relayed to deckhands on the ferry and to any driver with a window open. I am made welcome instantly and bid *Have a good one* as I disembark – though two seagulls squatting on a bollard give me a cold eye.

Bolivar Peninsula is a narrow strip some thirty miles long. The road bridge spanning Rollover Pass is the highest point. Much is marshland and a haven for water birds. A grey heron stalks the rushes. A scattering of developments faces the beach. Pillars raise wooden holiday homes in offering to a stiff cold breeze. I imagine a hurricane tearing the houses free and spinning them inland: a scene from the *Wizard of Oz*.

Massive trucks roar east on Interstate 10 from Beaumont to Baton Rouge. The Honda 125 is a flea; I am a plump tick on the back of the flea; flea and tick quiver in the slipstreams. We escape north on State 165 towards Alexandria and Natchez. Louisiana is as flat as the Texas littoral; however, fields are green and the road runs for mile upon mile through loose woodland. Broad-leaf trees are faintly powdered with spring's emerald and wild flowers edge the road. Brilliant splashes of deep pink azalea mark houses tucked amongst the trees. Trailer homes are common. Many are old and shabby: backs broken, they sag at each end, as do old abandoned wooden ships beached on the mud.

Christian churches painted in gleaming white serve or are served by a bewildering assortment of congregations. Is there a true difference between the dozen or more Baptist sects? Enough over which to divide a small rural community? Or merely sufficient to keep a pastor in food? Methodists and Independent Methodists, Seventh Day Adventists and Lutherans; best of all, the Church of Christ. What are the rest? Such exclusion, such splendid arrogance of faith. I prefer roadside diners advertising fresh catfish and fries.

I park between two Hollywood cop cars gleaming in the parking lot beside tired pickups and a black sedan. Four fat, pink County Sheriffs sit at one table; a fat family party celebrating a birthday occupy another. The rest are fair haired manual workers. This is the South; I expect Afro-Americans. Maybe Afro-Americans are kitchen help.

A blond waitress with a broad backside finds unbelievable that I have never tasted catfish. I suggest that English ponds and rivers are too cold.

The fish is served in crisp batter and in vast quantities. The fries are a mountain. I sit alone at a table. I expect a fellow diner to say *Hi* and ask where I've come from or where I'm headed. Nothing – not even from the four sheriffs for whom asking questions goes with the job.

I pay and am starting the bike when a big man in a white apron runs out with a visitor's book and a ballpoint. How was the catfish? Good, I say and print my name and Colwall, Herefordshire, England. End of conversation...

I have cruised, on this journey, the Beagle Channel and the Madeira River, crossed the Amazon, Orinoco, Panama Canal and Rio Grande (a muddy trickle). This evening I ride across the Mississippi into Natchez. The Southern states are a fine market for white paint: first the churches, now a casino disguised as a paddle steamer. Life is a gamble. So is the afterlife. Pick your Christian sect or pick your number on the roulette wheel.

I pick the Day Inn and hit a twenty per cent discount for Oldies.

NATCHEZ
Wednesday, 26 March

Natchez is pretty-pretty. Trees shade Southern houses. Southern houses have pillars. Pillars are romantic. So is the South, gentlemanly and gallant. Both Hollywood and Southern tourism project this image. Visit an old plantation house, inspect the slave hovels; tourists go home happy having flirted with history.

Sadly, it is too recent a history for time to have softened the evil. My grandfather was born in 1864: slavery existed in the South. Racial segregation continued into my adult years ... And Jews were banned from resorts and great hotels, not only in the South, but in New York City and Boston and Philadelphia and Chicago and San Francisco – *Restricted Clientele* was the euphemism. We knew of the Holocaust. We had seen films of Dachau and Belsen and of Ravensbrück where my Aunt Helen's sister was executed.

The white elders of the myriad churches here in the South were complicit as are the white Southern pastors of my generation. This is not company that I wish to keep. I had intended staying a day. No more … I rise early and ride the Natchez Trace Parkway.

The trail winds north through wooded hills from Natchez, Mississippi, to Nashville, Tennessee. Picture a private road through parkland to a Duke's castle in the Scottish borders – lengthened to 444 miles and not a single halt sign. Trucks and commercial vehicles are banned. Speed limit is fifty miles per hour: perfection for the small Honda. I ride in brilliant sunshine. Spring blossoms sparkle. Buds on broad-leaf trees uncurl. A white-tailed stag bolts across the road. An eagle scrabbles for height directly overhead. The eagle startles the hell out of me. It flies up the road well below treetops. Given time, I could count the belly feathers: the bird is that close – and big!

The road follows the wooded shores of a vast reservoir. A spur leads to a boat ramp and general store with a couple of petrol pumps. A dozen vehicles with boat trailers line one side of the car park. The storekeeper left his smile in the bedside locker. Perhaps he has toothache or had a fight with his wife.

Two men arrive in a pickup while I'm pumping petrol; they scoop minnows out of a tank for sale as bait. I report seeing the eagle.

The men say that I'm lucky; eagles are increasingly rare.

I hoped for breakfast and use of the restrooms. The storekeeper has been replaced at the till by an overweight wife who has forgotten to brush her hair. The restrooms are back of an abandoned diner; perhaps the diner isn't abandoned; possibly it merely looks that way. Breakfast can wait. I remount, ride a while. The countryside unrolls, Hereford cattle graze meadows glimpsed through naked trees. Wild flowers sprinkle the grass; azaleas and rhododendrons are in swollen bud. I am well muffled and sunshine offsets the chill. Bikers are a community in the US: every passing biker extends a hand as they pass. I pull into a lay-by and chat with a clean-shaved thirties on a gleaming blue 650 Suzuki. What a magnificent ride! What joy it would be to ride in summer shirtsleeves.

The trail ends and I head into Nashville…

Anyone who has tapped a foot or drummed a finger to Country & Western on the car radio is familiar with Nashville. It is a small town on a flat dusty plain, maybe a dozen streets, battered black Ford trucks, a bunch of lumber-floor saloons, a couple of theatres, a few last-decade recording studios manned by overweight white men who keep their pants up with red suspenders. We have been there, all of us, in our imaginations, watched a cowboy songster-hopeful drop off the Greyhound bus with his guitar and head for the Grand Ole Opry.

Hollywood has been at it again – deluding us. Reality is a big modern American city of glass and steel embraced by twelve-lane Interstate expressways. The red-brick buildings of Vanderbilt University dominate the high street (I had imagined Vanderbilt as East Coast Ivy League). The Grand Ole Opry is a minor also-ran. And I hadn't expected to ride ten miles from the city centre to find a motel room under eighty dollars. One night is more than enough…

TENNESSEE
Thursday, 27 March

I am due in Franklin, North Carolina, tomorrow. Franklin is the far side of the Appalachian Mountains. Today I ride east from Nashville on country lanes that dip and twist through green hills topped by woodland. The countryside is similar to my native Herefordshire. Cattle are the same breed. Even today's weather is a reminder of home with low cloud and spits of drizzle. Lack of hedges is the prime difference; erecting fences is quicker; as is building in timber as opposed to brick or stone. The houses are pretty when freshly painted, yet, to European eyes, lack substance. Agriculture has changed. As at home, fruit and vegetables have replaced dairy herds, hay barns superfluous. Our brick barns are converted into luxury homes. Barns here are timber; out of use, they rot.

My spectacles mist in the light drizzle. A narrow lane passes a clutch of small houses with sagging porches. Weeds clamber up rusting trucks and tractors, abandoned refrigerators, cookers, washing machines. Back home this would be a roadside gypsy encampment.

Three dark curls in a field are Latinos harvesting spring greens. In Herefordshire they would be East European and legal. Here they are illegals. *Get rid of them* is a popular cry. Truck farms would close, rural economies collapse. I stop at a diner and eat fried catfish served with fat fries. Three overweight women, belly-bulging from belted jeans, drink cola and eat fried food. One woman raps instructions in Spanish into a mobile phone, organising a squad of cleaners. Cleaning is Latino work.

With a population of 15,000, Athens, Tennessee, is a small, quiet, pleasant town situated at the foot of the Great Smoky Mountains. Tennessee Wesleyan College is a small liberal arts university – less than a thousand students – and provides that archetypal American amalgam of God, sport, education and the American flag. The forty-acre campus is two blocks north from Athens town square. Buildings are of red brick with the obligatory white pillars and surrounded by lawns. Old College Hall was built in the 1850s and is referred to as historic. Architecture is inoffensive. I stay at the Days Inn motel on Interstate 75. The motel is run by Gujarati and is equally archetypal of the United States; as is the diner specialising in barbeque chicken wings. Surely Tennessee is part of the South. Where are the Afro-Americans?

FRANKLIN, NORTH CAROLINA
Friday, 28 March

Athens to Franklin is a short ride. I am a little nervous as I circle the south-west tip of the Appalachians. I am invited to stay in Franklin by a friend made on the Internet biker site, Horizons Unlimited.

Jim Donaldson is more than a biker; he organises biker meets. Is he a Hell's Angel? A racist Red Neck? A right-wing Bushite Republican? Supporter of the United States Occupation in Iraq? Will he be enraged by my opinions, insulted? Will he swill Budweiser and bash me over the head with a bottle … Or throw me out of the house in mid-discussion? Were he a Brit and we were back home, I would have picked up clues. I am lost in the United States. I don't possess a social map.

He rides into the Wal-Mart parking lot astride a big-wheel knobbly-tired Kawasaki 650 fitted with top-of-the-range panniers. Impressive is my first impression: a six-six, all-American dressed in denim overalls and sporting a white down-to-his-chin Astérix moustache. A young sixty-nine, he is retired. To retain medical insurance, his wife teaches school in Georgia, a four-hour drive, where she rents a studio apartment close to the school. She and Jim spend weekends together, either in Georgia or at home, and during school holidays.

Insane? The health system in the United States is insane.

McCain, Republican presidential nominee, asked an audience whether they would rather enjoy the freedom of choice and excellence of the American system, the best in the world, or suffer British socialised medicine and wait months for an operation. McCain forgot to mention that we Brits have private hospitals for those who choose to carry private health insurance – or he deliberately deceived. Unlikely as McCain is an American hero. However he is old and naturally forgetful of inconvenient facts … Whilst we Brits are in agreement with our European neighbours in believing that medical treatment for all is a hallmark of civilised society.

FRANKLIN
Saturday, 29 March

A wooded hillside protects the Donaldson home at the rear. Below to the south lies a valley of green fields seen through a thin screen of silver birch. The house is comfortable rather than luxurious. The Donaldsons are a two-car two-bike family and twin double garages are Jim's joy. He and I have been out visiting two Harley bikers who recount a ride through Mexico and Central America. The bikers are middle-aged and married with kids, financially comfortable, on the School Board, etc., respected. The respect is important. These are law-abiding citizens. One is a judge.

They complain at having to wait in line at frontiers, traipse with their documents from window to window, fill in forms they can't read (they don't speak Spanish). They were caught speeding a couple of times and overtaking across the double yellow line. Breaking the law didn't concern them: this was Latin America and they were citizens of a superpower. They paid the cops off – thus reaffirming their opinion of Hispanics as venal. In our days of Empire, we Brits behaved with equal conceit. Nowadays we don't carry the same weight so most of us have learnt better. Perhaps that explains my sympathy for Mexicans who queue patiently at US borders. And why I understand Latin American anger at what they perceive as United States arrogance. Jealousy on my part?

A sun-shiny spring afternoon in the hills outside Franklin: rain has washed the air; tiny patches of pale pink blossom shimmer in sunlight on trees sprinkled with minute green jewels. Liz and Jim and I are on the deck at the rear of the Donaldson's home. Jim is introducing me to spud-gunning. The gun is made from plastic water pipe. Jim loads the eight-foot barrel with a plump potato and charges the combustion chamber with two squirts of hair spray. He spins the sparker: *Whoomph!*

That *whoomph* is spud-gunner heaven (think car crazies responding to the whining roar of a tuned Ferrari).

The spud flies high over a row of massive trees and I stamp and caper and slap my knee in juvenile glee. A well-fitting potato hurtles 300 yards. Accuracy? A barn door is a suitable target – or maybe the barn – a big barn.

Jim and I *whoomph* a sack of red salad potatoes while Liz watches with that look of kindly condescension. You know? The look all women keep in their armoury? The *Boys with their toys* look…

The Donaldsons are typical of the American heartland as portrayed by pre-sixties Hollywood – a Hollywood that didn't do black. They are decent folk, open, kindly, generous and honourable. Taller than the average European, they make a handsome couple. James Stewart would have made an excellent Jim, Liz played by Deborah Kerr.

In his early days, Jim was a staff photographer for *Time Life*. Divorce and custody of three children switched him to the construction industry. Liz inherited a 500-acre farm and they bred horses for a while – Pintos. Horses enjoy company; see them in a paddock, heads together. What do they discuss? Grass? Stallions? Mares? Horsemanship? Lightning killed the Donaldson's two best horses. My daughter's husband, Michael, lost two mares last year. How do giraffes survive?

FRANKLIN
Tuesday, 1 April

The Donaldsons have been introducing me to Southern cooking: fried chicken, corn bread, collard greens, black-eyed peas, grits. Grits are for chickens. The rest is great – especially the corn bread. So are the politics.

Jim and I are avid and cantankerous followers on television of the Democratic Party's presidential primaries. We are angered by the same crap, dismissive or suspicious of the same people, hope for an outcome of which we doubt the probability: Senator Obama…

We share other attributes. Jim has had triple-bypass surgery; I've had a couple of minor heart attacks. Jim has been in agony much of the past six months with a bad back; I suffered six months of back pain (the truck cured me). Jim has a long silver moustache; I have a silver beard. And we both enjoy toys.

A massive white Harley and the equally impressive Kawasaki bear witness to one of Jim's passions. I am privileged to sit astride the Harley.

Ride it?

No, thanks. Harleys weigh a ton.

FRANKLIN
Wednesday, 2 April

My tyres are shot. A man at Honda in Queretaro told me they are cheaper in the US. Yes, but you pay to have them fitted and availability is a problem: Honda 125s are a rarity in this land of super power. Jim checks via the *Yellow Pages* – no success. So we order a fresh set at a local bike shop for delivery in forty-eight hours. We leave my bike at the shop and I ride pillion home behind Jim on his trail bike. I hate riding pillion. Riding pillion surrenders your safety to a fellow biker. Bikers are adrenalin freaks. Risk is fun. Except for cowards. I am a coward.

Jim's approach to biking differs from mine. I put my trip together in under a week. Jim is a planner and he seeks perfection. He and Liz have toured the US and Canada on a Harley (they towed a custom camper trailer). Jim has explored Mexico with friends and ridden south through Central America to Panama. He wants to complete his long distance biking with a ride through South America. He has divided his future trip by nations and files information in a leather folder.

Triple bypass and his back have forced a downsize from the Harley – I don't consider the Kawasaki much of an improvement. One pannier is already full with spares; tools and a medical kit fill the second. A steel top-box and more of what Jim thinks of as essentials crowd the workbench. Jim and I are mature citizens (mature in age) and our legs have lost much of their thrust. I wouldn't attempt lifting Jim's bike on to its stand. My advice to him is to ride a bike for which spares are available on the road. True, I am being wise after the event. I bought the Honda because it was cheap and because I drive a sixteen-year-old Honda Accord back home that has never betrayed us.

Jim and Liz have been showing me the beauty of North Carolina. Spring has yet to blossom the forested mountains. Private roads to summerhouses of the wealthy spill trails of soil erosion through naked trees. Many of the incomers are Northerners by way of Florida, which they find too sultry in midsummer. Sweat wrecks their Florida golf game; their holiday homes wreck North Carolina.

Franklin and Ledbury in Herefordshire are both small country towns. Where do they differ? Sprawl is the easy answer. Distance from Franklin town centre to the Wal-Mart mall would take me halfway to Hereford. Trekking to either one of two bike shops is further and by our very English standards everything is new. Our cottage was built at a time when the Appalachians were Cherokee territory. President Andrew Jackson signed the Indian Removal Act in 1830: the Cherokee were herded 1,200 miles in winter. The trek lasted six months and one in four died.

Few of today's US citizens have roots in the Americas deeper than the last quarter of the nineteenth century: they avoid guilt for genocide and for expropriating the tribal lands of Native Americans.

FRANKLIN
Friday, 4 April

Jim rides me down to collect my bike from the bike shop – Long View Cycle Inc. Mike Townsend is the owner. A mechanic has serviced the bike, oil change, etc. Mike has written across the invoice: *Our contribution to the ride* – one more act of generosity.

Mike warns that the chain is about done and that the drive sprockets are worn sharp.

Will the chain get me to upstate New York?

Ride carefully…

I leave in the morning. This evening I sit in a comfortable arm-chair and watch with Jim the political news. I don't have a vote – unjust given that the UK's foreign policy is dictated in Washington. Obama is under threat for suggesting that the people of Pennsylvania are bitter at losing their jobs and take shelter in a gun and church culture. I shall ride through Pennsylvania.

Meanwhile I enjoy friendship and companionship and kindness. I have been a guest of the Donaldsons for a week. We have done nothing out of the ordinary. We have merely spent time together, enjoyed each other's company, explored our differences and our similarities. It has been a good time, a very good time. These are wonderful people.

APPALACHIANS
Saturday, 5 April

The Blue Ridge Parkway runs the length of the Appalachian Mountains north from Cherokee, North Carolina, 469 miles. Speed limit is forty-five miles per hour. Commercial vehicles are forbidden. Perfect for the ancient rider of a small bike who is fearful of trucks…

Cherokee Town is Native American tourism: mowed grass by the river beneath great trees in spring leaf, log-cabin fast-food outlets, Mom and Pop motels, native handicrafts manufactured in China. A gentleman riding a mower assures me that the Blue Ridge Parkway is closed, that it was closed yesterday. Sun shines. Gates are open. A Park Authority cream Ford pickup speeds by. Go for it…

Early spring and the Parkway climbs to over 6,000 feet. I wear three jerseys and a thick shirt over Alpinestar thermals, overalls, two pairs of nine-dollar waterproof trousers from Wal-Mart in Franklin, leather jacket, two pairs of gloves and Alpinestar boots.

The road climbs steeply out of Cherokee. Road verges are grey rock, pine trees and rhododendrons. The rhododendrons aren't yet in flower and I ride five or more miles before meeting a car. My feet, legs and body are warm. My cheeks freeze. So do my hands. I pull in at the summit viewpoint, dismount, beat my hands and sprint on the spot. Sprinting is an inexact term at my age, especially when swathed in layers of clothing. However I thaw somewhat and take photographs and say *Howdy* to a couple of fellow tourists warm from a heated motorcar.

The crunched-up ridges and peaks of the Appalachians march eastward to the horizon. A faint blue haze softens the contours and makes distant magic of the valley below where toy houses and barns crouch amongst stands of broad-leaf trees and beside small paddocks minutely spotted with dairy cows. Beautiful, magnificent, spectacular – oh, that it were a fortnight later, warmer, and the banks of rhododendron in full flower. Maybe another time ... and riding with Liz and Jim. That would be fun. In thinking of them, I feel my solitude.

Depression threatens. I heave a leg over the bike (no mean feat), kick the starter, settle into the saddle. A final wriggle of gloved fingers and onward again. A few days and I will be with my daughter, Anya, lie on the carpet and goo and coo at the baby, talk horses with Michael, admire the foals. Then home to England, my own bed, Bernadette, the boys, my daughter-out-of-law and Charlie Boo. Depression lifts. Life is good. I am immensely fortunate.

I stop a dozen times to photograph the mountains and wish that I owned a wide-angle telephoto lens. A sign warns of a diversion: no barrier so I ride onwards. Fool...

The barrier is twenty miles beyond the sign for the diversion. The diversion was to the right. At the barrier there is a lane to the left. The lane twists down through forested mountains. Appalachians are Hillbilly territory. Hillbillies are vicious degenerates in need of an orthodontist. I was taught this by Hollywood. Remember *Deliverance*? Trees drip. Shadows twist into scary shapes. I ride very slowly and with great caution.

The lane leads to a lush narrow valley and a T-junction. I carry a road atlas inside my jumper for extra protection against the wind.

I brake and unzip my bomber jacket. Where I am doesn't exist – or the atlas is in code. I don't have the code. I turn right and hit a further T-junction. Right leads to a church. Left gets narrower and turns to dirt. I am about to be raped or murdered. True, the only person in sight drags a mower behind a red tractor across a horse paddock. And the Hillbilly houses seem in fine repair and are considerably grander than those few in *Deliverance*.

I stop by the paddock, heave myself out of the saddle and wait for the driver to approach. He shuts off his engine – both a sign of friendship and that he can afford a sound battery. In the old days a Native American would have raised a hand and said *How* – or carved my scalp into a belt decoration. More Hollywood education…

I wish the tractor driver *Good day* and ask for directions back to the Parkway. He appears unsurprised at being addressed by an Englishman on a Mexican-registered motorcycle and he was born with good teeth or has an excellent orthodontist. A rock-fall has blocked the Parkway. The only road round the fall is loose dirt and mud – not to be ridden by an old man on a town bike. I can retreat to the Parkway and return to the diversion or circle back to the highway. Retreat is ignominious.

I am a brave British adventurer riding through Indian/Hillbilly land. These lovely green valleys offer cool summers and glorious mountain views. Perfectly groomed houses set in greenery are second homes for the wealthy who bypassed Florida – or third homes for those who took the Florida route. The Indians have long gone, as have the Hillbillies.

I stop at a petrol station and a gleaming Lexus 4×4 pulls up. An Afro-American and a white man dismount. I check the atlas with them. They aren't familiar with minor roads. The Afro-American has the soft clear diction of an up-market bond salesman. This is the South and he is the first Afro-American I have seen since fleeing Nashville. Is he investing a small fraction of his Wall Street Christmas bonus on a summer home? Seeking deliverance for his family from summer city pollution?

My deliverance is from *Deliverance*…

I backtrack to Ashville, take Highway 40 to Morganton, then north to Lenoir on Route 64. Crazy to retreat into this vast semi-circle? Probably. However what remains of my mind refuses to grapple with the map and Highway 40 requires a minimum of navigation. True, trucks are vast; slipstreams buffet a small bike. Buffeting does nothing for my bladder control: such are the minor handicaps of old age.

Now I am in Lenoir at the Comfort Inn and tapping the keyboard while sprawled on a king-sized bed. Carpets are being renewed which may explain the hotel's unpleasant odour. The television weather channel warns of a cold front moving down from the north followed by heavy rains and flooding on the East Coast. The screen fills with snow shots from Michigan. At least tomorrow will be fine. I set the alarm for six o'clock.

BLUE RIDGE PARKWAY
Sunday, 6 April

I am so close to the end of the ride. I load the bike under an overcast sky and take Route 321 out of Lenoir into the Appalachians. The cold grows bitter on the climb back to the Blue Ridge Parkway. Add wind chill and my fingers freeze. Paulo in Ushuaia fitted protective cuffs to the Honda's handlebars; the cuffs were torn off in the accident. Dumb fool that I am, I never replaced them.

The road is being widened. Giant dozers and hydraulic diggers munch chunks out of the mountain. Patches of wet slippery clay transform tar into a bobsleigh run. Massive dumper trucks pant on my tail. Frightened? Scared to bits…

I pull in at a petrol station café and wrap frozen fingers round a steaming mug of black coffee. Breakfast is two eggs sunny-side up, bacon, hashed potatoes. I share a table with two locals, lank-haired and with noses they wipe on their shirt sleeves; their conversation is unintelligible. Yellow hard-hats occupy the other tables. Two women work a stainless-steel hot plate. The smaller is younger and pregnant. Grease fumes from the hot plate rouge her cheeks (or does she have a fever?) and her nose drips. I am a little anxious as she breaks my eggs on to the hot plate. What makes the eggs splutter?

Zoning laws are foreign to North Carolina: property rights are sacrosanct and citizens have the right to do what they wish on their own land. Guard it with guns. Turn it into a shooting range. Or a bombing range. Build a cottage, tower block, incinerator.

Blowing Rock is a pretty village for affluent summer residents. Early April is out of season and shops and restaurants are shuttered. Blowing Rock is dead. So are my fingers. I beat my hands on my thighs a while, then take a right up through pine forest gouged for summer mansions and reach the Parkway. The cloud has lifted and the mountains are blue with cold. So am I. I work hard at admiring the view. I work hard at imagining trees in leaf, rhododendrons and azaleas in flower, the tiniest smidgeon of spring blossom. Beautiful? Yes. And enjoyable if wearing two pairs of thermal socks and driving a reliable car equipped with a fully functioning heater. This is bad weather for a biker – even a biker wearing heated leathers. Cold is cold is cold…

The Blue Ridge Parkway relates the history of white occupation. Here camped explorers, traders and Military expeditions. Historic cabins and campsites mark their progress. A century or two of rain and stormy weather has washed away the blood of conquest. Cafés and a hotel cater for tourists; campsites have hot and cold water and power points for recreational vehicles (camper trucks). Ancient trading posts (1850s) sell tourist tat. *Log-cabin* is the architectural style and signposts are varnished slices of tree trunk. Very tasteful…

What makes me cynical?

The pretty-pretties of a colonial power that boasts that it is rooted in freedom and democracy?

Or merely that the intense cold makes joy impossible?

Cafés are shut. So are the Minerals Museum and the urinals. I pass two cars in one hundred miles. My bladder demands a halt. Numb fingers search desperately within layers of clothing for a cold-shrunken male organ with which to urinate behind the tasteful log-wall of a shuttered Trading Post. Leaping and capering in the deserted parking lot restores a modicum of circulation that lasts a few miles before I am forced down off the parkway in search of catfish heaven.

Back in my youth, blue-collar Brits queued at the chippy most Saturday nights for fish and chips wrapped in newspaper. Thick soggy batter encased a stale chunk of greying cod; chips oozed grease. Today's preference is for equally vile fast food: sweet-and-sour with fried rice, chicken tikka, doner kebab or a Savaloy sausage. These are my musings as I shelter at a corner table in a jerry-built roadside diner in the Appalachian foothills on the border of West Virginia.

Lunch hour and the diner is packed with locals. These are country folk and polite; they don't stare at the fat old man off a Mexican mini-bike. Double doors keep the heat in. A mothering waitress helps prise me out of my bomber jacket and I shed a couple of jerseys. Warmth seeps through the remaining layers and my hands stop trembling. A woman at the next table interjects that we are suffering a cold front. Yes, indeed…

The waitress serves coffee and takes my order. She is medium young and blond and has a genetic advantage in remaining slim or avoids fried catfish in crisp batter accompanied by equally yummy fries. The servings are vast. Plump outriders escape on to the tablecloth. Add tomato ketchup and my plate is soon a redoubt within a scarlet-spattered war zone.

I feel good. I ponder on the politeness of people here, their friendliness. And I ponder at their lack of curiosity. Or does questioning a traveller breach etiquette? Are people nervous of what opinions they might encounter, nervous of betraying their own opinions, nervous of disagreement?

South of the Rio Grande, I would be in a discussion. The discussion would begin with the standard interrogation. How old? Where have I been? How does my wife feel at my being away? What do my children think? Which country did I like best?

We would drift into accounts of the economy and on into local politics; inevitably, someone would denounce President Bush as ignorant, arrogant and stupid – and denounce the United States as racist.

In the Appalachians, I have met only one Afro-American. That was yesterday, the up-market dealer in up-market bonds, the driver of a 4×4 Lexus. Or was he an FBI agent or a lawyer with the IRS – or a holidaying hit man? Or chauffeur for his ill-dressed Caucasian-American companion?

I have no idea.

People south of the Rio Grande are close kin culturally to Europeans. They are familiar to me. A few minutes' talk and I can write a reasonably accurate summary of their education and place in society.

Our sharing of language with the United States provokes a delusion of commonality. Dig a little deeper and we are very different.

There are those who believe me brave in undertaking this journey. I judge myself stupid. To exchange the warmth of the diner for the heights of the Blue Ridge Parkway – definitely stupid. I wish to write that the Parkway is beautiful. If so, I am soon too cold to notice. Low grey cloud envelops the mountains. A lone black turkey cock scuttles across the tar in search of a new winter overcoat. I ride with my left hand beneath my backside. The right hand freezes.

I last an hour on the Parkway. Thin drizzle mists my safety spectacles. I take a left down to the foothills and ride a further hour before pulling in at a petrol station. A woman serving coffee directs me to an upright heating unit. I lay both pairs of gloves on top of the heater, unzip my bomber jacket, press my chest against the heater and sip coffee. I am in a small town; it seems impolite to ask the woman serving coffee which town. A weatherman on television points to bands of downpour sweeping south from the Great Lakes. The rain won't hit till late evening. I could find a motel. Or I could ride a further couple of hours. Riding gets me closer to the end, to my daughter. I ride.

Route 42 crosses Virginia horse country: a land of hills and lush pastures, white farmhouses, white stables and white fences. Goshen and Staunton are red brick. Drizzle turns to light rain. Trees drip. I drip.

Tired is reasonable: I am tired. Cold is reasonable: I am cold. I am also wet and miserable. I have no right to be miserable. This ride is a privilege. I am one of the fortunate. So smile, Old Man, smile as you ride into Harrisonburg.

European cities have an obvious geographical purpose. Lesser inland US cities are confusing. Why were they founded in this particular stretch of emptiness? Where is the centre? What logic propels developers to clump skyscrapers wall to wall in a country of unlimited space? And why site the skyscrapers in these few city blocks rather than 200 metres left or right? And where do I find a hotel? I enter Harrisonburg on a minor road; for a motel I need the Interstate. Rain mists my spectacles.

I pull in at a petrol station beside a black Buick sedan. The driver is an Afro-American woman dressed (that bit that I can see of her) in artificial furs. She owns four teenagers – surely sufficient hell in an automobile without being asked for help by a miserable old Brit on a bike seeking a bed.

The teenagers compete with her in giving directions. My younger sons might understand the teen-speak. The mother recognises my bewilderment and accepts the impossibility of keeping the teens hushed long enough for a sensible conversation – even if the drenched old Brit on the bike is capable of rational communication (doubtful). 'Follow,' she says, 'I'll drive slow.'

She makes a U out of the petrol station and heads right across town to a Ramada Inn.

Many people have aided me on this journey. Few of them will read this account – and expressions of gratitude come easy. Yet I know of a future. I will sit on a bench in our Herefordshire garden, enjoy those few days of sun offered by our English summers and be better warmed by remembered evidence of so much kindness in a troubled world.

Management, reception and cleaners at the Ramada Inn, Harrisonburg, are Gujarati. I long for a curry made with fresh spices. I negotiate a moderate discount on the room rate. The weather channel shows heavy rain moving southward towards Harrisonburg. Rain will be followed by a cold front. Is a cold front colder than the cold I have already suffered up on the Blue Ridge Parkway?

I strip, turn the heating up and drape wet clothes over chairs and over the air-conditioner. Bliss is basking in a hot bath and contemplating the menu of a newly opened Thai restaurant. Spicy shrimp with fresh coriander…

HARRISONBURG, VIRGINIA
Monday, 7 April

Fierce squalls thrash rain against the windows of my room at the Ramada Inn. The Honda, sandwiched outside between an RV and a double-cab truck, seems very small and somewhat bedraggled – even a mite reproachful. It is accustomed to overnighting in hotel lobbies and seventeenth-century Spanish colonial patios: the Ramada Inn parking lot is a come-down while the king-sized bed is a sybarite's delight. I suffer a twinge of guilt – and worry that the Honda will avenge itself; worry that the chain won't hold up, or that a worn tooth or teeth on the sprockets will offer insufficient purchase for the chain.

However, this is not a biker day. It is a day for catching up on correspondence and my journal, for planning the final stage of the ride and for watching television news. And for sprinting (slowly) for free breakfast across the parking lot to the main building.

Later I watch coverage of the presidential primaries. Both Senators Clinton and McCain attack Senator Obama for describing working-class men of the Pennsylvania Valleys as bitter. According to Senator Obama the cause of their bitterness is the closure of the mills and mines – the men have lost their jobs. However, *bitter* is an insult – being bitter is un-American. Describing the unemployed as bitter proves Senator Obama an elitist (I am quoting Senators Clinton and McCain).

I am an outsider. What would I know?

Evening: the wind has dropped. Rain continues. Tomorrow will be dry – and cold. I am suffering a head cold. I am scared that the infection will move down to my chest. I am scared of United States medical bills. So are most citizens of this country.

Should I hole up here in Harrisonburg until the cold front passes? Or should I make a dash for my daughter's in upstate New York? Such weighty matters require energy. I call the Thai restaurant and order spicy prawns. Eleven months on the road – I'll be in need of a prawn detox.

TOWARDS WASHINGTON, DC
Wednesday, 9 April

I leave the comforts of the Ramada Inn, Harrisonburg, soon after first light and ride the Interstate north towards Harrisburg. I am riding through a gently up-and-down horse country of green meadows, white fences and woods. The sun shines – less watery as the morning progresses. Washington, DC, is to the east. I intend stopping a night in DC and visiting the Vietnam Memorial. I also want to be safe at my daughter's, to have this ride done with. To survive.

As I ride, I cogitate. I checked the chain before leaving the Ramada Inn. It is very slack and I am a little anxious, not only regarding the chain. I have survived the cities of Hispanic America without mishap. I understand Hispanic American cities. I am sensitive to invisible frontiers that divide safe from dangerous – and the moderately safe from truly terrifying.

Washington, DC, does politics, shootings-for-sport and carjacking

– so the media reports. Jim Donovan visited on his Harley and had police warn him that he had taken a wrong turn, was in the wrong barrio and should get the hell out fast.

The Honda won't do fast.

I wish to see the Memorial.

I don't feel in immediate need of a personal memorial.

And I am running short of funds.

The Appalachians are behind me. Washington, DC, is a rock thrown into a vast economic puddle. Ripples flow outward. White clapboard houses are bigger, better maintained. Mercedes, BMWs and Porsches are common as flies on a Third World butcher's slab. I catch glimpses of red-brick mansions sheltered by parkland. Riding stables abound, paddocks protected by white picket fences. Horses are as plentiful as handguns and bear the same romantic mystique. I am crossing the political heartland of the Land of the Free, whose early heroic presidents, General George Washington and Thomas Jefferson, were slave-owners.

The slaves have rebelled.

Reap and weep.

Or move to the suburbs and gated communities…

The cold front hasn't yet hit. I weep with a head cold. Sneezing fogs my spectacles. Signs point to Monticello – slavery as romantic, all those loyal darkies, *Gone With the Wind*. Is my head cold responsible for my dark mood? Or my fear of riding through DC?

I imagine DC as a city to which wise people travel by train or plane. They take cabs to their hotel or to friends' homes and venture forth by cab or with a guide (preferably armed).

I have a young friend in DC, Elizabeth Bergner. We met this trip in Cartagena, Colombia. Elizabeth is making a career change from Peace Corp volunteer. She shares a house with the like-minded, mostly met on her travels. I would enjoy listening to their experiences and to their opinions. Sadly, Elizabeth is away at a wedding. And the Vietnam War Memorial would be out of place at this point in my journal. Memorials are epilogues…

I travelled deserts in my youth, was shot at, broke free of ambushes. In my thirties I rode trucks the length and breadth of the Indian subcontinent and, in later years, drove and rode horseback across much of Afghanistan, mislaid my false teeth in a mountain stream, hid from Russian gunships. Now I am old – and a scaredy-cat. Or grown more sensible? Washington DC can wait. I crossed the Appalachians on Route 211. I bypass Washington on Route 15.

Road signs point back into recent history: Harpers Ferry, Gettysburg; signposts, in the Land of the Free, to a war in defence of the rights of gallant slave-owning Southern gentlemen. Perhaps I am obsessive. However, I have become accustomed to such accusations in journeying through Hispanic America.

Spain is the historic evil taught to white Protestant Anglo-Saxon England and the United States: Spain, Catholicism and the Inquisition.

The first laws in defence of the freedom of the native population and of universal human rights were promulgated in Spain by Charles V in the sixteenth century ('New Laws' 1542, 1543, 1544). The laws were seldom observed.

US President Andrew Jackson ordered the clearing by force of the native population from its lands in the nineteenth century (Removal Act, 1830).

Evil knows no monopoly.

I speed slowly north through Harrisburg before turning east on to Route 209, which will take me through the Pennsylvania valleys to Kingston, New York. Cross the bridge over the Hudson, ride through Reinbeck, Red Hook and Pine Plains, turn left on to Johnny Cake Hollow and up the track to Duchess View Farm and the Metropolitan Stud. I shall hug my daughter, admire my new grandson, park the Honda in the stables – total joy. How far? Approximately 270 miles. Can I make it today? Maybe…

I ride a short stretch north from Harrisburg before turning

eastward through the Pennsylvania valleys. Massive trucks roar by on the Interstate. The trucks strike me as symbolic of US power: blunt, heavy, no requirement for subtlety. Engines thunder; massive tyres add their own roar. Air is the enemy. Ram it out of the way. I shrink on to the petrol tank and struggle to steady the bike against the slipstream. Here comes the next and the next. In passing, they give me the space prescribed in the Highway Code. No more, no less, and no communication. My bike is too small for this land of giants. I am unimportant, a harmless bug. A very small bug…

I fancy myself an expert on truck drivers. Mexicans are the most humane. See a small bike on the road and Mexican truck drivers pull wide. They salute on the klaxon, wave. Peruvians and the drivers of Ecuador are equally friendly; meet them and they say *Hi* with a flash of headlights. I write here of drivers away from the Pan-American Highway. The Pan-American is a high-speed steeplechase track. National borders are the obstacles. Trucks queue for hours, sometimes days. Frustration seeds hostility. Keep your distance…

Forgive me for writing further of danger and truck drivers. My friends in Dallas judged my journey mad or suicidal. They warned of Mexican drivers, of crooked cops and crooked border officials. Mexicans in Veracruz added bandits to their warnings. So I progressed, country to country, each peopled by homicidal truck drivers, murderous terrorists and bandits, drug addicts, degenerates and deviants. Chance acquaintances expressed amazement at my survival.

I encountered only kindness.

On occasion, arrogance made me resent the kindness … As with cops in Peru who stopped me every twenty kilometres as I crossed the desert in a sandstorm.

Hey, grandfather, are you OK?'

They were nursemaiding me. Me! A survivor of ambushes in the Ogaden, of Russian gunships in Afghanistan. I felt belittled.

I stopped for lunch at a truck and coach halt in the Peruvian desert and chatted half an hour with the waitresses. Two cops ate at a table against the far wall. They departed. I asked for my bill. The cops had paid. This is my *Thank you* to the Peruvian police. Nanny me any time you choose…

Pennsylvania's mining and mill towns are imprisoned in narrow valleys: Tremont, Minersville, Port Carbon, New Philadelphia. Broken-backed trailer-homes hide in dripping birch woods beneath a low grey sky. Battered pickups, abandoned automobiles and soon-to-be abandoned automobiles are fashion statements. Shop windows are boarded up. *For Sale* notices thrive on small red-brick and clapboard houses and sullen teenagers gather on street corners to cultivate a tobacco habit. So were the Scottish Borders created by the Thatcher government in the eighties, mills shut, mines closed, a lost generation of kids. Bitter? Yes, indeed …Though Senators McCain and Clinton claim that bitterness is un-American.

Tories in Scotland ceased to exist.

What future have Pennsylvania Valley Republicans?

What future do I have? For bikers, this is unfriendly weather. Oh, for a little global warming…

Midday, the sky clears. The country grows more open, bigger fields bordered by good woodland, wealthier. Shiny automobiles pack the parking lot of a diner. The diner is low and light and new and built to last half of a short lifetime. I finger-comb my hair before entering and struggle out of a wet bomber jacket. Sunday lunch and tables are full. Uniformity in dress is obligatory. Gap or Old Navy is the choice in male tailoring. A smiling waitress with good teeth seats me at the counter and asks, 'How are we today?'

Cold and hungry.

In England waiting is obligatory. This is the US and coffee comes by instant magic. I cup the mug in cold fingers. I must look a little weird; too fat for a scarecrow, but, yes, a little weird: three short-sleeved jerseys over one long-sleeved jersey, all tucked inside two pairs of outsized rain-proof pants yanked halfway up my chest, two sets of broad suspenders visible, red and grey.

What is he? A pessimist? Maybe. But weird, definitely weird.

Country Brits would show their suspicions. Here bland faces hide any curiosity.

Or maybe I'm invisible.

Sweat, malt vinegar and stale oil is the perfume of the English chippy. I prefer the US odour of chemical air freshener. I doubt that I can reach my daughter's today. One more night in a motel and the journey is done. From the start I expected to give up somewhere along the road – admit that I was an old fool, that the journey was too tough. All in all, I am well content.

Route 209 joins the main highway south of Stroudsburg. Sunday hasn't kept truck drivers off the road. I open the throttle to max in hope of not being run down. Full throttle on the flat is around sixty miles per hour. A heavy machine gun fires a burst under my backside. The chain has snapped. The chain will entangle the wheel spokes. The wheel will collapse. I'll be catapulted on to the road. I'll have two seconds watching a truck's tyres before I get squashed. Totally squashed. Smeared. Except the bike comes quietly to a halt at the road edge.

I sit a while before dismounting. The sun shines. I breathe carefully and inhale the scent of pinewoods bordering the highway. Trucks thunder.

What am I going to do? So close, yet so far…

I prise the chain free, drape it over the crutches and push the bike fifty metres to a side turn. Do I push the bike onward until I find a village? Or do I wait in hope of a miracle? The miracle appears in the guise of a red Honda 4×4 driven by a typically friendly young man with short hair and dressed in standard Gap. Sunday and bike shops are closed. He suggests I park the bike a hundred metres down the road behind a church where it will be safe. He will drive me to a motel in Stroudsburg.

I imagine, as I push the bike, attempting to push a Harley or Gold Wing. I would collapse.

I park the bike behind the church. The young man in the Honda opens the passenger door. The rear is loaded with waders and rods and fishing tackle.

He asks where I come from.

'You rode that far on that small bike...' He shakes his head in semi-disbelief. Then, 'There's no sense leaving the bike out here. I have a trailer at the house...'

We drive through semi-suburban pinewoods country. His home is on a rise, dark-stained cedar, white window frames, perfectly maintained. Azaleas and rhododendrons are in bud. His parents live nearby. So do his in-laws. He works for the electricity company, maintenance on high-wire pylons. He and his wife have a first baby. They were at church this morning. His wife gave him the afternoon off to go fishing.

City folk are moving into the neighbourhood, building weekend and holiday homes. City folk complain if he keeps a pig or his chickens crow. We have the same problem back home. An ancient yew tree has been massacred on our lane. Neighbouring women complained that the tree cut their light. The tree was there before they bought their cottages. It was there before they were born. It was there before their parents were born.

We hitch the trailer to the Honda, collect the bike. Stroudsburg is a fifteen-minute drive. I attempt to give thanks, ask for an address.

'It's nothing,' my saviour assures me. A nothing miracle of generosity and so typical of my few weeks in the United States...

I set out on this journey through the Americas in 2006 from Providence, Rhode Island, the home of my ex and her son, Jed. I travelled south by train to Dallas and Don and Jane Weempe and adventured with the Boys with Bikes and was saved from disaster in Amarillo by the Angel of the Bourbon Street café (all described in *Old Man on a Bike*). Now, riding north in 2008 I was saved first by the wicked Muslim at the Texas petrol station, enjoyed the hospitality of Terry, Ed, Carol and Peter in Galveston. I have been pampered in North Carolina by Jim and Liz and aided by Mike Townsend at the Long View Cycle shop. Now I ride towards my daughter in

Duchess County, New York. Encountering such kindness, such generosity, why dare I be so critical of the United States? Why do I feel more at home, more secure, in Hispanic America?

Gujaratis run the Stroudsburg motel. The portly receptionist was born in Gujarat and attended art school in England before emigrating to the United States. He paints in his free time and shows me a painting of a goddess in profile on a black background, lots of gold leaf and gold dots.

Why did he move to the US?

In England, he worked for the couple who own the motel. They moved to the United States. The wife is British Gujarati, a university graduate. Does she enjoy the US?

Opportunities are greater – the motel business. Work hard for a few years and you are established financially.

I sit in the motel lobby and drool at the lush scents of curry seeping from the owners' quarters. A giant enters, giant in height, giant in shoulders, giant in belly – late fifties and losing his hair – stained jeans, stained sweatshirt, scuffed work boots. He leans against the reception counter. The counter quivers. So does the receptionist.

I am inspected by the giant.

'You look depressed,' he says. 'The type of depression that goes with needing crutches and owning a small bike with a broken chain…'

I plead guilty to the ownership and admit the depression.

The giant extends a massive hand, hefts me to my feet. 'Let's go get it fixed.'

I remark timidly that bike shops close on Sundays.

'We'll open them…'

A second giant, equally muscled and vast of belly, sits at the wheel of a grey truck. They are members of the Boilermakers Union. They are boilermakers from infancy – maybe even in the womb. Years have faded the Union badges tattooed on their massive biceps. They are refurbishing a power station. The first giant is the boss. The second is responsible for health and safety. The sidekick tells me pay is good

– that it needs to be: boilermakers don't survive into old age: asbestos kills them. The power station here is packed with asbestos that needs removing. The giants have a work gang of forty men.

The boss directs his sidekick round the block to a small, brick-built bike shop. A notice on the door proclaims the shop closed.

Elderly Brit blimps don't hammer on shop doors on a Sunday evening.

Boilermakers do. The door quakes in its frame and trail bikes tremble behind the shop window. I dread a burglar alarm, cops, jail…

We progress to a diner/bar; the giants have been in Stroudsburg a week and have integrated with the bar crowd. The crowd is male designer stubble. Dress code is check shirts or sweatshirts, jeans and baseball caps. We are hunting the bike shop owner's home number. I plead that tomorrow would be fine. The giants are unstoppable. They are on a mission (imagine a two-man blitzkrieg).

None of the bar crowd has the number. One of them suggests Jack has a wrecked Honda: *Jack, you know, guy with a stringy beard? Works at the gas station. The bike's there in the back.*

I am being negative in doubting that the bike would be a 125. Negativity never stopped a blitzkrieg…

However, giants require regular sustenance and we eat before hunting for gas-station Jack – eat as in mountains. One waitress is fun. The other is wary of giants and the sidekick is flirtatious. He has undergone multiple divorces. Born in South Carolina, he has a home on the beach.

Boss giant is a bachelor and owns homes in Queens and in upstate New York twenty miles from my daughter's home. If we can't get my bike fixed, he suggests I take the bus and he will drop the bike off at Anya's at the end of the month.

They ask where I live. I tell them Herefordshire, that we have a small cottage but a large garden. The sidekick adds a further mountain of fries to his plate and asks if I do much hoeing. He and the boss are keen on hoeing. I say that my wife prohibits hoeing, that hoeing is bad for my back.

I have surprised the hell out of him. He orders mammoth wedges of pie, flirts with the waitress. The waitress giggles and flounces off. To the boss he says, 'Remember those two hoes we met up with in Charlotte?'

Jack at the gas station is stringy of body and of beard. He has wrecked teeth and a wrecked Honda 750. I am welcome to the chain. The chain is way too big. Wal-Mart is the next stop. Work at the power station requires a multitude of keys; the boss wants the keys hung on fish hooks on a board in the works office. The sidekick drives and talks of boilermakers and how he is one of a dying breed. Modern kids won't get their hands dirty.

Mexicans?

Mexicans are rude and lazy and pretend that they don't speak English.

The boss and I wait in the truck while the sidekick buys fish hooks.

The boss says, 'Never met a Mexican who wasn't polite and a worker...'

My friend Don, a Dallas Good Ol' Boy, would agree with the boss. All the workers in Don's construction business are Latinos.

The boss curses himself for not thinking clearly; I have less than 200 miles to ride and a new chain is unnecessary. Easy to repair the old. For sure, one of his men on the job will have a spare chain link in his toolbox. The boss will have a mechanic come by in the morning – around ten o'clock.

STROUDSBURG, PA
Thursday, 10 April

I sit in the lobby of the Stroudsburg motel, eat breakfast and read the paper. A third giant arrives at ten o'clock. The boss giant has sent him to fix my bike.

Has he much experience of bikes?

Never had one. Too dangerous. However machines are machines. Patience and logic are the only requirements. He squats on the sidewalk and studies the bike a while, planning his moves before dismounting the chain cover to remove the broken link and a further link from the chain. He refastens the chain with a removable link from his toolbox – fifteen minutes and the bike is ready. I am in his debt – and in debt to the boss giant for his kindness.

The boss is a type I recognise and admire from earlier travels through Africa, the Mid-East and the Indian sub-continent: a type of US expatriate. You find them in the oil fields and in engineering, agriculture and construction. They possess great energy and are extraordinarily competent in diverse fields. Decision doesn't scare them. They act where we Brits would set up a committee to come to an indecision. And they treat all men as equals – race and religion notwithstanding. Perhaps this lack of prejudice drives them abroad. They are uncomfortable back home. Home is too small. Both the boss giant and Don Weempe are typical of the breed: Joe Brown (my host in Granada) is another – good men in every sense…

Nature is what the US does best. I have ridden the Natchez Trail and the Blue Ridge Parkway. Now for the Pocono Mountains. Route 209 follows the Delaware, one more name conjuring a romantic view of history.

I leave Stroudsburg under an overcast sky. Bitterly cold, I stop at Wal-Mart and buy an outsize pair of ski gloves to wear over my other gloves. The ski gloves keep my hands warm for a few kilometres.

I will finish this journey today – gratefully finish. I have been scared often – here, in the US, of falling ill. Not scared of illness. Scared by medical costs. We Europeans carry a plastic card that gives us free health treatment anywhere within the European Union. How good is the health treatment? Very good. Senator McCain asks voters which they would prefer: European waiting lists or US freedom of choice. Freedom for whom? For Senator McCain who enjoys senatorial health insurance and a billionaire wife and doesn't know how many homes he owns. Yeah, Yeah, Yeah…

Cold, cold, cold. Yet the route is beautiful. The two-lane highway follows the wooded banks of the Delaware. Mountains rise to my left. Dressed in spring-green this would be wondrous. Now the naked trees seem frozen in their stillness. Skinny branches drip at the border of a patch of bald plough. I stop a while; beat my hands on my thighs and watch two men cast for trout in clear waters. The fishermen wear waders; the river drags white water eddies round their thighs.

A barrier closes the road midway through the State Park. The detour winds through woods and a narrow valley. Trees part to a scattering of clapboard houses, a couple of churches, a jail – or perhaps a downmarket holiday camp? The lane climbs again out of the valley before dipping to the river. Clouds break and sunlight glistens on wet tar and on the clear waters of the Delaware. Joy is instant.

I stop in Milford for coffee and a Subway chicken sandwich. Sun shines. Woods fall back. The country opens. Route 209 crosses Interstate 84. I ride the frontier of New Jersey. How many states have I crossed? This has been a journey of calculations – kilometres to miles, litres to gallons, distance into minutes – anything to pass the time while crossing the vast emptiness of Argentina or central Brazil, any distraction that took my mind off my aching butt. Next trip I will buy a custom saddle. Next trip? I'll be 76. What am I planning? I'm crazy…

The terrain of the past two days was familiar in scale and history: a land of valley and hill, mill and mining towns, scattered villages, small fields and woods. Cross the state line into New York and everything is different. Development seems haphazard. The peripheral rash of abandoned stores and warehouses, multi-pump petrol stations and fast food outlets is the United States portrayed by Hollywood. Pimped-up trucks, automobiles and pickups are protagonists. People are redundant: a bag lady, hoods cloaking a black or brown or white face, baseball caps, faded jeans, slouched walk, scuffed trainers. Pennsylvania was an aberration.

I feel the Hudson River as a frontier between old and new, between the United States that is foreign to me and the United States with historic and cultural ties to Europe. I take the correct road round Kingston to the Hudson River bridge. I am home east of the river. Anya and I have toured every lane, visited each small town – Rhinebeck, Red Hook, Millbrook, Millerton – stopped for coffee here, shopped there, visited Anya's doctor, browsed the bookshops, collected a cat from the vet, ordered a Chinese takeaway.

Pine Plains is a few blocks each side of a crossroads. Houses are white weatherboard in lawned yards, upstairs and downstairs, a few pillars, cedar-shake roofs, sash windows and dormer windows – cute to an American, and to me. The brick restaurant on one corner of the crossroads is French-owned. The food is reasonable.

Nothing much happens in Pine Plains; nothing much happens back home in Colwall. Of equal size, they are good sane places in which to sink roots.

I ride in sunshine. My hands are warm and the Honda purrs contentedly as we coast the country road. In my early youth this was a land of small dairy farms. Two centuries or more of toil created fields from hillsides. Agro-Industry has put the farms out of business. Hill fields have surrendered to second-generation birch woods spotted with weekend homes. Valleys are given over to hobby farms and horse farms. White-painted post and rail fences enclose horse paddocks, white houses, white-painted stable blocks. Even the dirt has been deodorised.

Why so bitter?

Not bitter, sad.

Sad at the waste of labour dedicated to future generations, a cold funeral pyre of dreams for a better life: such was New England's fate. Walk the woods and you find remnants of its dry-stone walls, relics of a nobler culture.

Take a right after Pine Plains, swoop into the next valley. The farm road is on the right. The road runs uphill between dark-stained post and rail fences to the homestead. Farmhands wave. A chestnut mare turns to watch. I park outside the office between the stallion pens. The journey is done. Anya pushes open the door from her and Michael's duplex. Anya is small and immensely beautiful. She carries her baby, my grandson, in her arms. I am a real man, an intrepid adventurer: blame the cold wind for my tears.

DUCHESS VIEW FARM
Friday, 11 April

There is a difference between a love letter and a letter of love. A love letter is written to a lover. This book is a letter of love – and of gratitude to those who made my journey possible; those who picked me up and nursed and mended me when I was broken; sent me on my way with courage restored. It is dedicated firstly to Graciela Abbat Agostinelli – and to her ex-future *novio*, Fernando – to Pepe Gonzalez the one-legged orthopaedic surgeon – to all the residents at the Hostel Argentina, the oil workers of Rio Grande, my cousins in Buenos Aires – yes, the people of Argentina, a people who proudly portray themselves as tough and macho yet are such softies. They are immensely kind, immensely generous and immensely thoughtful. Oh that they had better politicians.

My treasured friends, I have waited to write to you until the journey was done. It is your journey. Had I failed, I would have betrayed you.

ACKNOWLEDGEMENTS

To name all those who have helped me on this journey has taken three hundred pages. However let me name a few: Pepe Gonzalez, Graciela and the Hostel Argentino crowd in Rio Grande; my cousins, Brian and Carmen Deane and John Nelson in Buenos Aires; Joe Brown and Gillian Lythgoe in Nicaragua; in Guatemala, Eugenio and Monica Gabatto, Jim and Olga Hazard; the Donaldsons in North Carolina; above all my brother, Antony, whose support made the journey possible.